THE CANONIZATION
OF THE
SYNAGOGUE SERVICE

UNIVERSITY OF NOTRE DAME
CENTER FOR THE STUDY OF
JUDAISM AND CHRISTIANITY
IN ANTIQUITY

Number 4

The Canonization of the Synagogue Service

Lawrence A. Hoffman

UNIVERSITY OF NOTRE DAME PRESS

NOTRE DAME   LONDON

Copyright © 1979 by
University of Notre Dame Press
Notre Dame, Indiana 46556

Paperback edition 1986
ISBN 0-268-00756-X

Library of Congress Cataloging in Publication Data

Hoffman, Lawrence A. 1942–
  The canonization of the synagogue service.

  (Studies in Judaism and Christianity in antiquity;
no. 4)
  Bibliography: p.
  Includes index.
  1. Jews. Liturgy and ritual—History. 2. Prayer
(Judaism) 3. Geonic literature—History and criticism.
I. Title. II. Series.
BM660.H63   296.4   78-62972
ISBN 0-268-00727-6

To my parents
Manuel and Ida Hoffman
zikhronam liverakhah

Contents

Acknowledgments

ACKNOWLEDGMENTS ARE NEVER EASILY COMPOSED. ONE SHOULD LIKE TO write for pages enumerating the many many people whose abundant help has been abundantly appreciated. I have never lacked for teachers, and they all should know that this book is partly theirs.

Unable to record all my mentors, I must at least mention those who have opened my eyes to the excitement of Jewish liturgy; this is a liturgical work, after all.

Leon J. Liebreich, *'alav hashalom*, introduced me to the subject. Unknowingly, he taught me to smile when, some time later, people were to respond with quizzical incredulity upon hearing of my decision to take liturgy seriously. His syllabus to my introductory course was better than most books in the field.

A. Stanley Dreyfus is an overly modest scholar who always knows more than anyone around him realizes. He has ever encouraged me by his faith in my abilities and by his very person. He is a noble personality and a genuine lover of his people's prayers.

It is Jakob J. Petuchowski who demonstrated the incredible depth and breadth of Jewish liturgy. His own writings reveal that it is philosophy, theology, poetry, politics, and so much else. Above all, he has cared: cared for the discipline that scholarship demands; cared for the courage to say what he believes; cared for my welfare in difficult times. Without his patient guidance, this book would not be.

The aura of scholarly excitement that envelopes the liturgical faculty at the University of Notre Dame cannot go unacclaimed. It is sui generis and captivating. Bill Storey and Joe Blenkinsopp were particularly encouraging to me. Charles Primus was a demanding, knowledgeable, and superb critic. James Langford has assembled a remarkable staff who have been unfailing in their concern that this book be published on schedule with the care and expertise that only those adept in the fine art of publishing can appreciate. To Ann Rice who has overseen the project I owe many thanks.

Writers need not acknowledge their family, but I wish to. My wife,

Sally, is no liturgist, but her prayers for me have never been lacking. It is I who should have prayed for her during these years of research and writing.

My parents, Manuel and Ida, whose memory is indeed a blessing, were my first and best teachers. What I am they taught me to be; and to them I dedicate this work.

Introduction

THE MODERN STUDY OF JEWISH LITURGY CAN BE TRACED BACK TO THE *Wissenschaft des Judentums*, an intellectual movement whose significance far surpasses what is suggested by a mere translation of its name. Yet translation tells us something. As the name implies, the *Wissenschaft* was a scientific movement, and a product of Germany, in the early years of the nineteenth century. Its subject was Judaism, and no Jewish source was beyond its purview.[1]

Its proponents were, by and large, products of a premodern, traditionalist milieu which had exposed them in their youth to an intensive study of rabbinic sources. The spread of the Enlightenment, however, allowed—even impelled—these men later to acquire the scholarly attitude and methodology then typical of German academia. Thus was born the "Scientific Study of Judaism": a synthesis of two worlds; the application of a particular discipline learned as an adult to a body of knowledge mastered as a child.

Underlying this enterprise was the assumption that the Jewish heritage was a product of the same immutable laws of development that shaped any other culture. Since Jewish literature from the ninth century on was known to have contained prayer books, and since the literature of even the earliest epochs displayed the existence of devotional prose and poetry, liturgy—though not yet a formal discipline—was included as one of the many cultural building-blocks deserving of scientific attention.

So Jewish scholars devoted to *Wissenschaft* began the arduous task of sifting through texts, comparing manuscripts, collecting and identifying sources, and, above all, restructuring the world's concept of what Judaism was. Slowly but surely, the fruit of their labor was disseminated to the public in what still remain classic explications of almost every conceivable facet of Jewish culture, including liturgy. The *Wissenschaft* treatment of prayer was like the *Wissenschaft* treatment of everything else: methodical, positivistic, textually oriented, remarkably thorough, obsessed with detail.

Yet for all the monographs that were produced on the origin of specific prayers, the general subject of liturgical canonization was not systematically investigated. To be sure, Leopold Zunz (1794–1886), a founder and outstanding personification of the *Wissenschaft* movement, recognized that liturgical

1

canonization had occurred. And he went about describing it in his own unique way. By collecting and identifying an inordinate number of liturgical manuscripts and tracing their characteristic features (particularly the selection of poetry they displayed), he was able to differentiate specific rituals and to suggest how the synagogue service had evolved from its relatively simple origins in antiquity to the abundance of richness that marked the worldwide spectrum of rituals in his own day.[2]

But the usually meticulous explication of which Zunz was capable is not to be found in his *Ritus des synagogalen Gottesdienstes*. To be sure, there is no end of detail, and even a general hypothesis regarding the existence of two basic rituals from which all later ones stemmed. But Zunz was really not interested enough in his subject to pursue it fully. He saved his critical acumen for other studies, like rabbinic *midrash* and medieval poetry. Here he contented himself with enumerating some basic causes for ritual diversity,[3] without, however, applying his criteria precisely and comprehensively even to explain the codification of his two hypothetical ritual prototypes. His work remains a classic study of ritual classification rather than an investigation of the process of ritual canonization.

Zunz's failure to investigate the canonization process can surely not be blamed on the man himself. His prodigious mastery of rabbinic sources and his ability to utilize them selectively are obvious on any single page of the thousands he penned. But the times through which he lived could not be mastered as easily as the manuscripts with which he worked. And the times had yet to identify liturgy—the stuff of Jewish worship—as a discipline independently worthy of study by a "scientist."

Just as philosophy had for so many years subsumed, in undifferentiated form, the several disciplines of the social sciences, so the historical study of rabbinic sources was still perceived as encompassing many subtopics which still, today, have not emerged as subjects in their own right. Thus Zunz and the many superb scholars who followed in his footsteps saw liturgy as but another aspect of rabbinics, all of which was to be treated from that philological perspective which they took to be true science. Assuming the essentially literary nature of prayer texts, they systematically compared manuscripts in an effort to uncover a presumed *Urtext*, a basic and original composition of each and every prayer, which, it was assumed, had been altered by time.[4] Their focus, then, was not on the social process of canonizing a set of existent prayer texts, but on identifying the original circumstances which engendered each particular text, seen in itself.

Through the years, it is true, the philological school has produced some very valuable studies of prayer books as a whole—and we shall cite them in their place—but they are the exceptions rather than the rule. And their goal is the same, if not their focus. They too are dedicated to the reconstruction of the "original" text. They are merely an expansion of the subject from single prayers to prayer books. Naturally, no serious study would be possible without the scientific editions which such scholarship made available, but our ability to reconstruct the texts should not be confused with the knowledge of how and why they were constructed in the first place.

In recent years another school of liturgical investigation has come to the fore, the form-critical school, represented most forcefully by Joseph Heinemann. Form-critical analysis of liturgy has been to Zunz's philology what the Scandinavian school of biblical scholarship was to the documentarists who preceded them. In both cases their conception of antiquity and its cultural forms denies the very assumptions underlying the work of their predecessors. They maintain that the liturgy was long circulated in oral form; thus there is no single *Urtext* for which to search. "From all our studies," declared Heinemann, "it emerges very clearly that the very supposition of one single original form . . . is without foundation."[5]

So Heinemann posited an alternative presupposition: not one but many alternative texts used interchangeably in early worship. The authoritative role of the tannaim was now limited to the selection and determination of a progression of themes to constitute the official worship service. Individual worshippers expressed these themes differently, each in his own way.

This would constitute a remarkable degree of liturgical fluidity, and how it was eventually curtailed is a genuine problem from Heinemann's perspective, but Heinemann stopped short of confronting it. He recognized that its ultimate occurrence postdated the literary evidence available in the Babylonian Talmud. It was, therefore, beyond the parameters he had set for his own study, which was, after all, prayer in the time of the tannaim and the amoraim. But he did state that the process had occurred, and, significantly, that it was typical of Babylonia, not of Palestine.

One should not, however, carry the form-critical critique too far. The tannaitic achievement included at least the successful normalization of the most basic liturgical themes, and probably—though the extent is hard to determine—some formal requirements of blessing structure to which individual blessing texts complied. The very genre of worship response which we call the blessing—as opposed to, say, the psalms, or the ad hoc biblical prayers of Hannah or Solomon—is the product of the early rabbinic era, though we may be unable to isolate the particular time within that era when each individual rule regarding this genre was conceived. The tannaim spoke regularly, albeit without unanimity, about short and long blessings, eulogies (or *chatimot*), and so on. So at least the cultural forms of standard rabbinic worship and the vocabulary for discussing and developing them were largely determined by the year 200.

There was also conceived by then the complex of institutions and professional roles which we identify with rabbinic worship patterns: the synagogue as the locus of the daily fixed public prayer; specialized conceptualizations, such as the *sheliach tsibbur* (lit. the congregation's agent or messenger; i.e., the prayer leader, at least for the *tefillah*); *'over lifnei hatevah* (lit. to pass before the ark; i.e., to lead the *tefillah*); *pores 'al shema'* (to lead the *shema'*); and so on. So by the end of the tannaitic period, a relatively fixed synagogue service had been achieved, in the sense that certain persons attended certain institutions at certain times to recite certain prayers.

The essential question is how determined these prayers yet were, and here an objective reading of the tannaitic and amoraic literature seems to support the assumption that within broad thematic guidelines, creative interpretation was common. It was probably less so as time went on, but even late literary strata testify to no dearth of innovation. The Babylonian Talmud lists not one but several private prayers which the rabbis said after their main prayer, the *tefillah* (*Ber.* 16b–17a). There are not one but many confessions for Yom Kippur (*Yoma* 87b). Several times Rav Papa (4th cent.) notes the variety of customs regarding a particular prayer and suggests that no one is more important than another, so that we should say all variants or choose any we like (*Sotah* 40a, *Ber.* 60b). Rabbis of the second and third centuries know of something called the *birkat hashir* (Blessing of Song), but cannot decide exactly what it is. They offer several alternative texts, and the Talmud accepts them all as equally acceptable. Even the *yotser*, the first blessing preceding the *shema'*, is by no means a fixed entity by amoraic times, for the amoraim discuss the possibility of people confusing the evening and morning renditions, and accept such "error" as satisfactory (*Ber.* 12a).

One finds not only differences of opinion among the rabbis themselves, but even regional customs, now quite universal, of which amoraic masters profess absolute ignorance. In one case (*Ta'an.* 28b) Rav is amazed at the Babylonian practice of reciting only a partial *hallel* (Pss. 113–18) on certain festivals; in another the notable Rav Ashi himself is invited to say the *kiddusha' rabbah* (lit. great *kiddush*) while he is visiting a certain community away from the academy, and he has no idea what the townsfolk are talking about (*Pes.* 106a).

So there is justification for conceding not only that the Talmud delineates no all-inclusive set of prescribed wording for prayers but even that it lacks evidence of the logically prior step: rabbinic consensus on what prayers there are for which common words might be sought. Beyond a common vocabulary that signifies a generally accepted framework in which licit worship might proceed, the rabbis could come to little agreement on what was proper and what not. This is a liturgical license which modern standards might even brand as chaotic. The majority of rabbinic debates end in no clear decision at all, and there is no evidence to indicate that even those debates which are resolved had any success in converting popular practice one way or another.

But what a different picture we get in the next stratum of Jewish literature. The amoraic, or talmudic, period is traditionally said to terminate around the beginning of the sixth century. Eventually there develops another Jewish society in the same Babylonian locale, but with different social forms, and a correspondingly unique political and economic infrastructure. The new period is known as the geonic age, its name being taken from the title of the chief religious leader in Babylonia, the gaon. Exactly when this new epoch dawned is open to question, some scholars postulating a beginning as early as 589, and others arguing a date as much as one hundred years later. Both schools of thought rely on medieval historiographical evidence, which, however, varies, so that scholars have had to estimate the degree to which they wish to side with one or the other historical tradition. The interim period, however long it may have endured, has been known as the saboraic period, but it is difficult to define with any precision who or what that period entailed. The first reliable data, therefore, derive from the geonim, and are mostly in the form of what are known as responsa, geonic answers to questions received from Jews in far-off communities.

Now, even if one assumes an early dating for the beginning of the geonic period, there is still no geonic literature dealing with prayer until quite late. The first gaon to be regularly represented in the formation of responsa is Yehudai Gaon (757–761), the head of an academy situated in the center of learning at Sura. Yehudai's gaonate coincided with the rise of the Abbasid Caliphate and the removal of the Moslem capital from Damascus to the new city of Baghdad. As the center of Abbasid culture now shifted to Babylonia, geonic cultural development increased dramatically. So from Yehudai on, there are abundant responsa demanding some liturgical practices and prohibiting others. Since these geonic communications, unlike previous talmudic parallels, tend to state the law clearly and decisively, admitting no variation, and since they assume a stance of absolute knowledge regarding the divine mandate, we can speak of these responsa as forming the first step in the geonic codification of the service. We shall see that Natronai Gaon (853–857), especially, seems to have been concerned about liturgical disorder, and that it was his successor, Amram Gaon (857–871), who carried the pursuit of conformity to its logical conclusion by compiling the first prayer book known to us. Roughly half a century later, Saadiah Gaon (928–942) issued his own order of prayers, and it is likely that Hai Gaon (998–1038), too, wrote a prayer book. The geonic period, then, produced a sustained effort to harness liturgical novelty by introducing a standard rite.

That this effort really was one of canonization is clear from a comparison of the dictionary definition of the word with the tenor of the geonic communications. One of the many acceptable definitions of *canonization* is "to sanction or ratify by, or as if by, ecclesiastical authority."[6] That the geonim were in fact sanctioning or ratifying the liturgy is abundantly clear. The questioners usually ask whether a given practice is admissible or not, and the responsa either assent to it or argue against it. The geonic perspective, moreover, is that of "ecclesiastical authority," if by the term we mean people claiming the right to speak for the entire population of the faithful, in this case, the Jewish people wherever they may happen to live and pray. Scholars of Judaica have often been hesitant to use the word *canonization*. But the canonization of, say, the Old or New Testament, by synagogue or church, is not functionally different from what we are studying here: the attempt by religious authorities—in our case the geonim—to certify certain expressions of religious life as divinely mandated, and to rule out others as errors.

Certainly there did develop a canonized liturgy just as there was a canonized Scripture. In both cases, certain prayers or readings were deliberately omitted even though their existence was known and even treated as worthy of inclusion by some parties. Indeed, the process in both cases amounts to a calculated decision regarding which of the available options to sanction as official doctrine. As all scholars have made clear, current Jewish rites are largely dependent on geonic prototypes, so we would have to say that the attempt to provide a canonized liturgy was ultimately successful. Only ultimately, however. Indeed, this study is devoted to determining the extent to which success was won within the time confines of the geonic age.

My goal, then, was to study the geonic attempt at liturgical standardization. Given the variety of communications from rabbinic leaders in Babylonian academies, dating from the middle of the eighth to the eleventh century, my intention was to determine the extent to which any or all of them reveal an intention of codifying prayer; to compare and explain any discrepancies between geonic opinions, and, finally, to diagram the process by which codification proceeded and the success which it had at the time. Eventually that process became clear. Before describing it, however, a word should be said about the methodology on which my study's validity depends.

Methodologically it was desirable to introduce some objective criterion by which to measure the degree to which codification was or was not a desideratum at any given time in the geonic period. Such a criterion should also help us to isolate the particular historical circumstances which made codification seem desirable. Since the very concept of canonization presupposes the selection of "satisfactory" liturgical formulas out of the great range of alternatives available, and the branding of certain other, competing formulas as unacceptable if not actually heretical, one particular criterion was quick to recommend itself. Sifting through all the known liturgical responsa, I extracted only those in which a gaon cites liturgical formulas disapprovingly. Such formulas were presumed to represent liturgical variants in geonic times, some relatively new, others of ancient vintage, but all used by one group or another in the Jewish world of that era.

The next step was the determination of the group or groups which used the responses in question, and against whom the geonic polemic must, either directly or indirectly, have been intended. To this end I relied on chronologically parallel but nongeonic sources, which apparently emanated from groups that were not in the geonic orbit of influence. The first such group to come to mind, though not necessarily the most significant, is the Karaites, who had definitely become a schismatic element in the period in question. Fortunately the presumed founder of the sect, Anan ben David (8th cent.), left us with his own work, *Sefer Hamitsvot*, which provides some idea of his liturgical practice. The same is true of other, later, Karaite authorities. I also consulted the ancient Palestinian service so far as it is known to us from published genizah documents. These, along with reports in classical sources regarding differences in custom between Palestine and Babylonia, made up an adequate sampling of Palestinian rabbinic rather than Babylonian rabbinic customs. Palestine did, after all, represent the other major liturgical stream of influence within the orthodox Rabbanite world of the time, and it was not inconceivable that the official representatives of the Babylonian rite were canonizing their own ritual in direct opposition to that other traditional claimant to Jewish authority. Thus, each liturgical response condemned by a gaon as noncanonical was compared with contemporary usage by these two other rival groups: Palestinian Rabbanism and Karaism. The degree to which this evidence proved conclusive will be discussed as each individual problem is encountered.

It might be objected that the canonization of the Babylonian synagogue service had as its object groups other than Jews—that a polemic was intended against Moslems, perhaps, or Christians. One would therefore have to include samples of Moslem and Christian prayer in the sampling of possible adversaries who prompted the fixing of Jewish liturgy. That is a possibility, certainly, and other researchers may carry on where this study leaves off, by making comparisons across religious lines. But one would assume that the major polemical thrust of any group's leaders is first and foremost against serious rivals for authority within the same group, not against foreign religious traditions which had long been seen as distinctly separate and different. The history of Christianity, for example, is replete with evidence that the many attempts to establish orthodox doctrine and practice had as their objects of concern not Jews or Moslems but precisely those subgroups within the church itself who offered alternative and potentially acceptable interpretations of Christianity. In the early days, Judaism and paganism in their several shades were potential rivals of Christianity, so one may find them relevant to canonization considerations. But after the church emerges as a clearly distinctive religious tradition, it is rivalry within the church itself which evokes charges of heresy.

Thus one would expect geonic concerns with proper Jewish behavior to reflect similar splits in the Jewish community. Though the general fact that the whole drama was being acted out in a Moslem world of a certain character must be borne in mind, we should not be intent on looking for objects of geonic ire in the non-Jewish world. Rather, we should proceed as we would with any other religious culture in the throes of defining orthodoxy, assuming those aspects of culture which are deliberately declared noncanonical by the authorities to be potential Jewish alternatives representing a group claiming to be Jewishly authoritative. Thus the steps in the canonization process are directly related to the institution of the gaonate, the extent to which it encountered rivals, and who those rivals were.

One more preliminary caveat is the reminder that we are discussing a time period of roughly 280 years: from Yehudai's advent to the gaonate in 757, the beginning of the period for which sufficient evidence for this study can be found, to 1038, the date of Hai Gaon's death. The historical changes within this period are considerable: the consolidation of the new Abbasid Caliphate in Baghdad, revolts by rival dynastic claimants like the Tulunides and the Fatimids, the birth and growth of Karaism, the changing fortunes of Palestinian Jewry, the growth of young Jewish centers in Europe and North Africa, the rise and fall of the gaonate itself—all these are hallmarks of the centuries in question. The responsa which discuss the potential canonicity of a given liturgical form fall within very different eras and represent the particular pressures generated by the specific period which evoked them. So the opinions expressed in the responsa, even regarding the same issue, are not homogeneous either in content or in emotive quality.

It is very important to realize, then, that the geonic age need not, indeed should not, be viewed as an unchanging epoch. The degree to which the authority of the geonim was accepted altered with the times, as did the specific groups against whom the geonim had to contend in their effort to achieve liturgical consensus. In sum, the evidence in the chapters that follow reveals a trifold division of the geonic period, with each of the three sub-periods displaying its own typical attitude toward canonization.

The first period extends from the middle of the eighth century to some time late in the ninth. This was the period in which the geonim attempted to consolidate their authority. Inheriting the liturgical freedom characteristic of the amoraic age, they narrowed the limits of acceptability, codifying Babylonian practice and trying to impose it elsewhere. Here, their major rival was Palestinian custom, which, if anything, was even freer than what the Babylonian had been, and was entrenched in various places as both long-standing and ideologically rooted in ancient Palestinian sources. Thus, for over a hundred years we find responsa attacking Palestinian liturgical options in characteristically harsh language while defending staunchly what was emerging as the typical Babylonian practice in the geonic academies.

By the tenth century, however, a change was occurring. As we enter the second period, we find a gaon, Saadiah, whose background was, in part, Palestinian. His liturgical polemic is directed not against Palestinians but against the Karaites, whose denial of rabbinic Judaism posed a threat to Rabbanites in both Palestine and Babylonia. But Saadiah's attack on this schismatic group was at the same time a defense of rabbinic worship mores, so his responsa, and his prayer book, are a demonstration of the rationality, the logic, and the general propriety of rabbinic liturgy. Saadiah freely mixes Palestinian prayers that would have been anathema to his predecessors in period 1. But he becomes most exercised over lapses in grammar, sloppiness in poetry or form, and, in general, any usage that contravenes the norms typical of the Moslem aesthetic which marked his day.

Period 3, finally, comprises the late tenth and early eleventh centuries. Though anti-Karaism is still a bias, a more overriding concern is the sorry state into which the gaonate has fallen. By now local Jewish centers have arisen throughout the world, each independently pursuing its own pulsating life while ignoring the one-time titular heads, the geonim. So the responsa of period 3 address themselves to reestablishing at least the theoretical authority of the Babylonian leaders. In so doing, the geonim of this period abandon all pretense of imposing their own liturgical practice on others. Satisfied with being consulted, and, in the process, economically supported, by the rising young Jewish communities elsewhere, they adopt a lenient stance toward liturgical diversity, liberally accepting differences in custom whenever possible.

Yet when all three periods are over, genuine canonization of liturgical practice has occurred. The geonim of period 1 clearly demarcated certain rules, prayers, and practices which, to all intents and purposes, comprised a Babylonian rite. Period 2 had little effect in changing it; and period 3, if only through the vast number of responsa generated by its liberal stance, made available great amounts of data regarding the Babylonian way of worship to far-flung Jewish communities which accepted this knowledge with reverence, and used it as a basis for their own worship.

1: The Passover *Haggadah*

THE PASSOVER HAGGADAH MAY SEEM A STRANGE PLACE TO BEGIN. IT IS THE daily liturgy, after all, which forms the nucleus for all the alterations and expansions which characterize the Sabbath and holiday prayers. We could have begun there and proceeded through Sabbaths and festivals, concluding with the liturgy for nonsynagogue settings: life-cycle, Grace after meals, and the Passover *haggadah*.

But for a variety of reasons, it is advisable to begin with the *haggadah*. For one thing, the *haggadah* generated a particularly extensive debate, so we have extant a relatively large and representative selection of geonic comment relating to it. This rich reservoir of responsa has been augmented by a comparable abundance of genizah material and considerable scholarly discussion. Moreover, the issues underlying the debate on the *haggadah* seem to have loomed very large, the arguments becoming exceptionally vitriolic. So the various geonim can here be seen at their starkest extremes. More than any other liturgical unit, the *haggadah* and its attendant debate represents a microcosm of the geonic contribution to liturgical fixity. Though the entire picture will emerge only after our whole study has been completed, the general conclusions will be evident from some observations on the *haggadah* alone.

Unfortunately, a veritable labyrinth of data must be sorted out, bit by bit, before the picture becomes clear. We shall move back and forth from one gaon to another, in and out of different controversial prayers and customs. But the picture is there, even if it does demand careful development. We shall see Saadiah (d. 942) and Hai (d. 1038) debating a heretical addition to the *kiddush*; Natronai (d. 858) and Amram (d. 871) apparently excoriating the Karaites for their *haggadah*; and authorities from Yehudai (d. 761) to Amram arguing over the benediction for washing one's hands at the conclusion of the *seder*. But the specifics merge harmoniously into a congruent image of three different approaches to liturgical fixity. Each one dominated geonic policy for a time, so each represents a separate period within the geonic age.

We begin with Saadiah. Saadiah Gaon was a particularly prolific, influential, and controversial personality. A native of Egypt who resided for a time in Palestine, he eventually emerged as the first non-native Babylonian to

10

occupy the gaonate at the most illustrious academy in Sura. Saadiah had already proved his mettle as a polemicist by successfully defending the Babylonian prerogative to set the yearly calendar against rival Palestinian claims to the contrary. As gaon he was to put his argumentative talents to use against the Karaites, whose denial of the oral law threatened the very validity of the geonic mandate, and against the exilarch, the lay Jewish representative to the Baghdad caliph. Throughout his tumultuous career, Saadiah wrote avidly, composing legal decisions, poetry, philosophy, and a grammar.[1] He also wrote a prayer book.

The history of Saadiah's prayer book is almost as bizarre as its author's life is colorful.[2] Though known and cited regularly by medieval rabbinic authorities, only one relatively complete manuscript has survived. In 1693 it was donated to the Bodleian library; there it lay unrecognized until 1851, when the famed bibliographer Moritz Steinschneider discovered its contents. Still, no significant monograph appeared on it until 1904. Its author, Jonah Bondi, hoped to publish the prayer book, but died before he could do so. The three scholars who eventually did edit the volume saw their effort delayed by almost a quarter of a century due to the political barriers of World War Two and the premature deaths of would-be collaborators. So Saadiah's work was not actually printed until 1941—and even then significant parts were missing. The main corpus has been supplemented by later genizah discoveries,[3] though we still lack sections, including part of the introduction.

But what we do have of the introduction includes Saadiah's avowed purpose in composing his prayer book: the correction of a ubiquitous state of liturgical sloppiness. In contrast to the many improprieties and seeming neglect which he saw as marking the actual worship of his time, Saadiah postulated an original and, therefore, pure liturgical corpus of prayers predating the Roman destruction of the Temple (70 C.E.). Saadiah would restore Jewish worship to this pristine state. He would identify and proscribe all formularies which diverged from the original enough to confound the purpose for which the prayer had been intended in the first place. That, at least, is Saadiah's claim.[4]

But Saadiah went further than that. He did not limit his objections to prayers whose present form invalidated their presumed original purpose. A survey of his prayer book reveals three distinct criteria regularly employed in the determination of whether a prayer should be included or omitted from Saadiah's official liturgy.[5] First, he rejected any modification in the prayers which would result in "injury to the formal structure of the blessing—its opening with *shem* [i.e., the name of God], and *malkhut* [i.e., reference to His kingdom], and its concluding with *shem*—or to the formal framework created by the combination of these blessings."[6] Secondly, he opposed any alteration which might "change the intent of the blessing itself and transfer it to another ideational realm."[7] Finally, he looked askance at the use of "any blessing not mentioned in the Talmud."[8] To be sure, realistic compromises were necessary,[9] but in general Saadiah wielded these criteria with careful precision.

Now, one of the prayers to which Saadiah objects strenuously is a particular version of the Passover *kiddush*, the introductory reading for the *seder* ritual. He explains his opposition to the formulary in his accompanying comment *'fsdth 'lrsm*, explaining, "There are many of our co-religionists... who say 'who created new wine' [*yein 'asis*] in [the blessing] 'who creates the fruit of the vine,' thus making it a long blessing, its eulogy being, 'Blessed art Thou, O Lord, sole exalted king, who creates the fruit of the vine.' It is forbidden to say this, and those who do say it *'fsdth 'lrsm*."[10]

The Arabic phrase *'fsdth 'lrsm* certainly represents Saadiah's objection to the extended *kiddush*, but unfortunately, scholars have not concurred on what he meant by the charge. Bondi, who first described *Siddur Saadiah*, translated the clause as "verderbe sie die Vorschrift," while Joel, who translated the Arabic of the standard critical edition, used the Hebrew phrase *bitel 'et haseder hakavu'a*, "nullifies the established order." A third alternative has been proposed by Naphtali Wieder, who understands Saadiah to be concerned that such a worshipper *meshaneh mimatbea' shekave'u chakhamim*, "changes the [blessing] structure which the sages established."[11] Wieder's suggestion would accord with Saadiah's charge that the addition converts a short blessing into a long one, and is fully in keeping with Saadiah's general opposition to alterations in blessing structure, one of the three general criteria postulated by Heinemann. So on the face of it, Saadiah, who permitted deviations elsewhere, would not go along with a common custom here, for it would have converted a technically short blessing into a long one, and he favored the retention of the traditional rules regarding blessing structure.

On the other hand, the very fact that he does allow alterations elsewhere suggests that other motives may have been involved here. We will understand them better if we first consider a parallel denunciation of this *kiddush* formula issued by another gaon of considerable fame, Hai bar Sherira (998–1038).

Reference was made above to the internecine rivalry between Saadiah and the exilarch, David ben Zakkai. Their acrimonious dispute resulted in no immediate defeat for Saadiah. After a brief period in which he was forced to live as a excommunicant—a gaon in exile, so to speak—he was reinstated in Sura, where he outlived his rival by two years, but for two years only, and Sura's greatness died with Saadiah. The renowned academy limped along until 944, under valiant efforts to keep the gaonate alive there, but then it was closed, and when it reopened forty-four years later, it was but a shell of its former self.

In the interim, the focus of geonic authority shifted to a rival academy, Pumbedita, an institution which paralleled Sura in the enjoyment of claims to antiquity. Despite interruptions occasioned by social and political unrest,

Pumbeditans traced an ongoing heritage of study back to the end of the third century.[12] The extent of its influence in the early geonic period is unknown but was probably quite limited. By the ninth century, however, it achieved parity with Sura, and now both Sura and Pumbedita could boast of having a gaon of international reputation who sent responsa to far-flung communities. So though Sura was closed in 944, the gaonate remained, in the person of the Pumbeditan chief authority, and despite unstable conditions there for the next two decades, Pumbedita emerged in 968 with perhaps the strongest leadership of the entire geonic period, Sherira Gaon (968–998) and his son, Hai (998–1038). Sherira and Hai's outstanding achievement in restoring the luster of the gaonate, as well as the circumstances which necessitated their frenetic activity, will prove to be most significant as we later attempt to explain their attitude to liturgical canonization. For the time being, however, we need merely note that their literary output was prodigious, and that they bequeathed to posterity a vast trove of responsa on all subjects, including those of interest to us.

We have extant two versions of Hai's responsum on the *yein 'asis* formula of the *kiddush*. The first (A) merely notes the author's awareness of the custom, and identifies it with certain specific communities.[13] Hai tells us in the other one (B), however, that

> Rabbinic custom is to recite certain blessings concisely. The custom of outsiders [*minhaga' lebara'ei*] is to expand them. But since they enjoy saying the lengthy form, it is permissible to expand the opening lines. For example, in the case of "who creates new wine which makes God and humanity happy."[14]

From (A) alone, we would assume our blessing to be a mere localism of certain communities. But (B) introduces a judgmental term for the people who say it: they are *bara'ei*, a term which implies that they were, at the very least, outsiders. Hai might have meant that they were geographically remote, but if so he should have used the word again elsewhere when he discusses other customs of such places, and he does not. Moreover, the places in question, though not cities rivaling Baghdad or Jerusalem in consequence, are not tiny villages either. So Hai probably meant that they were outside the normative rabbinic tradition as he understood it. They were beyond the pale, even sectarians, perhaps. Indeed, Judah ben Barzillai of Barcelona, writing roughly one hundred years after Hai, was utterly amazed at Hai's leniency toward these *bara'ei*. "I am absolutely amazed at this responsum," he declared, "which perhaps should not even be attributed to Hai. . . . He himself calls them *bara'ei*. . . . there may be a scribal error."[15] Modern scholars concur that *bara'ei* means "sectarians." Ginzberg says that their custom constituted a transgression of rabbinical law, and Lewin says categorically that *bara'ei* means *chitsonim*, "sectarians."[16] How are we to understand such incredible openness on Hai's part? Could a gaon really acknowledge the fact that a custom was heretical yet refuse to indict it?

Since Hai's responsum is phrased as a legal argument, it has been customary to explore Hai's thinking in terms of the legal issues involved. Thus, for example, it has been said that Hai could allow this particular structural alteration since it included the necessary concluding clause, the *chatimah*, or eulogy, "who creates the fruit of the vine," and therefore, technically speaking, constituted no legal alteration at all;[17] alternatively, that it was a technical violation, but that a precedent for its recitation could be found in the Babylonian Talmud's account of Rav Ashi's innovative recital of the Saturday morning *kiddush*, known as *kiddusha' rabbah*.[18]

There is, however, a serious problem in taking these legal arguments at their face value. That was precisely the approach which led Judah ben Barzillai to question the source of the responsum. How, he reasoned, could Hai, who opposed poetic insertions elsewhere, have countenanced this one? To which we may add the opposite question regarding Saadiah: How could Saadiah, who allowed poetic insertions elsewhere, have prohibited this one? Moreover, the legal bases are surely forced. In the first case, the genizah evidence indicates that the requisite three words of the traditional eulogy— *borei' peri hagafen*—were really not included; this sectarian wording actually replaced the standard eulogy, "who creates the fruit of the vine."[19] And in the second case, it is only Hai's imagination which conceives of Rav Ashi as having said these particular words. The Talmud's account cites no wording at all. Moreover, Hai was arguing from the case of the morning *kiddusha' rabbah* to the evening *kiddush*, two entities which are not necessarily identical. True, he was intent on claiming their equivalence, and he understood Rav Ashi's evident expansion of one prayer to provide grounds for enlarging upon another. But the real question is why he wanted to reason thus, particularly since he knew the latter-day practice to be sectarian, and therefore, by definition, beyond comparison with whatever it was that the leading amora, Rav Ashi, had done six hundred years earlier.

Surely the real reason is one generally passed over as secondary in the literature on the subject. Both Ginzberg and Wieder note, while discussing the legality of the issue, that the sectarian custom shows great similarity to a Karaite formula:

> Blessed is our God, King of the universe, who created the tree of vines, and, from its wine, made the heart of humanity rejoice; as it is written, [Ps. 104:15], "Wine makes mankind's heart happy, making the face brighter than oil."[20]

Now we understand why Saadiah's openness to liturgical poetic expansion elsewhere could not apply here. The Karaites, though tracing their origin to the middle of the eighth century, did not emerge as a force to reckon with until Saadiah's day. By the latter half of the ninth century, they had firmly established communities in Palestine, and much of Saadiah's geonic activity was directed at polemicizing against the Karaite heresy, which denied the authority of the oral law as well as its spokesmen, the geonim, and their Rabbanite counterparts elsewhere in the world. Though by the thirteenth century the purity of the Karaite liturgy was compromised to include much Rabbanite material, in Saadiah's day the group's liturgy was patterned carefully after biblical paradigm, while Pharisaic and later rabbinic practice was systematically eschewed.

But relations were rarely as acerbic between the followers of the two groups as between leaders. Despite clear demarcations in custom, there were several areas in which the two rival traditions might find their practices overlapping. Where the custom existed to embellish a blessing with poetry drawn from biblical prototypes, both Rabbanites and Karaites could well have recited blessings which were almost indistinguishable from one another. That seems to be the case here. Hai testifies to the fact that it is heretical, yet common among people whom he regards as Jews, not Karaites, even if misguided.

So we see a major difference between our two respondents in the attitude they take to the blessing. Saadiah, who dedicated much of his life to fighting the growth of Karaism, had no option but to rail against a structural alteration which transformed a rabbinic staple into a Karaite heresy. Hai, on the other hand, though, as we shall see, by no means impervious to Karaism, balanced his criticism with the recognition that this was not, strictly speaking, a "Karaite" formula, said, that is, *only* by Karaites. It was common, and people liked it. To censure it would have been to condemn a local custom of thousands of Jews whose forebears may well have been using such a blessing hundreds of years before the Karaites adopted a form similar to it. Hai permitted *yein ʿasis* because, as he himself said, people liked it.

We are now in a position to state some critical generalizations which will be reinforced again and again by subsequent examples in this study. First, the legal arguments the geonim advance are rarely sufficient to explain the stand they take. As with jurists in any system of law, the geonim come to their questions with ready propensities to interpret matters leniently or stringently, and to emphasize some principles at the expense of others. Opposition to Karaism was such a propensity. It is a very important key—though, as we shall see, not the most important one—to an understanding of Saadiah's liturgical rulings. With Hai, however, a more important consideration was the relative popularity of the custom in question. Why he should have cared so much to validate what the people liked is something we shall have to examine later, but his desire to do so is, at least in this case, beyond dispute. We see, then, a major shift in emphasis from Saadiah to Hai, exemplifying our second general observation: the principles which motivated the geonim varied from gaon to gaon. Yet they were independent of personal caprice. Both Saadiah and Hai represent their ages rather than the whims of an individual.

We have, therefore, caught a glimpse of the deciding factors for two

geonic periods rather than two individual geonim. Saadiah and Hai personify
these two periods, which crystallize in the work of these two outstanding
rabbinic leaders. There is also a third period, antedating the other two. It
culminates in the person of Amram bar Sheshna, perhaps the most famous
gaon, liturgically speaking, who occupied the Suran gaonate from 858 to 871.
He figures prominently in what is perhaps the most famous of all the liturgical
disputes in the geonic records. It is that dispute to which we must now turn.

Amram Gaon was the author of our first known comprehensive prayer book,
sent in the form of a responsum to Jews in northern Spain. It was compiled
precisely at the time that nascent Jewish communities were beginning to
blossom throughout Western Europe, and it was accepted readily as an authoritative guide for their liturgical conduct. Though Amram purports to be
the chief author of the prayer manual, he quotes several of his geonic predecessors with regularity, so that his *Seder Rav Amram* is a fine compendium of
geonic opinion generally, from the advent of Yehudai Gaon (757–761) until
Amram himself (858–871).

One of the geonic responsa which Amram cites is by his predecessor in
office, Natronai (853–858). It concerns the celebration of a variant Passover
service on which Natronai had heaped violent condemnation. The salient
features of this responsum are worth careful scrutiny for what they tell us
regarding the earliest geonic liturgical period, that represented particularly by
Amram.

> Rav Natronai said there are people who recite "who sanctified Israel" in
> the Passover *kiddush*, and then, when they finish "Why is this night
> different," say neither "We were slaves to Pharoah in Egypt" nor "In the
> beginning our ancestors were idolaters," but instead say from "Joshua
> spoke to all the people" to "Jacob and his sons went down to Egypt"; and
> then from "Blessed be He who keeps His promise to Israel" until "Go
> and learn . . ." Then they recite the entire passage, "A wandering Ara-
> mean was my father," saying the biblical verses as they stand without
> the accompanying *midrash*. Then they say "Rabban Gamaliel . . ." and
> "who redeemed us," and the *hallel*. This is very astonishing! Not only is
> it superfluous to say of one who follows this custom that he does not
> fulfill his religious obligation, but anyone who does so is a heretic of
> divisive spirit, who denies the words of the sages and deprecates the
> words of Mishnah and Talmud. All congregations are obliged to ex-
> communicate such a person, setting him apart from the community of
> Israel. . . . These people are heretics and scoffers who despise the words
> of the sages. They are the disciples of Anan—may his name rot—
> . . . who said to all those who went astray, whoring after him, "Abandon
> the dicta of the Mishnah and the Talmud, and I will make my own
> Talmud for you." They still persist in their error, and have become an
> independent sect. He [Anan] established an evil and iniquitous Talmud

of his own. Our colleague, Elazar Alluf from Spain, saw his book of lies, which they call *Sefer Hamitsvot* [*Book of Commandments,* and] how many errors it contains! So now it is necessary to excommunicate them, that they may not pray with Israel in the synagogue; and to set them apart until they return to the good, accepting the obligations to conduct themselves according to the custom of the two academies [Sura and Pumbedita, the two seats of the Babylonian gaonate], for all those who do not follow our practice are derelict in their duty. [21]

The deviations in this nonconformist *seder* are clearly given in our source. They include an expansion of the *kiddush,* the elimination of some rabbinic material normally used to introduce the midrashic core of the *haggadah*'s exposition, and the exclusion of that *midrash* itself, with, however, the Deuteronomy passage on which it is based being recited without homiletical interpretation. It is also clear that Natronai reacted very differently to this alteration in custom than did Hai in the responsum we just looked at. For Natronai, too, the issue was one of outright heresy. He even knows the group of heretics behind the practice, "the disciples of Anan—may his name rot—who . . . have become an independent sect." Natronai ruled not only that the practice was wrong, but that the group responsible should be excommunicated.

In favor of Natronai's analysis of the situation was the nature of the material omitted by the sectarians: it is all rabbinic. The celebrants skip over the two amoraic interpretations of degradation and begin their *haggadah* exposition with the biblical citation, Joshua 24:2; and they continue with Deuteronomy 26, again deleting the rabbinic elements surrounding it. Now, Natronai did not know very much about the Karaites, his only information coming by way of a second-hand report from a certain Elazar, a recent immigrant from Spain, who had reached the prestigious scholarly rank of Alluf in Sura. [22] He had shared his knowledge of the sect with the gaon, but the gaon gives no indication that he himself had ever met a Karaite or even perused Anan's *Sefer Hamitsvot.* Yet he knew enough to know that they denied the validity of rabbinic legislation, and, with no other real facts at his disposal, he mistakenly attributed this *haggadah* to them.

That his assumption was in fact mistaken is obvious from a second glance at the responsum. No Karaite would have recited the *ge'ulah* (the Blessing of Redemption) and the explanation of the Passover symbols. Both of these selections are tannaitic, not biblical, and the latter even carries the name of Rabban Gamaliel [II], a most outstanding tanna indeed. Natronai's incorrect identification has been recognized almost unanimously by modern scholarship. [23] So we may well look elsewhere for the source of the *haggadah.*

The critical realization for us is the recognition that these *seder* celebrants were by no means unrabbinic. They were at most "outsiders" in the same sense as the people Hai wrote about. Local deviation from geonic mandate was only as heretical as the individual geonim wished to see it. Everything depended on the degree of homogeneity required. The boundaries between valid and invalid liturgical custom were movable.

The contrary view, of course, is frequently encountered, both within religious traditions themselves, and in scholarly treatises which assume that the way those traditions present reality must correspond to reality. Since classical sources are often written by authorities whose institutional position necessitates their ordering of the religious community's actions according to some kind of rational criteria, they tend to present the religious situation facing them in static rather than changing terms. Everything is viewed from the perspective of a theoretical orthodoxy followed slavishly by an equally theoretical community of the faithful, who are sharply divided from the unfaithful by obvious deviations from the theoretical norm. To judge solely by authoritative sources, therefore, one gets the picture of a model community adhering to a carefully worked out pattern of beliefs and practices, with certain sectarians, numerically few and geographically scattered, operating beyond the bounds of acceptability. There is no middle ground. One is either within the circle of religious authenticity or not.

In fact, however, religious communities have not always been so neatly arranged. The religious community is rarely ever a single unified community, but several communities, who find themselves in accord on enough common issues to be able to identify themselves and each other as belonging to a common tradition and being related in some meaningful way to their "coreligionists" of the present. On any particular issue, though, a given subgroup may be quite independent, and if that issue is not a critical index of the overall group's definition of unity, no one will question its continued existence.

This is particularly true of worship practices in premodern communities where localisms dating back many generations are sanctified through years of use. The classical Jewish scholarship of the philological school (discussed earlier in this book) erred in accepting the authoritative definition of religious reality, and insisted on the existence of a single authoritative text from the very inception of rabbinic institutions. But there was no single normative authority that held sway everywhere; and even though men like Gamaliel II and Judah I must surely be credited with successfully imposing a considerable degree of uniformity, the parameters of orthodoxy still remained sufficiently broad as to include vast alternatives in the practices of many subgroups within the rabbinic Jewish community as a whole.

More than any other single event, it was the discovery of the genizah documents in the 1890s that provided the breakthrough for a full recognition of the liturgical variety in the geonic and pregeonic centuries.[24] At first, the documents unearthed were used to fit into the philological schema which postulated single authoritative and original prayer texts.[25] Since the fragments were of Palestinian provenance, they were presumed to be the originals on which later Babylonian variations were based. Other scholars, however, simply described the various texts as they found them, and eventually, despite certain hallmark phrases which seemed to be common to most of the documents, and could therefore be described as typically Palestinian, it became clearer and clearer that the scope of liturgical expression was even greater than had been assumed. It became correspondingly more difficult to assume a single Palestinian prototype, and instead one was forced to the conclusion that "in Palestine, the process of standardization was never completed."[26] How wrong Natronai was, then, in his perfectly orthodox structuring of Jewish communality into Rabbanites on one hand, all of whom followed geonic precedent and could be granted the imprimatur of propriety, and Karaites on the other, who stood boldly outside the realm of acceptability waiting to be read out of the ranks of the faithful. His own description of the *haggadah* of these "outsiders" indicates that they were not really "outsiders" at all, but simply members of some Rabbanite subgroup who knew the Mishnah and accepted rabbinic oral law, but followed their own age-old custom of celebrating the Passover *seder* according to local dictates.

One of the first significant publications of liturgical documents from the genizah was made by the eminent British scholar Israel Abrahams.[27] He recognized immediately that "some of the abbreviations described by Natronai as Karaitic are clearly of an altogether different character," and that he was in possession of "shorter and older versions of the *haggadah* which did not yet contain many of the elements which, in the Geonic form, constituted characteristic features" of the ritual.[28] (Abrahams's assumption still seems to be, however, that a single orthodox rite grew with time, and that all of his documents that were shorter in form must necessarily have been earlier. The belief that concise prayers evolve into lengthy ones was taken as axiomatic by philological researchers.)[29] Abrahams's find, along with others published subsequently, enables us to determine that the sectarian *haggadah* was really just a Rabbanite variant of Palestinian origin.

Natronai complained that the group in question omitted the amoraic debate on the meaning of *genut*, "degradation," that is, the two paragraphs *ʿavadim hayyinu* ("We were slaves . . .") and *mitechilah* ("Originally, our ancestors were idolaters . . ."). Abrahams's tenth genizah fragment does indeed omit these passages, as does another manuscript published by Goldschmidt, and considered by him to be the most ancient form of the *haggadah* text extant.[30] It is probable that Palestinians customarily omitted these two pieces, since our only known genizah text which has them is Abrahams's number 12.[31] But this fragment is demonstrably Babylonian, though Abrahams does not identify it as such. Throughout the geonic period there was considerable migration back and forth between the Babylonian and Palestinian areas, and settlers used to Babylonian liturgical customs organized synagogues with their own native ritual in areas where the preponderant practice was Palestinian. Abrahams's twelfth fragment derives from such a group. Its version of the Four Questions, for example, follows the Babylonian Talmud's recension of the Mishnah rather than the Palestinian one. All his other fragments carry the ancient Palestinian version, that is, three questions, not four, one asking why our meat must be roasted on Passover eve. Also, the question about dipping asks why we dip twice instead of once. But this fragment asks four questions, exclusive of the question about roasted meat, which is absent; and the question on dipping asks why we dip twice instead of not at all.[32]

Natronai also relates that these heretics say only the biblical verses of *'arami 'oved 'avi* ("My father was a wandering Aramean . . ."), omitting its accompanying *midrash*. This is what sounds most like a Karaitic trait, since Karaite liturgy is marked by an exclusive use of biblical verse, with a correspondingly scrupulous avoidance of rabbinic comment thereon. Moreover, we have no Palestinian fragment which omits the *midrash* entirely. But Goldschmidt's genizah text omits most of it,[33] and we know full well, from the evident variety characteristic of the Palestinian rite generally, that if part of the *midrash* could be omitted in one version, there is no reason to believe that the whole might not be excised elsewhere. Of course, in the absence of an actual text that does in fact omit it, we can only state the likelihood of this omission deriving, along with the rest of the *haggadah* in which it is contained, from Palestinian custom.

We are still left with Natronai's initial objection, the insertion of *'asher kiddesh 'et yisra'el* ("who sanctified Israel") in the *kiddush*. This too is in the Goldschmidt Palestinian fragment.[34]

In sum, we may conclude with Goldschmidt, "There is no doubt that the version which R. Natronai Gaon opposed was based on an early Palestinian custom."[35] And, we may add, he opposed it in particularly vitriolic language, a characteristic which, we shall see, he shared with his illustrious successor, Amram, who willingly incorporated the Natronai responsum into his prayer book. How different these two geonim are from Hai, who could recognize sectarian customs yet accept them because people liked them.

We are almost in a position now to summarize the characteristic features, at least in part, of the three periods into which this study divides the geonic epoch. We have seen Hai, Saadiah, and Natronai/Amram reacting in different ways to liturgical variations. One further source of dispute might be adduced here first, however, since it again indicates the type of harshness associated with the Natronai/Amram period, and suggests that it may go back as far as Yehudai Gaon (757–761). The issue is known technically as *mayim 'acharonim*, the washing of the hands after dinner. In this case, we deal with the custom as part of the *seder* meal.

The practice of washing one's hands after eating is debated at some length in the Babylonian Talmud. Though the actual practice was apparently universal, a disagreement emerged regarding the reason behind it, and consequently whether a benediction was to precede it. Centuries after the amoraic period, opinion was divided on the matter, and authorities in Western Europe were able to cite geonic opinions on either side.

A few of the geonim wrote that one should say a blessing over it, i.e., *'al rechitsat yadayim* [Blessed art Thou . . . who hast commanded us concerning the washing of the hands]. But the author of *Halakhot Gedolot* wrote that it is intended only for human needs [and not as a commandment, which would necessitate a blessing], it being on account of sodomite salt, so no blessing is necessary. Rav Amram wrote similarly, that one should say no blessing over it, neither in the wording of *netilah* nor in the wording of *rechitsah* nor in the wording of *shetifah*. [36]

Now the reasoning of the few geonim who advocated a blessing is not given here, but the majority, who opposed it, substantiated their views by a reference to sodomite salt. For them, the custom of washing was only a medicinal remedy against this salt. Since no religious duty underlay the custom, no benediction was to precede it.

Other than Amram, the identities of the parties to the debate are by no means clear. Those favoring the benediction are anonymous, and possibly not of major significance, or their names would have been preserved. It is hard to imagine a later authority lumping Amram, Saadiah, and Hai together, for example, as "a few geonim." The opposite side of the argument is represented not only by Amram, but by the author of *Halakhot Gedolot*, a major geonic legal composition, and since it is cited with regularity, we might pause for a moment to determine whether, and if so, how, this source should be used by us.

We have already seen the importance of Yehudai Gaon as the man who probably instituted the practice of large-scale responsa. He is also considered by some authorities to have composed a lengthy compendium of law known as *Halakhot Gedolot*. The book is organized so as to follow the order of talmudic tractates, enumerating the relevant commandments as they arise, and discussing geonic opinion regarding them. For years the standard reference version was the 1888 publication of Azriel Hildesheimer, but recently (1972) his grandson, of the same name, began publishing a scientific edition. [37] If we knew for sure that Yehudai had in fact authored this important collection, we would be in a magnificent position to ascertain his opinion of liturgical matters relevant to geonic canonization attempts.

Unfortunately, Yehudai's authorship cannot be assumed. For one thing, there is a great deal of confusion regarding extant recensions of the book; for another, our *Halakhot Gedolot* has been confused with other works cited by medieval authorities, so that it is hard to know for sure exactly what books the various citations are referring to in the first place. Finally, a completely different author has been claimed, a certain Simon Kayyara, whom scholars have placed at different locations and different times. Ginzberg, for example, maintains that "The real author of *Halachot Gedolot* is Rabbi

Jehudai."[38] But Assaf is equally sure that "*Sefer Halakhot Gedolot,* the most important book in the geonic legal literature, was composed by Rabbi Simon Kayyara [who] lived in all probability two generations after Rav Yehudai, so that his date should be set not before 825,"[39] a conclusion with which Hildesheimer (the younger) concurs.[40] In any event, the book, as we have it, is vastly expanded even beyond the time of Kayyara, so that it becomes very difficult to ascertain with any degree of certitude the particular subperiod within the geonic era, let alone the particular geonic author, to whom a given statement in the book should be attributed. Since our interest here is not the geonic epoch as a whole, but the particular periods which compose it, along with the given *Tendenz* of each one, it would be folly to utilize anonymous quotations from *Halakhot Gedolot.* Without other corroboration, there is no reason to believe that these represent the view of Yehudai, and it helps us not a whit to know that they are generally geonic if we do not know specifically which gaon it was who authored them.

Thus, in the case before us, Jacob ben Asher's testimony, stating only that the author of *Halakhot Gedolot* opposed the blessing, is insufficient as a basis for attributing the same opinion to Yehudai Gaon or to anyone else. Such a statement is indeed to be found in *Halakhot Gedolot,* but it is anonymous.[41] On the other hand, the thirteenth-century Italian authority Zedekiah ben Abraham says, in his *Shibbolei Haleket,* "Rav Yehudai Gaon explained that no blessing is required, since it [*mayim 'acharonim*] was instituted only on account of sodomite salt."[42] Here, not only is the gaon explicitly given as Yehudai, but the reasoning of sodomite salt is cited as well. Now it happens that the reasoning, though talmudic, is not given in *Halakhot Gedolot,* at least not in any of the versions collected by Hildesheimer. So Zedekiah did not get his tradition regarding Yehudai from there. If he learned about Yehudai's opposition independently, it may be that Jacob ben Asher did too, but believing that Yehudai was the author of *Halakhot Gedolot,* he cited his information in the name of "the author of *Halakhot Gedolot.*" If that be true, then in this case anyway, Yehudai was of a similar opinion to Amram, whom the *Tur* cites as also opposing the benediction.

Now we have already seen how Amram tended to echo his predecessor, Natronai, including Natronai's responsa regularly in his, that is, Amram's, prayer book. This general commonality of viewpoint is again evident in the case of *mayim 'acharonim.* An independent responsum informs us that Natronai called the practice of saying a blessing over the washing of hands after the meal "an error [*ta'ut*]."[43]

Moreover, Amram himself explains in his prayer book:

> A blessing [over the washing of the hands] is to be said only twice during the Passover *seder.* I hope you are not still practicing the foolishness which the rabbis in your location explained to Rav Sar Shalom Gaon, i.e., "At Passover, we say [three] blessings: '*al netilat yadayim,* '*al*

rechitsat yadayim, and *'al shetifat yadayim,"* . . . to which he responded commanding you regarding this great foolishness. [44]

Not only is Amram consistent here with his opinion recorded in the *Tur*, but he also cites the three blessings in use, using the identical three synonyms for "washing" known to the *Tur*.

In sum, Amram's opposition to *mayim 'acharonim* did not originate with him. His opinion of its "foolishness" goes back to his predecessor, Natronai, and, in fact, to Natronai's predecessor at Sura, Sar Shalom (848–853). And if, as seems probable, Yehudai was really responsible for the citation attributed to him personally in *Shibbolei Haleket* (and to his putative work *Halakhot Gedolot*, reported in the *Tur*), the opinion goes all the way back to Yehudai. We would then see an ongoing similarity in opinion stretching back from Amram to the beginning of a strong gaonate in Sura, that of Yehudai, a period extending from 757 to 871.

And, as in the case of the heretical *haggadah* which Natronai mistakenly assumed to be Karaitic, we have here yet another Palestinian custom, documented plainly by Abrahams's fragments. His seventh text, plainly Palestinian—the three questions follow the Palestinian Talmud's recension, for example—has three washings, with the same wording and the same order of the blessings given by Amram's quotation of Sar Shalom. [45] We have no way of knowing for sure who the "few geonim" were who sided with Palestinian custom here. But we do see that Amram and Natronai are again pitted against it, and that this anti-Palestinian bias was shared by Sar Shalom, and probably even by Yehudai. And we note, too, that the harsh language directed against the heretical *haggadah* is here paralleled by a disdainful reference to the alternative custom as "foolishness."

In sum, though only a fraction of the available evidence has been analyzed, [46] we are already in a position to make some general hypotheses regarding the breakdown of the geonic period into three segments, each with its own characteristic attitude toward liturgical license. The first period probably begins with Yehudai, and continues at least until Amram. Three successive geonim, Sar Shalom, Natronai, and Amram, are all explicitly associated with this position. It is marked by strong language and anti-Palestinian prejudice. By Saadiah, however, a new concern is evident; Saadiah, at least in part, was preoccupied not with Palestinian tradition, much of which he—a Palestinian himself—incorporated into his book, but with Karaite customs. And by Hai's time the focus again shifts, so that Hai is marked by a lenience equally as radical as Amram's intolerance.

Our task now will be to see whether the rest of the evidence bears out this hypothesis, to try to round it out and to see where other geonim stood on the issues, and eventually to explain each period's unique attitude toward the evolving liturgical canon.

2: Daily Liturgy

The *Shema* and Its Blessings

THE CORE OF THE LITURGY, OF COURSE, IS NOT THE HAGGADAH OF A SINGLE holy day, but the standard prayers of the daily service. And within that essential skeleton, two particular rubrics stand out: the *shema* and its accompanying blessings, and the *tefillah*, which follows.

Our current version of the *shema* is composed of three biblical readings (Deut. 6:4–9, Deut. 11:13–21, Num. 15:37–41), recited twice daily. Each recitation is accompanied by two preliminary blessings: the first emphasizes divine creation, particularly of light; the second celebrates God's selection of Israel, and the covenant at Sinai marked by His revelation of the Torah. A third blessing, the *ge'ulah*, follows the *shema* and emphasizes the exodus from Egypt as paradigmatic of God's salvationary work in history. A fourth blessing regarding divine protection is added for the evening recitation.[1] The *shema* as a liturgical unit is referred to by Josephus, and is therefore one of the few prayers which we know definitely to have been common before 70 C.E.[2] The data of the *tefillah* is somewhat harder to arrive at, since much depends on what is meant by the term. Gamaliel II is credited with putting the individual blessings in order sometime around the turn of the second century.[3] Yet insofar as we understand the term *tefillah* as a generic description of a particular form, that is to say, a series of blessings, largely petitionary, following upon the creedal affirmation of the *shema*, we may postulate a period of prior development, a gestation period in a sense, in which different orders of blessings were in circulation. Some scholars see this earlier manifestation of a *tefillah* going back as far as the second or third century B.C.E.[4] In any event, the *shema* and the *tefillah* were sufficently old as to have attracted considerable attention by both tannaim and amoraim, so that the geonim had no dearth of precedent to guide their own deliberations.

For some reason, it was particularly the *shema* that received the most generous treatment by the geonim. In fact, of all the liturgical controversies, it was probably these which generated the greatest emotion. Amram, whose prayer book—as we have already seen—is hardly noteworthy for tactful expression, saves his most vitriolic remarks for certain aspects of the *shema*.

24

And Saadiah, too, is renowned for his unflinching stand against a *shema'* variant.

The latter case regards an interpolation in the first blessing preceding the morning *shema'*, the *yotser*, or "creation" blessing. The phrase in question is, "May a new light shine upon Zion, and may all of us quickly merit its light." It is known technically by its first two Hebrew words, *'or chadash*.[5]

Our earliest source for Saadiah's remarks is in *Seder Rav Amram*, though it is obviously an interpolation there, since Saadiah wrote half a century after Amram died. We are told, in essence, that Saadiah inveighed against the recitation of *'or chadash* in the *yotser* on the grounds that the *yotser* does not refer to the future light of messianic days, while the *'or chadash* does. True, the blessing does feature the word "light" but only insofar as it symbolizes creation, not in any eschatological sense.[6]

> Thus said Rav Saadiah Gaon: Anyone who concludes the blessing by saying "May a new light..." makes a mistake, since the sages established this blessing not over the future light of messianic days, but over the light of the present which shines each day.... It would thus be fitting to silence anyone who mentions it.[7]

A parallel recension of this report, carried also in Amram's prayer book, agrees in every detail, but adds a legal-theological consideration. Saadiah reasons that reciting the insertion is tantamount to invoking God's name without cause (*motzi' shem shamayim levatalah*).[8]

On the other hand, there is a remarkable dissenting opinion attributed to Sherira (968–998). According to him, the "new light" referred to is not the messianic light at all, but simply a general expression signifying nothing in particular (*hazkarah be'alma'*). Moreover, Sherira maintains that Saadiah's strong opposition was never taken seriously either in Pumbedita or in Sura, even during Saadiah's own gaonate; both academies have always said *'or chadash*, Saadiah's view to the contrary notwithstanding. But Sherira concludes that if a worshipper were to omit *'or chadash*, he would lose nothing thereby.[9]

What is this "new light"? We can be sure that Saadiah saw it as a messianic symbol, since even Sherira, who argued that it was not, says so. Saadiah held, he relates, that "The precentor is not permitted to say, 'Let a new light shine upon Zion...' since the sages established this blessing not over the future light of messianic days but over the light which we see each day." In fact it was probably precisely because everyone knew the "new light" to be a messianic symbol that Sherira felt constrained to deny that interpretation. He personally favored including the phrase in the prayers, so he justified his practice by denying the identification on which Saadiah's objection had been grounded.

It is noteworthy that despite his own preference, Sherira displays the same leniency we have seen so far to characterize the approach of what we have called stage 3 of the geonic period, that is, the responsa of both Sherira and Hai. Both academies say *'or chadash*; they have always said it; and they apparently felt so strongly about saying it that Saadiah's minority position was ignored even by his own academy, and in his own lifetime. But Sherira tells his respondent he may do as he wishes.

Given the conflicting geonic intepretations of the "new light," it is not surprising to find still another interpretation of Saadiah's reasoning, this one attributed to Rabbi Eleazar ben Nathan of Mayence, a legal authority and liturgical poet of note, who flourished in the first half of the twelfth century.

> It is our custom and the custom of our ancestors to say, "Let a new light shine upon Zion," though there are some people who do not say it. Similarly, there is a geonic responsum which says not to recite it, the reason being that one should not say a blessing [here] over light of the future. But I, Eleazar, say that our ancestral custom is perfectly correct, since the blessing in question refers to the lights created during the six days of creation, that is, the sun, the moon, and the light which the Holy One, Blessed be He, stored away for the future. That is what is meant by "To the Maker of great lights" [Ps. 136:7]: i.e., the sun, the moon, and the light which He stored away in the future so as to make it shine for the righteous in the time to come, as it is written, "Arise, shine, for your light has come" [Isa. 60:1]. . . . And we pray that we shall be worthy of its light along with the righteous.[10]

So according to Eleazer ben Nathan, the "new light" is indeed eschatological, but it is the light reserved by God at the time of creation for the enjoyment of the righteous in the world to come. Since, however, it was created at the same time as the other luminaries mentioned in the prayer, we are entitled to include it here. Thus, Eleazer ben Nathan's dissenting interpretation displays the same motivation as Sherira's. He too wanted to say *'or chadash*, believing it to be an age-old custom which could not, by definition, defy tradition. The difference was that Sherira was willing to deny the messianic symbolism inherent in the phrase, but Eleazer ben Nathan was not. It was probably that very eschatological connotation that made him so unwilling to stop saying it in the first place. So rather than deny its future implications, he took recourse to a familiar rabbinic notion of the light for the righteous created from the beginning of time, and then reserved for use in the future. What could be a more fitting topic in a prayer designed to praise the Creator of light?

But Eleazer ben Nathan was guilty of misinterpreting Saadiah here. Saadiah certainly believed in the *'or ganuz*, the light stored away from the time of creation—he refers to it explicitly in a separate responsum[11]—but he was not referring to it when he spoke of *'or chadash*. By the "new light" he meant a light for Zion Rebuilt, an altogether different concept, as we can see from a glance at Saadiah's philosophical work, *Beliefs and Opinions*. When the Messiah comes, the Temple will be rebuilt, and "Then the light of God's presence will appear shining upon the Temple with such brilliance that all lights will become faint or dim in comparison with it. . . . Thus Scripture says, 'Arise, shine . . .'"[12] So for Saadiah this new light is not the light stored away from the time of creation, but the light of God's presence; it is not for the righteous after their death, but a source of illumination for the time when the Temple is rebuilt.

But Saadiah's intense opposition to the petition for "new light" now becomes more mysterious than ever. He not only believed in the concept but even included it prominently in his philosophical treatment of the days to come. Why should he have objected so firmly to including the notion in a prayer regarding God, the Creator of light? Elbogen argued, on the basis of his Palestinian fragments, that *'or chadash* was a Babylonian custom, and that Saadiah's opposition was intended as a defense of his native Palestinian practice.[13] But even Elbogen recognized that a minority, at least, of his fragments had *'or chadash* within them, and further research has shown that the diversity of Elbogen's sampling is typical of the genizah as a whole. Palestinians were not united on the matter. The presence or absence of *'or chadash* is simply not one of the characteristics by which one can judge a prayer to be Palestinian or Babylonian.[14]

The most remarkable fact about the whole debate is that just where we should most expect the controversy to be clarified, we are given no information whatever. Saadiah did compose a prayer book, after all; and he included a running editorial commentary to its prayers. Yet that *siddur*, as we have it, is completely silent on the matter. Surely Saadiah would not have omitted his views on *'or chadash* from his own prayer book! But apparently he had.

Only apparently however. In 1943 fourteen hitherto unknown fragments of Saadiah's *siddur* were discovered and published; and contained in them, at long last, was Saadiah's objection to *'or chadash*. His basis for rejection was *yfsd 'lm'ni*, the Arabic equivalent of the Hebrew *mafsid*, a phrase which the editor of the fragments, Naphtali Wieder, recognized as "the stronger of the expressions employed by Saadia." Saadiah took exception to its insertion because it "spoiled the original intention of the prayer," the criterion which we saw Saadiah specify in his own introduction.[15]

The only possible objection to this handy solution was that in the *ge'ulah* (the blessing immediately following the *shema'*), Saadiah included an insertion of the stylistic type which may be called a *kayem* formula. Such formulas, as we shall see later, were petitions for God to "establish" (= Hebrew: *kayem*) the future age of redemption. It was common for Palestinians to interpose such requests in the *geu'lah* benediction since its topic was the laudation of God for bringing salvation. But this too would constitute a petition inserted in a prayer of praise and, structurally, would be the same as the *'or chadash* being inserted in the *yotser*. Both examples would amount to instances of mixing logical categories, praise for the past and petition for the future, or, in Saadiah's philosophical-logical vocabulary, "spoiling the original intention of the prayer." Why, then, would Saadiah adopt the *kayem* petition in one prayer of praise, yet eschew the *'or chadash* phrase in another? Wieder explained:

> The *yotser* was instituted as a thanksgiving for the creation of the sunlight. An insertion in it of a prayer for redemption would constitute a clear change of subject. . . . For the same reason—change of subject—Saadya objects to the insertion of a prayer of deliverance in the eighth benediction of the *'amidah.* . . .
>
> The insertion of such a prayer in the *ge'ulah*, however, cannot be regarded as introducing quite a new subject, as the theme remains the same: redemption of Israel. It is for this reason that Saadya did not oppose the addition of the phrase, *keshem she 'asita nissim* [just as you wrought miracles] . . . in *'al hanissim* [for the miracles], although the latter was intended as thanksgiving for deliverance in the past.
>
> It is only in the eulogy, being the principal part of the benediction, that Saadya insists on the wording expressing precisely and accurately the main theme for which the benediction was originally instituted, namely, the deliverance from Egypt.[16]

To Wieder's exhaustive discussion, a footnote was added by Heinemann.[17] He modified the theory somewhat by holding that Saadiah's subject matter was limited to such topics as were endowed with enormous popular appeal, and might therefore come to overshadow the blessing's primary theme. Surely *'or chadash* was such a topic! How else explain the enormous sentiment behind its inclusion throughout the geonic age and beyond? Recall Sherira's claim that Saadiah was ignored (or disobeyed?) in his own academy, and even in his own lifetime; and later German rabbis arguing at such length to retain their popular custom!

A glance at the genizah documents indicates why such heated emotion should have been invested in so few words. Even those Palestinian texts which do not have *'or chadash* frequently display a short poetic expansion based on Isaiah 40:1, the same biblical promise with which we saw *'or chadash* to be connected by Saadiah himself; or, sometimes, just that prophetic line alone, pointing implicitly to the promise made explicit by the poem or the *'or chadash* petition.[18] All of these interrelated liturgical insertions are of the same messianic nature. They reflect a Palestinian tendency to express messianic hope in the *yotser,* and this Saadiah opposed, since logically it constituted a change of subject, which the common term "light" did not mask. The everyday light of creation was simply not the same as the future light which will shine on Zion. They should not be confused.

Now the overall significance of Saadiah's vehement rejection of the *'or chadash* petition is worth considering. This was, after all, not just a matter of passing fancy; at least neither Saadiah nor his successors considered it so. If Sherira be correct, the inclusion of the phrase was an old practice, antedating Saadiah, in both Sura and Pumbedita. How old is hard to say, since the evidence for *Seder Rav Amram* is equivocal. Scribal negligence with Amram's prayer texts is well known.[19] The manuscripts do not display '*or chadash*, but this could be because of Saadiah's objection which was inserted. The person who inserted it may well have acted on it and erased the phrase at issue. Natronai appears unaware of it, whereas Nachshon, Amram's immediate successor (871–879), seems to know of at least a variant version of it—*takhin* ("prepare") instead of *ta'ir* ("cause to shine").[20] If the attribution of Nachson Gaon (871–879) be correct, it goes back at least as far as the period immediately after the composition of *Seder Rav Amram*, and, though the *Seder* itself apparently omits it, we have already noted the generally corrupt recension of Amram's prayer texts, so the insertion may even go back to Amram or beyond.

Moreover, unlike Saadiah's other isolated responsa or the individual opinions recorded by him in his prayer book, this ruling remained a cause celebre for centuries. It was known all over Europe, and scribes inserted his words in recensions of *Seder Rav Amram* lest people forget it. In Spain, Saadiah's caveat was followed; it is found neither in our present Sefardic rite nor in the early ritual unearthed by Goldschmidt nor in the commentary of the fourteenth-century authority, David Abudarham.[21] In Germany and France the argument was still being waged, as we saw, as late as the twelfth century, so that both Solomon ben Samson and Eleazer ben Nathan had to offer justifications for it.

Yet the only general influence we have so far been able to isolate as being a formative consideration for Saadiah was the Karaite schism, and his objection to '*or chadash* seems manifestly to have nothing to do with the Karaites. The only conceivable connection would be its apparent opposition to the practice of mourning excessively for Zion, and would therefore be directed against the group of '*avelei tsiyon*, an ascetic sect known to us from about the middle of the eighth century; according to some authorities, this group was predominently Karaitic.[22] But since the Karaite liturgy and theology of Saadiah's time do not seem overly concerned with a concept of a "new light" which will shine on Zion, and since Saadiah himself validates the concept in his other works, it would surely be foolish to explain away his opposition here by a putative attack on the Karaites. Dauntless opponent of Karaism that he was, Saadiah was far too complex an individual for his every action to be explained away by one single political motive.

Surely the clue to his concern lies in his own admission, which we looked at earlier. Saadiah the philosopher, the rationalist, the logician, says he will oppose any alteration in prayer structure, and there is no reason to doubt his words. Still, we have yet to account for Saadiah's feelings about structural purity. Why was he intent on retaining homogeneity of concept within individual blessings? Why were prayers of praise and petition carefully to be separated one from the other? Why, in other words, was the canon of logical distinctiveness of concepts and prayer forms so vital to Saadiah that he should defy precedent and deny the validity of this simple insertion in the *yotser* blessing? Though the answer to this conundrum will have to await our marshaling of more evidence, the question's significance must be admitted now. We shall see later that the case of *'or chadash* is no isolated example of Saadiah's structural rigidity. It is only the most famous of many cases where this exceptional gaon strikes out against "irrational" practice, and this factor, his championing of liturgical "rationality," will prove to be more important than his battle with Karaism in our understanding of what we have called the second period of geonic liturgical canonization.

We turn now to the second blessing before the *shema'*, the *birkat hatorah*, or Blessing over the Torah. In our contemporary Ashkenazic rite, two familiar forms of this blessing can be found. Thematically they both deal with the same complex of ideas: God's selection of Israel, His love for His people, and the gift of Torah as the manifestation of that love. The two blessings are differentiated, commonly, by their opening words, *'ahavah rabbah* ("great love") for the morning, and the evening parallel, *'ahavat 'olam* ("eternal love"). The Sefardic rite, on the other hand, has only the latter formula in both places. As we shall see, these two alternatives far from exhaust the total scope of formulas still in use in geonic times.[23] Like so many other blessings dating from the tannaim, this one too was fixed early in terms of theme but varied widely regarding wording. Thus, the generic title *birkat hatorah*, or simply Torah Blessing, as I shall refer to it, is the preferable term of reference. As its name indicates, its function was to precede and introduce a reading from the Torah, in this case, the *shema'* itself.

There is no dearth of testimony to alternative *birkat hatorah* formulas for the geonic age. We possess, as well, documentary evidence of amoraic precedent, and considerable analysis in the secondary literature. It might be wise, then, to begin by citing the textual evidence, and only then to discuss scholarly opinions on its significance.

Though tannaitic sources record the existence of such a blessing, they do not indicate any precise wording. The Palestinian Talmud, too, discusses it only in terms of its generic term, *birkat hatorah*. In the Babylonian Talmud, however, both introductory formulas, *'ahavah rabbah* and *'ahavat 'olam*, are cited and traced to tannaitic times. The locus for the debate is the Mishnah's enigmatic dictum that two (unspecified) blessings precede the *shema'*, to which the amoraim quite naturally inquire, "What blessing does one say?" In part, the following discussion ensues. For purposes of later identification, we shall label it (A).

(A) Rav Judah said in Samuel's name, "It is *'ahavah rabbah*," and thus did Rabbi Elazar teach Rabbi Pedat his son: "It is *'ahavah rabbah*." A *baraita'* taught similarly: "One does not say *'ahavat 'olam*, but *'ahavah rabbah*." But our rabbis said *'ahavat 'olam*, just as it says [in Scripture, Jer. 31:3]: "With an everlasting love [*'ahavat 'olam*] I have loved you; therefore with affection have I drawn you." Rabbi Judah said in Samuel's name: "If one gets up early in the morning in order to study [Torah, thus necessitating a blessing upon such study, i.e., a *birkat hatorah*], if one has not recited the *shema'* yet, one must say a blessing [i.e., *birkat hatorah*], but if one has already said the *shema'* [and therefore, by implication, also the *birkat hatorah* which precedes it], one need not say a blessing, since one is exempt, having already said *'ahavah rabbah*."[24]

Thus, tannaitic precedent included both forms of the blessing. But the first-generation amora Samuel mentioned only one, *'ahavah rabbah*. Rabbi Elazar concurred with him, though we cannot tell whether Elazar was aware of the alternative.

The issue arises next in a question put to Yehudai Gaon. The question itself is irrelevant for our purposes, since it deals with the advisability of saying a *birkat hatorah* prior to the recitation of psalms, such recitation being a practice of personal piety and occurring after the conclusion of the statutory prayers. Yehudai's answer, which we label (B), reads,

(B) One need not say a blessing since one is exempt by virtue of having already recited *'ahavah rabbah* [as the normal blessing before the *shema'*, part of the statutory prayers already completed].[25]

Yehudai's rationale is a verbatim quotation of Samuel's advice contained in (A), but the fact that he uses it without altering the name of the blessing to *'ahavat 'olam*, or just using the generic *birkat hatorah*, indicates that Yehudai used *'ahavah rabbah*, probably precisely because of Samuel's ruling.

Yet Yehudai's ignorance of the later Ashkenazic practice of alternating the two formulas was not matched by his geonic successors. We have two separate accounts of how the system of employing both responses was instituted. Let us refer to them as (C) and (D). (C) reads as follows:

(C) By Rav Tsemach Gaon: As for *'ahavah rabbah* and *'ahavat 'olam*, there are places where people say [*'ahavah rabbah*, and places where they say] *'ahavat 'olam*, but Rav Jacob asked R. Chaninai . . . "Why do you say *'ahavah rabbah*, considering the fact that the Talmud says, 'A *baraita'* taught similarly: One does not say *'ahavah rabbah* but *'ahavat 'olam*, just as it says [in Scripture]: With an everlasting love, I have loved you'?" He answered them, "In the morning we say, 'With great love [*'ahavah rabbah*]' and in the evening . . . 'You have loved your people Israel with an everlasting love [*'ahavat 'olam*],' in order to fulfill our responsibility by using both of them." From then on it has been the custom in the academy and in *bet rabbenu* to say it this way.[26]

Now the first thing to note is that some confusion existed regarding the *baraita'* from (A). Our *Babli* edition (A) gives the exact reverse of (C). Indeed, the discussion in the *Babli* has more than a little confusion built into it. Rashi, for example, had a Talmud text with yet a third alternative.[27] And some geonim were of the opinion that not Samuel, but his contemporary Rav, had favored *'ahavah rabbah*.[28]

As for the dramatis personae of (C), since the identity of *bet rabbenu* is a matter of scholarly dispute, it is best left untranslated until a definitive interpretation is arrived at.[29] The gaon in question, Tsemach, could be either Tsemach bar Paltoi of Pumbedita (872–890) or Tsemach bar Chayim of Sura (879–885).[30] Since he does not cite Kohen Tsedek or Sar Shalom—see (D)—both prominent Surans (843–853 and 858–871 respectively), one might suppose that this is a Pumbeditan responsum, its author thus being the latter Tsemach (bar Paltoi), who was unaware of the Suran precedent. Moreover, the Chaninai whom Tsemach quotes could be Chaninai Kahana bar Abraham, also of Pumbedita (782–786). Alternatively, our Tsemach may be the Suran, whose opinion as we have it is excerpted and truncated to exclude the known opinions of Kohen Tsedek and Sar Shalom. Chaninai, then, would be Chaninai bar Huna of Sura (765–775), whose opinion was included because it was the earliest attempt to solve the problem by dividing the two formulas into a morning and an evening version.

But a similar apportioning of the two responses is ascribed to yet another gaon, Kohen Tsedek, and to two other Surans, Sar Shalom and Amram. We will call this communication (D).

(D)   Kohen Tsedek wrote that one should satisfy both opinions by saying *'ahavah rabbah* in the morning and *'ahavat 'olam* in the evening. Thus it is written in *Seder Rav Amram*, and thus did Mar Sar Shalom write, that they were accustomed from then onward to do so in the academy.[31]

Kohen Tsedek could be either Kohen Tsedek bar Abomai of Sura (838–848) or Kohen Tsedek bar Joseph of Pumbedita (926–936). If the reference to Amram and Sar Shalom is by him rather than by Abudarham, who combined his opinion with that of other geonim, then it would have to be the latter since the first lived too early. But this is by no means certain, and I suspect we have here a conflation of two or three responsa. So our Kohen Tsedek may be the Suran, a probability in the light of Sherira and Hai's opinion yet to be surveyed (E).[32]

Moreover, we would now be able to trace the decision directly from Kohen Tsedek of Sura (838–848) to his immediate successor, Sar Shalom, who says that from the time Kohen Tsedek made the decision, the academy has followed it. Amram recorded it in his *Seder*, and his decision was followed faithfully by the later gaon of Sura, Tsemach bar Chayim, who was questioned on the practice because of the variant *baraita'* reading which seemed to necessitate *'ahavat 'olam* in the morning.

We would then have an unbroken custom in Sura reaching back from Tsemach (879–885) to Amram (858–871) to Sar Shalom (848–853) to Kohen Tsedek (838–848) to Chaninai (765–775) and even to Yehudai (757–761).

There is, however, a final opinion, unmistakably Pumbeditan, which is puzzling in the extreme. It hails from Sherira and Hai. We shall call it (E).

(E)　Know that the custom of our academy from the very beginning until now has been to say only *'ahavat 'olam* both morning and evening. And in Mata Mechasya in Sura and in all their academies, they say *'ahavat 'olam* both morning and evening. The sole exception is one single academy, and it appears to us that it is where Mar Rav Kohen Tsedek used to be, and before Rav Kohen Tsedek it was similarly the custom there to say *'ahavah rabbah* in one place and *'ahavat 'olam* in the other. Certainly the tradition has emerged that we say not *'ahavah rabbah* but *'ahavat 'olam* . . . [as the Talmud relates]: "Rav Judah said in Samuel's name . . . one is exempt by *'ahavah rabbah.*" But since this is an individual opinion to say *'ahavah rabbah*, while our rabbis [the majority] said *'ahavat 'olam*, and since there is a *baraita'* which agrees with our rabbis, you should not say *'ahavah rabbah* but *'ahavat 'olam.* . . . Thus, since this is the customary practice, we ought not change it, and, to be sure, [such a change] would be a mistaken custom [*minhag ta'ut*].[33]

What are we to make of such diverse information? On the one hand, we have traced a distinct tradition of saying both formulas in the major academy of Sura, all the way from Kohen Tsedek, in the middle of the ninth century—and perhaps even from Yehudai and Chaninai, in the middle of the eighth—down to Tsemach bar Chayim (d. 885). Sherira and Hai, on the other hand, proclaim that the bifurcation of formulas was never customary in either major academy; they doubt that Sar Shalom could possibly have recommended it. Kohen Tsedek's responsum to the contrary is explained away by the fact that one little academy used *'ahavah rabbah* and that Kohen Tsedek was brought up there. Thus Kohen Tsedek was entitled to his solitary deviance from overwhelming tradition because of his own personal history, which gave him his own personal tradition as well.

And that rationale by Sherira and Hai is important. Apparently they were willing to admit that a gaon had differed, and done so with justice, simply because of his own personal tradition, grounded in the unique community of which he had been a part. Since, however, the respondents to whom the responsum was sent could not have been parties to such a minor localism, there could be no justification for them to say *'ahavah rabbah.* They should abide by the general rules of legal procedure, which, in this case, depended on the juridical distinction between the majority opinion and a minority view, particularly in light of the fact that the tannaitic *baraita'* in Sherira's text supported the majority. True, Sherira and Hai understood the talmudic account (A) to say that Samuel recited *'ahavah rabbah*, but the rabbis, who, by definition, constituted a majority, said *'ahavat 'olam* and in cases between an individual and a majority, one follows the majority. Thus, for the group sending the query at any rate, it would be a mistake (*minhag ta'ut*), to recite *'ahavah rabbah*. It would contravene both established rules of majority decisions as well as tannaitic precedent. In fact, given the latter factor, one is amazed at Sherira's lenient judgment of Kohen Tsedek. Could local tradition really be more important than tannaitic evidence? Plainly the root of the controversy goes back to our talmudic citation (A) and the *baraita'* found in it. But before concluding our analysis, we should compare it with prior scholarly discussion.

It was the eminent authority Adolph Büchler who first proposed a solution to our contradictory data. He saw the issue's genesis in conflicting customs of Sura and Pumbedita, each custom being founded on contrary talmudic recensions.[34] Yet Büchler did not see the confusion in the transmission of the *baraita'*! He proceeded on logical grounds to postulate a difference in the names of the amoraim mentioned.

Our printed text of the *Babli* (A) buttresses Samuel's opinion with that of the second-generation Palestinian amora Rabbi Elazar. But the Sheriran responsum understands *'ahavah rabbah* to have been the preference of Samuel alone, since it refers to him by the Hebrew word *yachid*, "individual": so Sherira could not have had the reference to Elazar in his text. On the basis of his Pumbeditan reading, Sherira naturally ruled against such a single individual in favor of the majority, the rabbis as a group, who say *'ahavat 'olam*. But despite Sherira's disclaimer, the sources clearly demonstrate (as our own analysis showed) that at Sura *'ahavah rabbah* was recited, at least in the morning. Surely the Surans would have ruled along with Sherira if their text had been the same as the Pumbeditan one. So Büchler inferred that their text differed from Sherira's, reading instead with ours, including within it Elazar's support for Samuel. Thus, for the Surans, Samuel was no longer a single opinion, or a *yachid*, and they could permit his practice. On the other hand, Sherira says explicitly that the Surans do not say *'ahavah rabbah*, and, as far as he knows, they never did. So sometime before Sherira, Sura must have discovered the error in its Talmud reading and changed its custom to accord with the Pumbeditan one. Now we know of one, and only one, Suran gaon who did indeed say *'ahavat 'olam*, albeit in drastically different wording in the body of the blessing following these two introductory words. That was Saadiah.[35] Büchler surmises that it may have been Saadiah who altered the Suran tradition.

Elbogen accepted Büchler's reasoning but went further. *'Ahavah rabbah*, unlike the shorter *'ahavat 'olam*, contains a messianic insertion, requesting the ingathering of the exiles.[36] Such a plaint seemed to derive from the diaspora, not from Palestine, so Elbogen identified the *'ahavah rabbah* formula as Babylonian, while *'ahavat 'olam* he assigned to Palestine. Mann concurred with Elbogen, since all the genizah fragments considered by him to be truly Palestinian displayed *'ahavat 'olam*.[37] Such thinking was entirely consistent with philological axioms which assumed short variants of prayers to be original, and with scholarly opinion at the time, which claimed greater originality for Palestinian formulas, which presumably were expanded when developed, centuries later, in diasporan centers.

Despite the meticulous legal and textual logic behind this position, though, there are some formidable problems which militate against its acceptance. How is it that Sura should carry a Babylonian tradition, and Pumbedita a Palestinian one? It was Sura, after all, which claimed a Palestinian, Rav, as its founder; while Pumbedita had not been established until close to the end of the third century, by Judah bar Ezekiel, not known for any fondness for Palestinian precedent. It was he who charged anyone returning to the homeland with a breach of divine commandment![38] And according to tradition, when Judah died and a struggle for succession arose, it was the candidate with Palestinian backing who was denied the position of authority. He went to Sura, where Rav Huna (Rav's successor), a relative of the Palestinian patriarch, felt so strongly about his ties that he ordered his body to be buried back in Palestine.[39] Indeed, if either of the two academies should have been careful to preserve Palestinian customs, it should have been Rav and Huna's Sura, not Judah's Pumbedita! In fact, if Goodblatt's assumptions regarding the nature of amoraic institutions be correct, it is anachronistic even to speak of fixed institutional, as opposed to personal, deviations in recensions of tradition, at least in pregeonic times,[40] and this network of personal relationships would be all the more decisive.

So we must consider any possible differences in the practice of the academies as being geonic, and, hence, consider the next step in the Büchler-Elbogen-Mann hypothesis: i.e., the pivotal position of Saadiah as the gaon who brought the Palestinian (= Pumbeditan) tradition to Sura. It is clear at least that Saadiah begins the blessing in question with *'ahavat 'olam*, but the rest of his benediction, including the all-important eulogy, resembles *'ahavah rabbah*, and is at least that much in keeping with the Suran tradition outlined above.[41] But the conclusive objection is our knowledge regarding Saadiah's judgment of *'or chadash*, which we analyzed above. Would the Surans have erased a centuries-old custom on the basis of Saadiah, whose opinion of *'or chadash* they ignored? And why would Hai and Sherira be so adamantly opposed to a custom which had its basis in a mere difference in talmudic reading? They do, on occasion, make a point of declaring the correct reading of various passages, but they rarely go so far as to call a custom derived from an alternative reading an error (*minhag taʿut*). Are we to believe that they knew all about the history and practices of both academies—Sherira is, after all, *the* historian of the period, and must have had access to Sura's records, particularly after Sura was closed in 944, when many scholars left

Sura for Pumbedita—but did not know of the variant reading in Suran Talmud texts? Finally, above all, one wonders why our version of the *Babli* reads as Büchler assumed Sura's to read, if it was Sura that admitted that its text was in error. If that were the case, the emendation should have been the other way around, with Sura striking out the reference to Elazar in deference to the Pumbeditans!

However the readings differed—and they may have differed, since Alfasi's version reads without Elazar's name—the distinction in custom did not necessarily stem from a textual variation. A less radical but more plausible reconstruction might be the following.

Given the fluidity with which prayer texts interchanged throughout the amoraic period and into geonic times, especially in Palestine, it seems likely that the introductory words 'ahavah rabbah and 'ahavat 'olam did not yet imply wholly distinct versions of the entire blessing. Both were key phrases introducing the theme of the blessing, the latter especially, since it had scriptural warrant (Jer. 31:3). But no single set of words for the benediction's body was necessitated by the selection of its introduction. Thus, for example, Saadiah was free to begin with 'ahavat 'olam but to conclude with wording typical of what we know as 'ahavah rabbah. Practices must have varied throughout both Palestine and Babylon, though Büchler may be correct when he says that Pumbedita tended to begin with 'ahavat 'olam.

Now we have seen tradition ascribe to Yehudai a particularly important role in the geonic chain of authority. It was he who wrote the first large body of responsa available to us, and he who was believed to have composed *Halakhot Gedolot*, the first post-talmudic legal compendium. Moreover, it was Yehudai who is said by some medieval authorities to have had a hand in the final revising of the Babylonian Talmud itself,[42] and once again (as we shall see), it is Yehudai who wrote to the Palestinians urging Babylonian precedent upon them.

If there was any competition between the two geonic centers of Sura and Pumbedita, it was surely of minimal significance in Yehudai's day. The overwhelming factor in his time was the changeover from Omayyad to Abbasid suzerainty, and the consequent shift of the center of Moslem power from Damascus to the new city of Baghdad. This was accompanied by the very coming into being of geonic hegemony, for without civil authority to support the institutional complex of gaonate and exilarchate, Yehudai's successors would have had as little influence as his predecessors. So for Yehudai, as for the entire Jewish population of Babylonia, any petty interacademic rivalry that may have existed was vastly overshadowed by the major historical accident that converted the Babylonian authorities into spokesmen to reckon with: the Abbasid dynasty and its support, both political and—through the natural process of converting Baghdad into the empire's hub—economic, of the aspirations of Babylonian Jewry. Indeed, Yehudai was himself a resident of Pumbedita, not Sura, when he was chosen to become the first significant gaon in this most significant of epochs. Institutional loyalty was of negligible importance then.

We shall later have occasion to look more closely into Yehudai's attitude toward the Babylonian Talmud, and the tradition that he is to be assigned credit in making it a central link in the tradition that began at Sinai and spread among Jews worldwide. For the time being we need simply note that if indeed Yehudai was still involved in its final redaction, it could by no means have been the completely edited version we have today. Nor, for that matter, should we assume that it was even known as a single legal corpus which could constitute the basis for subsequent Jewish law. We shall argue that it was precisely Yehudai who should be credited with establishing it as such an authoritative body of tradition. We may doubt very much, then, whether he was primarily concerned with a painstaking comparison of manuscript variations in order to determine the correctitude of a given reading. Thus, in the case of the *baraita'* in our text (A), the simple fact that Yehudai cited the Babylonian amora Samuel was of far greater consequence than the possibility (of which he was probably as yet unaware), that a *baraita'* within the same pericope varied between *'ahavah rabbah* and *'ahavat 'olam*; or that, technically speaking, Samuel was not the majority and should therefore be overruled by the rabbis who were. For Yehudai, the salient fact was that he had a tradition from his Talmud supporting *'ahavah rabbah*, and he quoted it, not, mind you, because he was the least bit concerned about the two alternative *birkhot hatorah* which we are investigating—remember, his questioner had asked him about an entirely different matter. His concern was simply to apply the Babylonian Talmud to every question of Jewish practice, and this he did by citing Samuel's dictum in regard to the question put to him. In all probability, however, he followed Samuel's example in his own prayers, as we pointed out above.

Yet both *'ahavat 'olam* and *'ahavah rabbah* remained current in various places, their use determined by local precedent. As the practice of limiting acceptable responses developed, itself a natural result of geonic centralization, talmudic canon formation, and the institutional structure of a gaonate which trained students, sent them abroad to advise Jewish communities, and encouraged them to request enlightenment on any matter of confusion, it was only a matter of time before geonim would be faced with the question of whether *'ahavah rabbah* should be the preferred form of the *birkat hatorah* or not. So Chaninai, Kohen Tsedek, Sar Shalom, and Tsemach were asked by Jews in different parts of the world what they should say as their prayer, and they gave the standard Suran practice, which was to satisfy both suggestions of the Babylonian Talmud, assigning one for the morning and one for the evening. Amram codified this practice in his prayer book. To be sure, none of these geonim utilize polemical language in their communications, since the matter was by no means emotionally laden. It was a request for information which they willingly gave, based on their own academy's experience. This difference in possible practice, in other words, had not yet become a controversy.

The first notion of controversy comes with Sherira and Hai, who proclaim their custom absolutely correct, deny previous geonic communications which imply otherwise, and explain away the known exception of Kohen Tsedek as a personal idiosyncrasy born of long-standing local tradition in his own academy. Now it should be recalled that when Sherira and Hai held sway, the academy of Pumbedita was for all intents and purposes the only one that counted. Sura had actually been closed some forty-six years, and reopened, we may imagine, only with Sherira's consent, and under his guidance. When he reports, therefore, that both Sura and Pumbedita say *'ahavat 'olam*, morning and evening, he is certainly to be believed. An entire generation had passed since the days when an autonomous Suran tradition existed. The scholars who peopled Sura's halls were Pumbeditans, now transplanted to the new academy, and they surely transferred Pumbeditan liturgical practice with them. It is also noteworthy that Sherira does not dissemble regarding Kohen Tsedek. He says that this gaon's custom of alternating responses was the age-old custom of his academy, and indeed it was. The academy was the old Sura, and the tradition was the one that went back through Tsemach, Amram, Sar Shalom, Chaninai, and Yehudai. But the Sura of Sherira's day, of which, by the way, Sherira speaks only in the present—it being a new institution for all intents and purposes—was not part of that tradition. The only remnant of the old Sura was what Sherira calls the "one single academy... where Mar Rav Kohen Tsedek used to be."

The fact remains that elsewhere Sherira does single out Sar Shalom for refutation. Sherira cannot believe that Sar Shalom authored the responsum in question. Why Sherira should have been so intent on this matter while willing to let Kohen Tsedek's precedent go unchallenged is a matter of speculation at best. But perhaps it had something to do with the fact that Sar Shalom's responsum (C), of which we have extant only the conclusion, "From then on, etc.," implied that the custom was accepted as widespread. As Sherira himself puts it: "We do not believe that Sar Shalom could have said that, since *'ahavah rabbah* is not said in Nehardea whether in the morning or the evening; nor in Ilam, nor Persia nor Medea."[43] So by Sherira's day, half a century after Suran practice had been superseded by Pumbeditan custom, Sherira knew of no place but one where the old Suran opinion still reigned supreme. That was the old Suran academy where Kohen Tsedek had once lived. But surely Sar Shalom was wrong in attributing the practice to the far-flung reaches of world Jewry.

The remarkable thing, of course, is that Sherira and Hai do not try to suppress the age-old custom at the academy where Kohen Tsedek used to reside. They believe it to be illegal, contrary to the law of majority versus minority, and opposed as well by tannaitic precedent. But they hesitate to condemn it, since it has local precedent on its side: not only Kohen Tsedek, but even those who lived there before him. We have seen these two great geonim in the late stages of the geonic period to be liberal so far, liberal, that is, in their willingness to accept alternatives other than their own as licit liturgical expressions, and they maintain their liberality now. Since that is the way people have prayed for generations (centuries?), the case is roughly equivalent to the *minhag bara'ei*, the sectarian custom of adding a phrase regarding *yein 'asis*, "fresh wine," to the *kiddush*. In that case they ruled that since the people like it, they may continue it. Here too, local custom remains the prominent consideration.

Another feature which is worth noting is Saadiah's preference for the introductory words *'ahavat 'olam*, despite his proclivity for a continuation of the blessing in words typical of *'ahavah rabbah*. We shall argue later that Saadiah was especially interested in grounding his blessings in biblical precedent, and that the opportunity to utilize a phrase from Jeremiah was appealing to him. Since Saadiah, temperamentally, was apparently perfectly capable of countermanding all available Suran precedent regarding *'or chadash*, there is no reason to assume he would be hesitant about demanding a similar alteration of custom here. Since blessings really were not fixed, and since both had talmudic support, he had no reason to avoid the alternative. Why he should have cared enough to choose the biblical model is a question we will have to face later in this study.

We may turn now to the third blessing in the *shema'* complex, the *ge'ulah*, or Blessing of Redemption.[44] This is actually only one of several blessings that carry that name, the others being the seventh blessing of the *tefillah* and the Blessing of Redemption that follows the first half of the *hallel* psalms recited during the *seder*. The last-mentioned we have already discussed as being part of even the "heretical" Passover rite condemned by Natronai, and we shall have occasion to discuss the *tefillah* Blessing of Redemption in the next chapter. Here our interest is in the blessing immediately after the *shema'*. To be precise, our interest is in a peculiar custom by which worshippers avoided pausing between the final words of the *shema'* itself and the first word of the *ge'ulah* blessing which follows it.

The custom goes back at least as far as the tannaitic period, since the Babylonian Talmud informs us:

Rabbi Abbahu said in Rabbi Yochanan's name, "The law follows Rabbi Judah, who said, 'One may not pause between "your God" [the last

words of the *shema*'] and "True and enduring" [the first words of the
ge'ulah].'" Said Rabbi Abbahu in Rabbi Yochanan's name, "What was
Rabbi Judah's reason? It is written [Jer. 10:10]: 'For the Lord your God is
true.'"[45]

The discussion then turns to whether or not the worshipper should recite the
word, "true" ('*emet*) yet a second time, as the introductory word of the
ge'ulah blessing, or whether his recitation of it as the last word of the *shema*'
will suffice. On this point there is no unanimity, but the conclusion of the
argument seems to imply that such a repetition is neither required nor even
proper.

Now it is this custom of adding the introductory word of the *ge'ulah* to
the end of the *shema*' which is the subject of a responsum from Hai.

> Rav Hai wrote that an individual, whether praying alone or in a congre-
> gation, should conclude [the *shema*'] with "I am the Lord your God.
> True." [i.e., '*ani 'adonai 'eloheikhem*, the last three words of the
> *shema*', and then the first word of the *ge'ulah*]. The prayer leader who
> completes his recital of the *shema*' and then says [in his reader's re-
> petition], "I am the Lord your God," does not follow a comely custom
> ['*eino minhag yafeh*].[46]

It is not easy to fathom the context to which Hai addresses himself, but it is
probably related to the rise of a numerological interpretation of the *shema*'.[47]
The *shema*' in its entirety (including the inserted line, which follows
Deuteronomy 6:4 but is itself not biblical) numbers 245 words. Sometime late
in the geonic period people were entranced by the coincidence of the fact that
if the prayer leader were to reiterate three words at the end of the *shema*', the
total number of words would then be 248, a figure equal to the number of
positive commandments and also the presumed number of parts to the human
body. The repetition of at least some form of the last line in the *shema*' was
already customary because of Rabbi Judah's instructions to join the end of the
shema' to the first word of the *ge'ulah*. Only if we presume the addition of this
word as part of the *shema*' to have been separate from the recitation of the
ge'ulah does the rest of the amoraic discussion regarding the relative wisdom
of repeating that first word again, this time as the introduction to the *ge'ulah*,
make sense.

What is striking, however is that neither Rabbi Judah nor anyone else in
the entire talmudic discussion of his remarks seems to have any numerological notion in mind. The whole procedure is merely a personal desire
to base a liturgical staple on a fortuitous combination of words that resembles
Jeremiah 10:10. Moreover, Rabbi Judah stipulated the addition of the *two*
opening words in the next prayer, not just one. But Rabbi Judah's remark
coupled with Babylonian amoraic assent did become common practice in the
academies apparently, and people there did conclude their *shema*' with the

first word of the next prayer, *'emet* ("True"). Postgeonic authors do not seem to question this custom.[48]

Hai's responsum comes ultimately from a fourteenth-century(?) codification of law in southern France known as *Sefer Ha'eshkol*. The author adds his own information regarding the practice in Spain and France. Taken together with what we have already seen, we now have no fewer than four ways of ending the *shema'*. Before continuing, we would do well to summarize them.

1. Talmudic practice: The individual says the whole *shema'* plus (at least?) two words of the next blessing. The precentor says the last few words of the *shema'* and the first two (or more) words of the *ge'ulah*. There is no numerology here. The number of words by individual or precentor is never 248 except by chance.

2. The practice today: The individual says the whole *shema'*. The precentor repeats the last two words of the *shema'* plus the first word of the next blessing, three words in all. The individual's 245 and the precentor's three combine to make up the necessary 248 words. For cases where there is no precentor, prayer books print three additional words of introduction which the individual says so that his own recitation can equal 248 words in total. Our practice satisfies Rabbi Judah's original desire to join the *shema'* to the *ge'ulah*, thus following the biblical precedent of Jeremiah 10:10, and it also satisfies the mystical requirement of making 248 words.

3. The custom addressed by Hai: Hai tells us what individuals should do, but does not entirely tell us what in fact they actually do, at least not in their congregational prayer. The precentor, however, is clearly in defiance of Rabbi Judah, since he repeats the last three words of the *shema'* but does not include the first word of the *ge'ulah*. This satisfies the mystics since any three additional words will make the total of 248; but not talmudic custom, since the *shema'* and *ge'ulah* are not joined on the model of Jeremiah 10:10.

4. The *'Eshkol* tells of a custom current in the thirteenth century by which the people repeat not the last three words but the three words before them, *liheyot lakhem le'lohim* ("to be your God"); and the author comments, *ve'eino minhag*, literally, "It is not custom."[49] His Hebrew wording, however, seems to be a shortening of Hai's own judgment on case (3). Hai said *'eino minhag yafeh* ("it is not a comely custom)." In all probability, the author of the *'Eshkol* came across a custom by which three words (for mystical reasons) were repeated. But the initial word of the *ge'ulah* was not one of them. Knowing this to be contrary to the original intent expressed by the Talmud, he looked askance at it. Finding a similar case (3) in which Hai had opposed the simple addition of words without regard to

talmudic precedent and labeled it an uncomely custom, the medieval author cited Hai, and then even borrowed Hai's verbal description of the custom in question.

So it would seem that Hai had no interest in either promoting or
opposing whatever mystical speculation there may have been regarding the
words of the *shema*. He held only that people should conclude their individual recitation of the *shema* with the inclusion of the first word of the next
blessing. That was the talmudic mandate. And he opposed a precentor's
repetition of three other words if those words did not include the first word of
the *ge'ulah*. To do otherwise would constitute "not a comely custom."
    Now the issue per se is not as interesting to us as Hai's categorization of
the deviance, betrayed by the linguistic choice made by Hai to describe it. We
have seen Hai refer to a *minhag bara'ei*, "a heretical custom"; and we have
seen Sherira and Hai describe *'ahavah rabbah* as *minhag ta'ut*, "a mistaken
custom." Now we find yet another practice of which Hai disapproves, probably because it runs counter to amoraic precedent, of which he says, *'eino
minhag yafeh*, "it is not a comely custom."
    Now the way people categorize experience is crucial to the action they
may take to respond to it. The decision in modern times to understand
political speeches as rhetoric rather than resolutions that may ultimately win
congressional approval, or to view certain information as headlines in the
local press rather than official government sources which might entail actual
court procedures, makes all the difference in the world to the casual bystander
at a political rally or the reader perusing the local newspaper. Both modes of
understanding communication, campaign rhetoric and newspaper headlines,
imply a certain freedom, even license, and warn the bystander not to do
anything about them. A certain latitude adheres to words and actions taken by
politicians on the stump and by reporters on their trail. What they do may be
wrong, but we suffer their errors under the understanding that propriety gives
them a certain right to make them. We may quibble, we may bristle, we may
even make public our antagonism when they seem to go beyond the pale of
good manners, but we rarely treat them seriously enough as to warrant taking
up the cudgels in outright defensive action.
    The labeling of liturgical behavior as *minhag*, "custom," is just such a
categorization which lends itself to a broad sanctioning of differences. Not
law, mind you, not dogma, nor Torah, nor morality, but just custom. The
custom may be laudatory or it may not. If the latter, to take our cases, it may
be "heretical," "error," or "not comely." But each such case was met by Hai
with the same degree of equanimity that we might employ upon seeing a
newspaper headline we do not like. The heretical custom was allowed because
people liked it. The erring custom could be continued since it had local
precedent. And as for our "improper custom" here, we simply do not know
what Hai recommended, though if he did advance any views toward enforcing

the talmudic ruling, we might reasonably imagine the author of the *'Eshkol* to have included the remedy, since he himself was struggling against just such a similar custom.

This relatively mild phrase, *'eino minhag yafeh,* "it is not a comely custom," implies censure to be sure, but censure in the form of mild displeasure, not dire opposition. It should be contrasted with the kind of language used by other geonim in the first two stages of geonic canonization, and especially the first. In those instances, as we shall see, it is not at all uncommon for the geonim to denounce the practices they disapprove of, labeling them foolishness, ignorance, illegality, or worse, and ordering that the perpetrators be silenced or removed from liturgical authority.

So, in sum, Hai is consistent here with his attitudes so far discussed. He is mild in his censure, open to novelty, and liberal in perspective. He categorized experience as customs which may run counter to what he himself knows or hears about, but which are rarely such as to require firm denial of authenticity. A custom, after all, may have on its side the countermanding weight of local appeal or time-worn usage, and these are matters not lightly brushed aside.

We should also note that once again Hai has opted in favor of an alternative which has as its basis a dependence on a biblical proof-test. As with *'ahavat 'olam,* Hai prefers to maintain liturgical practices which have biblical precedents. Here he is at one with Saadiah, who exchanged an old Suran custom of saying *'ahavah rabbah* for a version of *birkat hatorah* that began with *'ahavat 'olam,* part of a biblical verse. This tendency of the geonim of periods 2 and 3 of the canonization process will be discussed later.

We have yet one more debate on the blessings of the *shema'.* It concerns an unknown gaon's strenuous objection to an extension of the *ge'ulah* blessing in the morning service.

> There are people who extend the *ge'ulah* of *'emet veyatsiv* [the morning form of the blessing] with "May the Lord our God establish for us His kingdom, His might, and His glory." They continue extensively in this fashion and make alterations. [Is it permitted to do so] or not?

Thus far the question. The answer is,

> Thus do we see it. It is impossible that one should be allowed to do so, for two reasons. . . . And all the more is this so since [we do not say it] in the two academies and in *bet rabbenu.* We say only, "May the Lord reign forever and ever."[50]

The two stated bases for his objection are attenuated legal arguments dependent on the Babylonian Talmud and too long to reproduce here. Basically they amount to: (1) the additional clause would change what should be a short blessing into a long one; and (2) this blessing is a blessing of thanks referring to the exodus of the past, so an inserted petition for future redemption is out of order. This gaon's view is in noted contrast to that of Saadiah, who, as we noted in our discussion of the *'or chadash* controversy, was not opposed to a petitionary insertion here.[51] It will be recalled that Wieder thinks Saadiah accepted these insertions because they were on the subject matter of the benediction, i.e., redemption. He probably borrowed the idea of such insertions from Palestinian custom, with which he was well acquainted. At any rate, they were very common in Palestine.[52]

Now whether this gaon is a Suran or not, scholars are unanimous in recognizing the undoubtable link between his view and a similar admonition given by Amram in his prayer book.[53] Amram says:

> It is forbidden to add anything to "May the Lord reign" [*'adonai yim-lokh*], since there are those who err by saying what the sages did not institute, i.e., *biglal 'avot* . . . ["For the sake of the ancestors, save the descendants and bring redemption to their descendants"].[54]

In other words, Amram too was aware of people who admitted petitions for deliverance in this blessing on deliverance. True, the ostensible theme of the blessing was the deliverance of the past, the exodus from Egypt, and the verbal form of the final eulogy was the perfect, *ga'al*, implying past events alone which were being called to mind and praised. But liturgically speaking, past recalls present and anticipated future, liturgical time being unfettered by the rational boundaries of what was, what is, and what will (or might) be. In the first of the blessings of the *shema'*, celebration of the creation of light had become a cry for the future light that will shine on Zion. Even the second blessing, regarding the selection of Israel, the covenant of Torah granted in the wilderness on route to the promised land, was provided with an inserted petition to "bring us standing erect to our land" once again. And so, too, the third blessing; though technically but a blessing of thanks for miracles past and a credo of faith in the God who wrought them, it was converted into a call for deliverance in the future. The usual form of these inserted petitions took the form of a verbal variant of *kym*, to "establish" or "bring about," and pleaded for God's establishment of His might, kingdom, glory, and holiness.[55]

The prayer cited by Amram, however, is phrased in an altogether different style, omitting the usual referrents to deliverance (kingship, might, glory, etc.), but pleading for redemption on the basis of the rabbinic theological concept of *zekhut 'avot*, "merit of the ancestors." This doctrine holds that the pious forebears of old bequeathed the fruit of their work to future generations. If the latter are not worthy of deliverance in their own right, they may draw upon the merit inherited from the worthies who preceded them.

Yet despite its formal distinctiveness, thematically it represents an expansion identical to that of the more usual *kayem* petitions. They are all very natural extensions of thought, from thanksgiving for things past to petition for similar things in the future. Why Amram should have selected the one in this blessing for negative comment when he was not at all upset by similar expansions in the blessings preceding the *shema'* deserves our scrutiny.

The only other gaon who mentions this blessing, and whose opinion must be considered in any attempt to systematize general geonic attitudes, is Saadiah. He has no comment regarding the blessing, but he did write his own *siddur* and therefore had to come to terms with it. We know he opposed the parallel insertion (*'or chadash*) in the first blessing because it constituted a clear change of subject matter, transposing light from its original denotation of the natural heavenly luminaries created at the beginning of time to a symbol of deliverance. On the other hand, he included the insertion for the ingathering of the exiles in the second blessing since, as his somewhat unique wording of the blessing makes clear, he considered the promise of the return to Zion to be intrinsically related to the covenant celebrated by the blessing as a whole.[56] Similarly, one would expect him to have no reason to object to petitions for salvation in the third blessing, where salvation was in fact the predominant theme. And in fact he includes them, first in the form of a *kayem* petition[57] and elsewhere in a variant of the blessing known to Amram. It reads, "For the sake of the ancestors you saved the children, and brought deliverance to their descendants."[58] Yet he limited the latter addition to the *ge'ulah* blessing that succeeds the *shema'* on Friday night (probably to enhance the occasion of the coming of the Sabbath), and changed the tense of the verb from the imperfect *toshiya'* to the perfect *hosha'ta*, thus making it refer to the past, like the rest of this blessing of thanksgiving.[59]

The origin of *biglal 'avot* cannot be documented with certainty. Amram and the anonymous gaon know it is not Babylonian, but it does not appear in the truly Palestinian genizah fragments at our disposal either. It is found in the earliest Italian rite (Codex Turin), but early Italian worship borrowed freely from both Babylonia and Palestine, and even, we may assume, from local liturgical innovation, since the rite as we know it does not predate the eleventh century, and by that time Jewish communities in southern Italy had produced many scholars and poets of note. So its inclusion in the Italian rite, though suggestive of possible Palestinian origin, is not conclusive.

On the other hand, we have far from exhausted the potential of the genizah, and we may yet discover a Palestinian fragment which does bear *biglal 'avot*. Moreover, of all the Babylonian geonim, only Saadiah, the native Palestinian, uses it. And finally, it does, after all, seem to parallel the Palestinian *kayem* formulas, since it comes at the same place in the service and carries the same message. So Ginzberg is probably correct when he states, "I have no doubt that *biglal 'avot* also is part of the Palestinian rite."[60]

In sum, the *ge'ulah* of the Palestinians was marked by insertions for future redemption, since in their view—as their eulogy to the prayer shows—

the *ge'ulah* was referrable not only to the past: they concluded their blessing
with *tsur yisra'el vego'alo*, "Rock of Israel and its Redeemer," a reference to
God's eternal presence as redeemer in history. Amram and the anonymous
gaon, on the other hand, argued from the perspective of Babylonian ritual,
where the ge'ulah was seen as a reference to the exodus alone, and was to be
concluded with a eulogy couched appropriately in the perfect tense, *ga'al
yisra'el*, "who saved Israel." But Saadiah, a former resident of Palestine, and a
native of Egypt, where Palestinian ritual was in common use, saw no reason
to preclude petitions for deliverance within a prayer on the same theme.

In this issue we have seen geonim of period 1 (Amram and, probably,
the anonymous Suran) and period 2 (Saadiah) being thoroughly consistent
with their opinions elsewhere. The former, intent on centralizing Judaism
around Babylonian custom and norm, wish to canonize worship procedure by
declaring illegitimate the only existent alternative source of potential precedent: the age-old practice of Palestine. Thus Amram opposes *biglal 'avot*, and
does so with characteristic peremptoriness. Saadiah, however, of stage 2,
includes this Palestinian custom since it in no way alters the basic theme of
the blessing, though, grammarian and logician that he is, he prefers a form
reading entirely in the perfect so as to harmonize with the general thrust of the
ge'ulah's message.

Time and again we shall return to Saadiah's concern for grammar,
linguistic precision, and biblical style as paradigm, but first we should turn to
the *shema'* itself. Since it is a biblical citation, no argumentation over its correct phraseology was possible. But the manner in which it was said occasioned
vociferous debate, and, along with the Amram/Natronai opposition to the
heretical Passover *haggadah*, it shows Amram at his most uncompromising
when it comes to Palestinian alternatives. Together with what we have seen
elsewhere, it establishes the *Tendenz* of period 1 without question.

No passage better typifies the militancy of stage 1 than Amram's discussion of
whether one ought to stand or sit during the recitation of the *shema'*. It was
important to him because Palestinians stood while Babylonians sat. Amram
devoted more space in his *Seder* to this issue than to any other. Naturally, he
phrased the entire discussion in typical legal format, but it is perfectly clear
that it is the Palestinians on whom he wishes to vent his wrath; he says so,
explicitly. Some background, however, will be of help in following the legal
reasoning which clothes Amram's remarks.

The question of prayer etiquette is as old as prayer itself. Since the
shema' is one of the oldest staples in the liturgy, questions about saying it
properly can be found in every stratum of rabbinic literature. One of the
questions that vexed the minds of the rabbis was whether to stand or sit during
the recitation of this all-important prayer.

The question seems to have been answered in two mutually exclusive ways by the two outstanding schools of rabbinic opinion of the first century C.E., the Hillelites and the Shammaites. The key phrase begging for interpretation comes from the *shema* itself, Deuteronomy 4:7, which instructs us plainly that the *shema* should be spoken "when thou liest down and when thou risest up." Thus, both schools had long agreed that the *shema* was intended for dual recitation each day, both evening, "when thou liest down," and morning, "when thou risest up." But an argument occurred over the possibility of learning not only the time of recital from these lines, but also the manner of recital.

The Hillelite position was that the lying down and rising up in question were not to be taken literally. They were mentioned merely as indications of what one would typically be doing at the times in question. When the times actually arrived, one was to continue standing, sitting, lying down, or whatever one was doing, simply pausing momentarily to say the *shema*. The Shammaites, however, did take the language literally; thus one should stand during the morning recitation and lie down during the evening reading.

Now we know very little about how prayers were conducted during the emergence of the synagogue service, the determination of its basic rudiments, and what I have called the earliest stage of its codification (before 200 C.E.), the one dealt with by Heinemann and most of the philological school of thought preceding him. What little we do know suggests only that a member of the praying group led his fellows in the recitation of the *shema*. This was discovered as early as 1906 by Ismar Elbogen, who also postulated that (1) the leader led the *shema* from his place, and (2) the recitation was done antiphonally. Though scholars have argued with this description from time to time, the overwhelming sentiment has been to accept it, with, however, a slight emendation here and there.[61]

Whatever the case originally, however, by geonic times a clear distinction had emerged between the Babylonian and Palestinian traditions. The Palestinians stood for each recitation, while the Babylonians sat during both. Clearly the distinction had little or nothing to do with the ancient Hillelite-Shammaite controversy, since both sides were Hillelites in theory and had been for centuries. Moreover, neither custom is a logical outgrowth of either of the two classical positions. A true Shammaite would presumably have asked people to stand in the morning and sit in the evening. A true Hillelite would have answered that no dogmatic regulation was binding in either case, as long as the worshipper recited the prayer in the bodily posture in which he found himself at the time.

Now Amram takes up the cudgels against the Palestinians, who stand. He accuses them of being Shammaites (bad enough), and poor Shammaites at that. He draws a caricature of them as being overly fastidious about prayer posture when those who are really meticulous in matters that count know enough to sit during the *shema*. He hurls every imaginable insult at them, drawing freely on rabbinic and biblical dicta to support his position; and when such support is not forthcoming, even by virtue of misreading the context in which the text was originally composed, he lets his invective stand unsubstantiated. The total discussion runs several pages. But the following selection gives a representative picture of Amram's position.

> People in the two academies [of Babylonia] and in all of Spain [where Amram sent his responsum]—may all of them be remembered for a thousand meritorious rewards and blessings, for they are all filled like a pomegranate with [knowledge of] Torah and [fulfillment of] commandments; their works are becoming, and they are stringent regarding the examination of food to discover what is forbidden, and the ritual immersion of menstruants, and everything which calls for stringency. But they recite the *shema*ʿ sitting! As for those people who say, "We follow the custom of the land of Israel [by standing]," do we not read in the Palestinian Talmud [P.T. *Ber.* 1:7, 3b], "A tanna taught, 'A heavenly voice emerged, saying both [the Hillelites and the Shammaites] are the words of the living God, but the law follows the Hillelites forever'?" Moreover, in the same discussion in the Palestinian Talmud [we read] that before the heavenly voice emerged, [and one might conceivably have followed the Shammaites,] it was ruled that one who acts so stringently as to take upon himself the stringent rulings of both schools [choosing in every issue to accept the least lenient ruling, and thereby following no single school of thought consistently], of such a one Scripture says, "The fool walks in darkness," and one who adopts the lenient ruling [in every case] regardless of school is evil. Rather, one should either follow the Shammaites in both their lenient and their stringent rulings, or the Hillelites in both their lenient and their stringent rulings. [Thus, standing both for evening and morning recitations would in any event be prohibited.] But in any case, after the heavenly voice emerged, the law [was fixed] eternally according to the Hillelites, and all who transgress the words of the Hillelites deserve death. In the Babylonian Talmud's discussion of that very same law [*Ber.* 11a], R. Nachman bar Isaac said, "All who follow the words of the Shammaites deserve death. . . . all who alter [the law] are called habitual sinners."[62]

And this is not all. Elsewhere in the discussion Amram refers to the Palestinians, who follow neither the Hillelites nor the Shammaites consistently, and asks rhetorically, "Could there be any foolishness [*kesilut*] greater than that?"[63] and, "How can it be that they are so mistaken?"[64] In sum, "Those who appear to be imposing stringent standards on themselves by saying that they accept the Kingdom of Heaven [i.e., say the *shema*ʿ] standing are guilty of piling error upon error, foolishness, ignorance and nonsense" (*taʿut vetaʿut beyadam vehedyotut veborut veshetut*).[65]

We have finally completed the arduous, though rewarding, task of surveying the *shema'* and its blessings. Surely our results substantiate those arrived at in our analysis of the geonic comments on the *haggadah*. We noted earlier that there were three periods in the geonic canonization activity, the first being best personified by Amram and Natronai, the second by Saadiah, and the third by Sherira and his son, Hai.

We saw period 1 to be militant, fond of harsh language, and opposed particularly to Palestinian alternatives. We hoped to be able to trace this attitude back beyond Amram, wondering if it went all the way back to Yehudai. To some extent we have done that, though the evidence is far from complete. At least, however, we know of a Suran tradition from Yehudai to Amram regarding *'ahavah rabbah*, and we see several of the geonim in the intervening years taking anti-Palestinian positions. Certainly Amram, regarding standing during the *shema'*, and Natronai, regarding the heretical *seder*, seem to be in complete agreement of motives and criteria.

Period 2, that of Saadiah, still requires considerable attention. We have seen him to be opposed to *'or chadash* yet in favor of petitions for salvation when the subject matter of the blessing involved seemed appropriate. Yet he changed the tenses of verbs and seemed overly concerned with picayune grammatical and logical differentiations. Certainly our observation that Saadiah was not interested in anti-Palestinian polemic has been borne out, since he regularly took stands unrelated to geographic rivalry. Yet beyond our conclusion at the end of chapter 1 that even though the Karaites were his enemies, some other more general understanding of this man's driving impetus need be sought, we have not advanced very much. We need to know much more about Saadiah and the environment which claimed his attention. The key will be seen to lie in his attention to biblical precedent and proper grammatical and linguistic usage.

Period 3, that of Hai and Sherira, has received more than enough evidence to substantiate what we tentatively proposed in chapter 1. We have seen these two geonim conceptualizing their liturgical experience not by law but by custom, frowning on various matters but rarely declaring them illicit. Their reputation as moderates has certainly survived.

We may now turn to an analysis of the *tefillah* and the *kaddish*, both significant prayers in geonic days. Though the number of writers and their emotional investment seem hardly to rival what we have seen so far regarding the *shema'*, the evidence must nevertheless be analyzed and included in our overall portrait of geonic canonization activity.

3: Daily Liturgy
The *Tefillah* and the *Kaddish*

The Tefillah

IF THE SHEMA ͨ AND ITS ACCOMPANYING BLESSINGS REPRESENT THE CREEDAL affirmation of the Jew, the *tefillah*, which follows them, constitutes the petitionary prayer par excellence. Attempts to reconstruct its origin are numerous despite the fact that the paucity of primary data seems clearly unable to support with any surety the details of any theories to date. We do know that Josephus seems unaware of the prayer, but in all probability the *tefillah* went through two readily recognizable stages, only the second of which can be seen as an institutionalized rubric such as we have; and there is no reason to distrust the tradition (*Meg.* 17b) that ascribes that institutionalization to Rabban Gamaliel II at Yavneh, somewhere around the turn of the second century C.E., and therefore too late for its effect to have been felt by Josephus, by then living in Rome, far from the scene of Judean creativity. The same source posits also the existence of some earlier form of our prayer, but even if there be some truth to this supposition, it is very difficult to know what is meant by it, and how far back into antiquity this first stage of the prayer reaches—whether, for example, Ben Sira 51 should be seen as an authentic echo of an early *tefillah*.

Even limiting ourselves to the second stage—after Rabban Gamaliel—there are many unanswered questions. Following Heinemann, it seems to me that though the prayer now became a staple daily liturgical portion with specifically stipulated petitionary themes officially arranged in orderly sequence, there still remained great differences among the tannaim as to the requisite number of blessings and the wording thereof. It may be that blessing topics were settled upon, and even some sample eulogies which seemed more representative of the prayer's basic intent than others. Yet even here it is hard to imagine a final and absolute crystallization until after the promulgation of the Mishnah. First-generation amoraim still debate such elementary issues as whether a blessing must address God in the second person and whether His name and Kingship must be included (e.g. *Ber.* 12a, 40b). So only in the amoraic period did certain eulogies or key phrases slowly become typical of

Palestine, while others came to represent Babylonia. Moreover, the number of the blessings eventually varied too, Palestine generally expressing the mandated themes in eighteen discrete blessings, and Babylonia in nineteen.[1]

One would expect this most significant of prayers—it was called *hatefillah*, after all, "THE prayer"—to have occasioned considerable diatribe. Compared to the *shema'* and its accompanying blessings, however, there are remarkably few disputations regarding the daily recital of the *tefillah*. As far as this daily *tefillah* is concerned, our sources speak of controversies on three matters:

1. The ninth blessing, *birkat shanim*, literally, "the Blessing of Years," but actually a plea for agricultural prosperity.

2. The last blessing, *birkat kohanim*, or "Priestly Blessing," a remnant of the Temple cult, when the priest dismissed the people by intoning Numbers 7:24–26; thereby invoking God's name on them.[2]

3. What is loosely called *birkat shalom*, or "Blessing of Peace." This is actually an extension of the Priestly Blessing, the latter being no blessing at all, stylistically considered, but merely biblical quotation. Thus at some point in tannaitic times it was expanded into the benediction genre favored by the rabbis, outfitted with a eulogy, and declared fit for recitation by a lay leader of prayers. Different forms exist for different services, and, following Heinemann's general reconstruction of the state of the liturgy, we may presume our two surviving examples (*sim shalom* = "grant peace"; and *shalom rav* = ("great peace") to be only a fraction of a larger selection of similar renditions no longer extant.[3]

We have already alluded to the debate on *birkat shanim* in our discussion of Saadiah's liturgical criteria. The problem is discussed thoroughly by Heinemann in that context.[4] At issue was an inserted petition for salvation, "Call into being, for your people, a year of deliverance and salvation" (*vetikra' le'amkha shenat ge'ulah viyeshu'ah*), which Saadiah opposed as a secondary theme likely to overshadow the primary subject of sustenance. This is consistent with Saadiah's attitude to *'or chadash*, and another example of the application of his second criterion, to disallow intrusions which might significantly alter the basic theme of the blessing itself. As such, his defiance occasions no surprise to us.

To the relevant genizah citations given by Heinemann, those adduced by Marmorstein might be added. Marmorstein reviews eight manuscripts of *birkat shanim*, and states:

> Of these eight texts, 1, 2, 5, and 6, represent the Palestinian rite; 3, 7, and 8—the Babylonian. The chief difference between them is that the latter have no reference to future redemption; the former have. This is one of the chief differences between the Babylonian and Palestinian texts of the *'Amidah*.[5]

We might note in passing, then, two significant points. The first is that Saadiah, who included Palestinian precedent elsewhere, as in the case of *biglal 'avot*, was by no means consistent in his geographical bias. His *tefillah* text, for example, is typically Babylonian, carrying nineteen, not eighteen, benedictions. (Saadiah was, after all a leading scholar in Babylonia when he wrote his *Siddur*, and would ultimately become the gaon there; moreover, he achieved his reputation originally by siding with the Babylonians when Ben Meir, the nationalistic Palestinian leader, challenged the Babylonian right to set the Jewish calendar.) So Saadiah, a native Palestinian but converted Babylonian, is syncretistic with respect to different rituals, and here he saw a logical reason to disallow the Palestinian penchant for requesting salvation in a prayer dealing with agricultural fecundity.

But this Palestinian fondness for requesting salvation should itself not go unnoticed. We have seen it in the *ge'ulah*, both in a variety of *kayem* formulas and in *biglal 'avot*; and now we see it again in *birkat shanim*. Just on the basis of the limited evidence of this study, the Palestinian desire to insert petitions for salvation presents itself as a worthy subject for further research. It seems, indeed, a hallmark of Palestinian theological uniqueness, cutting across the great diversity of liturgical formulations that constituted the daily prayers of the Palestinians.

Two grammatical points, one connected with rabbinic exegesis, mark the geonic discussion of *sim shalom*. *Siddur Saadiah* reads, "Bless us all, as one, in the light of Your countenance." Now the word "one" is the masculine *'echad*, and Saadiah remarks that he has deliberately selected it, rather than the feminine equivalent, *'achat*. He tells us that he is actually following a previous ruling to that effect by Sar Shalom, who held that the masculine *'echad* was called for, since its referrent is masculine, i.e., Abraham. As proof for this contention, he cites Isaiah 51:2, *ki' echad kera'tiv*, which is to be read in this context as, "[Look to Abraham;] I called him one."[6] Thus for Saadiah (and Sar Shalom) this blessing would be understood creatively as: "Bless us all, like Abraham, with the light of your countenance."

We should note, too, that once again Saadiah's concern is biblical precedent and grammatical consistency.

Now it is this very same prayer, *birkat shalom*, that provides Saadiah with yet another opportunity to exercise grammatical precision. All manuscripts of his *Siddur* agree on the fact that the Hebrew version of the English petition we have just quoted is *uvarekheinu kulanu ke'echad bime'or panekha ki meme'or panekha. . . .*[7] The word for light, then, appears twice, the first time with the preposition *beth*, "in," and the second time with the preposition *mem*, "from." In both cases, however, the manuscript evidence is unanimous on Saadiah's selection of the Hebrew noun *ma'or* for "light." Indeed the word does mean "light," but Saadiah's use of it here is diametrically opposed to his own responsum (carried elsewhere) which reports his vociferous insistence that the proper word for "light" is not the Hebrew *ma'or* but the alternative shorter form *'or*.

> When the prayer leader reaches *sim shalom* . . . he should say *ke'echad be'or panekha*, and not *'achat*; and similarly *ki be'or panekha*. He should not say *me'or panekha*. In our presence in the academy, and in all of Babylonia we say *ki be'or panekha natata lanu*, etc., and anyone who says it this way practices linguistic precision, since Scripture writes [Prov. 16:15]: *be'or penei melekh chayyim* ["In the light of the king's countenance is life"]; and it is written [Ps. 89:16]; *be'or panekha yehaleikhun* ["They walk in the light of Thy countenance"]. Thus said Saadiah.[8]

How careful Saadiah is in his citations here! He is not content to select just any biblical proof-texts with the word *'or*; he carefully culls only those which relate light to the divine countenance. It is quite amazing, therefore to find his actual prayer book utilizing the alternative *ma'or*.[9] Since Saadiah is generally careful to follow biblical precedent in his concern for linguistic precision, and since his *Siddur* reflects later scribal activity whereby his own preference is frequently exchanged for words or phrases with which the scribes were familiar, it is probable that Saadiah's real opinion is carried in the responsa, not his prayer book.

So Sar Shalom's original point was both grammatical and exegetical. He understood *'echad* to refer to Abraham, and therefore demanded the masculine pronoun, as opposed to what must have been a frequent error of many worshippers who were unaware of the rabbinic allusion. Saadiah, the grammarian, reiterated the lesson, adding another of similar substance. Basing his grammatical preference on biblical usage, he opted for *'or*, not *ma'or*, as the correct nominal form. Again we see Saadiah at his best. As a grammarian who based his preferences on biblical example, he was without peer among the geonim. But we are still in no position to explain his concern, and for this we await the totality of the evidence.

We come now to the controversy over the Priestly Benediction.[10] As already stated, the familiar threefold blessing of Numbers 6:24–26 was a regular staple of the Temple cult. The rules governing its usage are given in verses 23 and 27.

> Speak unto Aaron and unto his sons, saying, This is the way you shall bless the children of Israel. . . .

> So shall they put My name upon the children of Israel and I will bless them.

During the Second Commonwealth, regardless of any synagogue worship that may have transpired outside the formal institution of the Temple, it was the Temple activity which was vested with primary religious authority and charisma. It was in that context, therefore, that the command of Numbers 6:23–27 was carried out. Since the officiants in the Temple were priests, no question arose as to whether a nonpriest might legitimately fill the priestly role so obviously addressed to (and limited to) Aaron and his sons, the priestly progenitors of the Bible.

But the demise of the cult in the year 70 evoked that very problem. Now the leaders of worship were generally nonpriests, and there loomed the potential desacerdotalization of what had once been a priestly prerogative. Should laymen be allowed to bless the people as the Aaronides once had?

As with so many other liturgical customs, this dilemma was solved in different ways by different communities. The Babylonians generalized the priestly prerogative to any prayer leader and allowed the Priestly Benediction to be recited daily by lay leaders. But the Palestinian communities omitted the actual Priestly Benediction if no priests were available to say it. In such cases only a symbolic priestly recitation occurred, by which the lay leader recited the instructions from the biblical narrative (vv. 22—and, perhaps, 23—and 27) but omitted the actual blessing (vv. 24–26). Thus only the instructions to the priests would be read, and the biblical wish to limit the actual act of blessing to priests could be scrupulously upheld.[11]

Both geonic prayer books are alike in following Babylonian precedent here. Amram and Saadiah clearly give lay readers the right to recite the Priestly Benediction in its fullness.[12]

Once again, then, Amram championed the Babylonian tradition against the Palestinian, not a surprising fact in the light of what has been said here so far. But Saadiah's decision to follow Amram's precedent deserves some attention. Since, as we have seen, Saadiah follows both traditions from time to time, it may be that he opted for the Babylonian custom here at random, or perhaps this was so popular a custom that he could not have done otherwise. The latter is improbable when one considers that elsewhere—*'or chadash*, for example—Saadiah does not shrink from attacking popular preference; and although the former may be the case, we are at least entitled to look for some purpose beyond what would otherwise amount to meaningless whim. Especially is this true with a personality like Saadiah, who is nothing if not punctilious about individual decisions of even the most minute impact.

We have so far seen Saadiah reacting strongly in two directions. The first is his antipathy to his lifelong foe, the Karaites, who were just beginning their age of glory in Palestine. The second was a rather general observation that Saadiah scrutinized language and logical structure very closely, preferring linguistic phraseology found in the Bible. Certainly he does not take the biblical instructions to Aaron literally here, and in that sense he opposes his general tendency to look carefully for biblical precedent, a characteristic that marks his decisions elsewhere. It makes sense, then, to examine the Karaite liturgy to see whether Saadiah was reacting against that. As we have said, the Karaite liturgy was then restricted to biblical citations, and thus it normally has little or no relation to Rabbanite prayer. But our case here is starkly different. Since it is a biblical prayer with which we are dealing, and an important one at that, the Priestly Benediction; we might well expect it to find its way into the Karaite liturgy as well as the Rabbanite.

Now our knowledge of Karaite worship comes from several sources. The most important one is Anan ben David's *Sefer Hamitsvot*, referred to by Natronai in his ninth-century excommunication of the sect. There are, in addition, several comments offered parenthetically by the numerous Karaite scholars who led the sect's golden age in Palestine in the tenth and eleventh centuries, the most notable being Kirkisani, the sect's historian, some of whose work is now in translation.[13] From a later period, but still carrying reliable information about the past, we have Judah Hadassi's *'Eshkol Hakofer*, an encyclopedic work written in alphabetic acrostic and partial verse, emanating from the new center of Karaism, Constantinople.[14]

A methodical synopsis of early Karaite liturgy was composed by the pioneer scholar Jacob Mann.[15] Mann's account of Anan's ritual leaves two things absolutely clear. The first is that the differentiation between Priest, Levite, and Israelite was no anachronism for him. Postdestruction Rabbanite Judaism maintained the separation too, but only in a few symbolic forms. For Anan, however, the entire choreography of his service emphasized the strict demarcations of class and status that the Bible itself had intended, and that had, in fact, been carried out in the worship activity of the Second Temple. Thus, for example, there was a special bench for the priests, while Israelites were seated in a special area apart from the priestly classes, so that "Anan endeavored to make the synagogue resemble the Temple as much as possible."[16]

Naturally one would expect Anan also to make sure that only bona fide priests blessed the people, and indeed he did.[17] So we may be correct in seeing more than just personal whim behind Saadiah's choice of Babylonian precedent here. If he knew of the Karaites' literal interpretation of the biblical command and their attempt to maintain the class divisions of Temple days, including the prerogative of the priest alone to bless the people, we can well understand Saadiah's giving the right of invoking God's blessing to every prayer leader, as was the custom in Babylonia.

In this case, then, we find Amram acting in character, prohibiting Palestinian practice; and Saadiah deciding the same matter in the same way but for other motives: a desire to refute the liturgical claims of the Karaites.

The Kaddish

The *kaddish* is one of the most fascinating prayers in all of Jewish liturgy. Though greatly loved and therefore much discussed, we still know very little about how, or even when, it came into being.[18] It is generally considered to be tannaitic or even Pharisaic in origin, and to have some thematic similarity with the Lord's Prayer. Its use in the synagogue service has varied considerably. Originally it was probably a concluding prayer to a sermon delivered on the occasion of the reading of Scripture, but as time went on it insinuated itself into several parts of the service, and in a variety of forms, including one in which scholars and students of Torah are singled out as particularly deserving of reward; and another, the best-known form, the mourners' *kaddish*, which, in the popular mind at least, was at times considered efficacious in relieving the soul of a loved one from eternal punishment and transferring it to the realm of heavenly bliss. It is the first paragraph of the *kaddish*, however, that is basic to all synagogue usages and, along with its accompanying response, is assumed to represent the essential kernel to which various additions and alterations were made. The *kaddish*, then, consists of an introductory paragraph of praise and of hope in the coming of the Kingdom, a congregational response, and several appended units. The addition occurring immediately after the congregational response is the one which especially attracted geonic attention because of a particular word in a series of words, all roughly synonymous, expressing the sentiment, "May He [the Lord] be praised." That Hebrew word is *veyitkales*.[19]

It is none other than Yehudai, the earliest gaon in our sample, who first discusses the term, prohibiting it on the grounds that its connotation is ambiguous: it can designate not praise but derogation. "I have found," says the author of *Shibbolei Haleket*, "in the name of Rabbi Yehudai Gaon, that one should not say *veyitkales* since we discover it to be a derogatory expression."[20]

Amram, however, gives us the following report:

> Before me in the academy, we do not say *veyitkales*, not because it is a derogatory expression, but because we heard that our teachers used to say that one is obligated to say seven words of God's praise here, corresponding to the seven heavens. Those who do not say *viyitkales* reason that since they have said *yitbarakh*, that word added to the next six words, totals seven. Those who say *veyitkales* claim that since they interrupt [the list of synonyms] by saying *'amen* after *yitbarakh*, they still require seven [and thus must include *veyitkales* along with the other six]. Neither way of doing it amounts to an error.[21]

Amram's point can be appreciated only by a glance at the structure of the *kaddish*, and an appreciation of the notion that the seven words should parallel the number of heavens.

The first paragraph of the *kaddish* is composed as a call to praise God, and contains concepts both similar to those in the first section of the Lord's Prayer and in the same order.[22] There then follows the doxology, or community response: "May his great name be praised unto all eternity!" Next there appears the verb *yitbarakh*, "May it [or He] be blessed [or praised]." Finally we find six synonyms for *yitbarakh*, and in the case under discussion, yet a seventh, *yitkales*. Thus, the total number of synonyms, including both the first (*yitbarakh*) and the last (*yitkales*), is eight. The difference, however, between the first one and the others is that the first must have been associated with the doxology which immediately precedes it. Indeed, looking at that word as an integral part of the congregational response, one is struck by the possibility that the response was couched in parallelism, so that it properly should read:

(1) *yehei shemei rabbah mevorakh le'olam*
(2) *le'olmei ulemaya', yitbarakh*

or, in English,

(1) *May his great name be praised forever!*
(2) *Forever, may it be praised!*

In that case the first of the eight synonyms which comprise the next part of the *kaddish* is technically not part of the list at all, and, in fact, it may have preceded the list in time, the list being appended later, building upon the final word of the response by adding a series of synonyms for it.

In any event, whether it be true that the original *kaddish* extended beyond what is generally considered the congregational response to include the first word of the next line, people in Amram's time considered there to be some differentiation between the word and the words following it. As Amram expressly says, people customarily said *'amen* after *yitbarakh*.

Now the concept of seven heavens was common to the Hellenistic world, and Judaism too assumed it. The Mishnah mentions it, as do several tracts attributed to certain mystics whose goal was to proceed through the heavens by inhabiting the last heaven.[23]

By Amram's time the assumption of seven heavens and the corollary that one ought to include seven terms of divine praise to correspond to them was well established. Amram does not take issue with the theory. Indeed, he explains the dichotomy of practice in terms of its common acceptance. Since some people wish to count all the terms, including the first, *yitbarakh*, they omit the last, *yitkales*; others note that they say *'amen* after the first, and reason that their count should commence only after that disjuncture. Thus they start counting with the second term in the list and need the last to make seven. Amram himself follows Yehudai's view—though for different reasons—and omits *yitkales*. (In fact, only because he is aware of Yehudai's responsum does Amram say explicitly that his reason for omitting the word has nothing to do with any derogation that may be inferred from it.) Who the others are he does not tell us, since he has no quarrel with them. Both groups adhere to the same theoretical basis for deciding, and the alternative custom is acceptable to the gaon.[24]

The issue emerges again in a surprising report from Hai. An extract from a Pumbeditan *siddur* from the days of Tsemach bar Paltoi Gaon (872–890) displays the *kaddish* without *veyitkales*,[25] yet Hai, a Pumbeditan himself living about a century later, is of a different mind, going so far as to demand the word's inclusion.

> One is obligated to say *veyitkales*, and it is fitting to say it, since the *kaddish* is said regarding the future, the time when our God will rule over His world and extirpate every idol and false image.... At that time, He will cause the horn of David His servant to sprout for Israel His people, in the coming of the Messiah . . ., and when they are arrayed for battle, our God will emerge and fight for them.... Thus [the prayer] says *veyitkales*, it having the linguistic denotation of armaments, and "helmets of brass" [I Sam. 17:5, *vekhova* *nechoset*], for which the Targum reads *vekulsa* *dinechasha*.[26]

So for very interesting theological reasons, Hai mandates the inclusion of *veyitkales*. Basing his understanding of the term on an Aramaic translation of I Samuel 17:5, he sees it as heralding the great war of the Lord which will usher in messianic times.

But we are not only obligated to say it; it is also, we are told, fitting that we do so. Surely this latter information seems superfluous. If we are obligated, certainly the prayer must be fitting. Hai must have included this extra comment to counteract the earlier opinion of Yehudai, which attached negative connotations to the word. Just as Amram had felt it necessary to deny Yehudai's charge, so too did Hai.

This opinion is bolstered by another responsum by Hai on the same subject. It refers explicitly to the word's semantic ambiguity.

> You asked about *chazzanim* [prayer leaders] some of whom say *veyitkales*, and some of whom do not. Thus it appears to us: *Yitkales* in the talmudic idiom is used to imply praise, whereas in the biblical usage it can imply either praise or derogation. Whether one bases oneself on biblical language or on talmudic idiom, one should say it, and anyone who does not say *veyitkales* makes a mistake.[27]

So Yehudai's objection really was still an issue, and one is impressed with the sophistication of Hai's response. Knowing there is merit to the objection, he traces the word's double entendre to different literary strata. Biblically it is true that the word sometimes functions derogatorily; but talmudically the word is given a new, praiseworthy denotation, and consequently, in Hai's opinion, it may be employed in the *kaddish*.

This controversy is discussed at length by Büchler,[28] who offers the following explanation. V*eyitkales*, according to him, was included by Palestinians, and was therefore combated by Yehudai when he found its use infiltrating into Babylonia. Eventually Sura adopted this Palestinian custom, though Pumbedita did not. Since Hai says in his responsum that various *chazzanim* act differently on the matter, Büchler contends that Hai did not even recognize the issue at first except as a "variant fluctuating custom," and intervened only to end "verbal quibbles" brought on by Karaites ever ready to find an excuse to lambast their foes' ignorance. No other Pumbeditan gaon even mentions the term. Its Palestinian origin is demonstrated by its presence in one manuscript of the eighth-century Palestinian work, *Massekhet Soferim*.[29] Furthermore, *veyitkales* was a favorite term of the *merkavah* mystics, who were responsible for its being brought to Babylon in the first place.

But as Büchler himself notes, an eleventh-century Palestinian text of the *kaddish* does not contain *veyitkales*,[30] and other genizah material from earlier times varies.[31] Besides, why would Sura adopt a custom which Yehudai, its founding gaon, had condemned? And Büchler does not account for Amram's statement that he, personally, also omits it; Amram was certainly a Suran! Moreover, we do not know that people "quibbled" over every word of the *kaddish*, and even if they did, Hai's normal procedure would have been to say, at most, "It is fitting to say it." For Hai to have declared obligatory a pointless case of "verbal quibbling" is inconsistent with the picture of Hai emerging from the evidence of his other liturgical decisions.

In fact, on the basis of Lewin's eleventh-century document mentioned above, Ginzberg repudiates Büchler's theory and offers one of his own: it was, he says, merely a case of scholarly debate, of no particular consequence whatever.[32]

But an alternative reconstruction may be warranted. What seems like a "verbal quibble" to us was usually not so to religious authorities in the thick of battle. How many "heresies" have depended on a "verbal quibble"? And how many Supreme Court decisions, even today, are determined by a word or phrase being read one way or the other? Moreover, to say that a geonic debate has no particular relevance is to beg the question and admit in effect that we have failed to unearth whatever relevance there was.

There are at least two issues here, not necessarily related. At least they should not be confused. The first is the very natural tendency of a gaon like Yehudai, beginning an arduous process of canonizing Babylonian custom, to avoid liturgical language which might, by virtue of its potentially negative implications, cast doubt on the divine service for which he stands. The second is what appears to be a very real role of the *merkavah* mystics, whose doctrine of the seven heavens is attested 'as accepted lore by Amram.

A full treatment of these mystics is beyond the scope of this study, and, in any event, still dependent on much initial research into the sources, work not yet done. In fact, despite the fact that the basic study on the subject was published as long ago as 1893, and that monographs and books of considerable importance have been written by many noted scholars,[33] we still know surprisingly little about the *merkavah* influence on the liturgy.

There are, however, some salient facts that emerge from these studies and are significant here. The group emerged out of the Hellenistic milieu of the second century C.E., if not earlier. Basing their theology on the cosmology positing seven heavens (and perhaps eight),[34] they conceptualized God as seated on His throne of glory (or *merkavah*) and surrounded by angels constantly praising Him. Worship's purpose was to praise God similarly, and to escape the fetters of worldly habitation in order to break through the barriers of the various heavens and see God in His splendor. This psychic journey occasioned considerable danger, particularly at each entry into a new heaven, and would-be travelers were outfitted with secret lore (gnosis), and proper incantations that would prove effective in protecting one from madness or even death at such moments of crisis.

It was not petition, then, or even prayers of thanksgiving that were the hallmark of the mystic's liturgy. Praise was all. Like the angels in Isaiah's vision, the human worshipper was intent on praising God, while ascending through heaven after heaven in search of the ultimate throne of glory. Moreover, it was not the content of the words that mattered so much as the manner in which they were pronounced. Like mantras, they were a means by which a worshipper could transfer his mind from cognitive considerations to affective alteration of one's total perspective. Legend, in fact, regarded even bodily posture as a recommended means of achieving the perspective required if one was to ascend the celestial spheres.[35] It was not the liturgy's semantic meaning, therefore, but the method by which it was recited that counted.

So words which have different meanings when translated into English ("praised," "adored," "sanctified," "lauded," etc.) were regularly strung together by the mystics, without, however, any necessary thought about their cognitive significance. They were all synonymous of the general picture of praising God, and were never meant to be analyzed into their fine differences of meaning. Said together, one after the other, perhaps even repeated time and again, one could reach beyond oneself to the holy vision that beckoned. It was Bloch himself who recognized, in his original monograph, that mystical liturgy tends to have synonyms piled up together; and that their meaning is insignificant, content being secondary to effect.[36]

But traditional scholarship has not taken kindly to the possibility of widespread Jewish mysticism as a formative entity in the decisive tannaitic period. Drawing an a priori distinction between non-Jewish gnostics and "rational" Jewish rabbis, a general assumption is made in which the regnant personalities of the Second Commonwealth are seen as remote from mystical pursuits. From time to time one hears that Hillel or Akiba had some mystical leanings, but the idea that this mysticism was a significant motive in rabbinic development has hardly been broached. Yet Scholem has pointed out that mysticism need not be irrational.[37] So we would be guilty of enormous prejudice if we were to limit our search for the *merkavah* mystics to but a few individuals, by definition beyond the pale of normative rabbinic develop-ment. It would be far more beneficial if we were to ignore the misleading term "mystic" altogether and focus our search on any and every rabbi of the period, asking only if the man involved is reported to have said or done anything that implicates him as a personality with *merkavah* leanings.

I do not say "*merkavah* group," note, since in fact there was no such group, if by group we mean the usual sociological definition of an aggregation of individuals who organize together by virtue of seeing themselves somehow apart from the masses around them. In fact we have no record whatever of *merkavah* organizations, cells, meetings, leaders, social structure—nothing that a student of human organizations would point to as illustrating the development of a group. We have instead legends about rabbis, some well known, like Yochanan ben Zakkai and Akiba;[38] a literature detailing visions of people who attained the mystical vision; and prayers galore illustrative of *merkavah* values and *merkavah* style. So we should speak not of the *mer-kavah* "group," but of a *merkavah* "tendency" to which many a rabbi may well have leaned at one time or another.

Thus there is no reason to limit the *merkavah* influence on the liturgy to fringe elements, a prayer here or a line there. Nor need we assume their influence to stem from people outside the mainstream of Judaism, or living at times and places beyond the reach of more rational tannaim and amoraim. More likely is it that the *merkavah* tendency is evident in many places in the prayers, awaiting only the glance of the unbiased observer to be pointed out.[39]

The most obvious examples, however, are those which deal with *kedushah,* "holiness." Aside from whatever English translation or interpreta-tion one wishes to assign this highly discussed Hebrew word, to the mystics it implied the essence of what they were about. It is used in apposition to other similar terms (in the *yotser,* for example, or the *kedushah*) and implies the generic concept of praising, sanctifying, lauding, exalting, etc. It is what the angels do in the paradigmatic case of Isaiah 6:3; it regularly concludes the visionary accounts in the *merkavah midrashim;* and it figures prominently in more than a few central prayers in the Jewish liturgy.

So in our case, Büchler's evidence for the word *yitkales* being favored by the mystics is convincing. It was one of the many terms regularly employed to describe the angelic praise of God in their recitation of the *kedushah* of Isaiah's vision.[40] In fact the *kedushah* in its many forms was a favorite prayer of theirs, based as it was on that very vision. But they were also interested in the *kaddish*, as Amram's comment suggests, and this should not surprise us, given the fact that (1) the terms *kaddish* and *kedushah* are etymologically related, and (2) the theme of the *kaddish* is the same as that of the *kedushah*: praise of God and His ultimate kingdom. We may even expand the conceptual framework that unites these two prayers by emphasizing their common vision of God as King, an image suggested by His sitting on the throne of glory. Both *kedushah* and *kaddish* reach their climax in the vision of the Lord reigning over His creation.[41]

If more proof were needed to establish the intimate connection of *kaddish* and *kedushah* in terms of their common mystical tendency, one might simply note that they developed in the same milieu. The *kaddish* functioned originally as a short prayer accompanying a sermon and a session of study.[42] And the same origin is given for a form of the *kedushah*, the *kedushah desidra'*, in a celebrated responsum by Natronai.[43] The very title confirms Natronai's historical account, since the noun *sidra'* was the term used in Palestine for the weekly lection.[44] Not for nothing does the fourth-century Babylonian amora Rava, while discussing the woeful state of the world, where tribulations increase daily, remark, "What maintains the world? The *kedushah desidra'* and the *yehei shemeih rabbah de'aggadeta'*!" That is, the *kedushah desidra'* itself and the response to the *kaddish*, still connected in Rava's mind with its original context, the *'aggadah*, or lore of the preacher. *Kaddish* and *kedushah* alike were prayers of ultimate hope; hope of seeing the divine vision and of experiencing the coming of the Kingdom.[45]

As an integral part of rabbinic Jewry rather than some splinter party, these people of mystical tendency were not averse to study. In fact, they had their own favorite formula, *lamdeini chukekha* ("Teach me your statutes"), which they recited to attain perfect knowledge of Torah.[46] So as regular students of Torah, it is not surprising to find them elevating their favorite prayers, including our *kaddish*, to essential parts of the liturgy accompanying the act of study. In fact, this entire discussion was prompted by Amram's description of the piling up of adjectives in the *kaddish* and its association with the seven heavens, a perfectly reasonable situation if one accepts the portrait of the mystics as painted here.

Originally the *kaddish* may have ended at the first word of the phrase, *yitbarakh*, as part of the parallelism of the congregational response. The congregation may have responded with the first line, to which the preacher answered the second, and the congregation again responded with their *'amen*.[47] But the mystics' tendency to pile up synonyms and their natural interest in this prayer led to the addition of several synonyms, not always the same to be sure, content being secondary to effect, and thus the differences in our manuscript samples;[48] but one word which occurred frequently was *yitkales*, and Yehudai was asked about the propriety of including it.

Now Yehudai may well have known that one synonym was the same as another as far as the mystics were concerned, or he may have been completely impervious to mystical intentions. In either case he felt no need to substantiate the use of a word which might cause some embarrassment, and he was quick to abandon it. On the other hand, he may actually have opposed the freewheeling attitude toward the liturgy that marked the mystical additions to many prayers. Recent scholarship has shown, for example, that Yannai, one of the leading classical *payyetanim*, the poets of Palestine who composed so much poetry to be included in the standard prayers, was much intrigued with *merkavah* speculation;[49] and we shall see later that Yehudai was intransigently opposed to such poetry, probably because its unfettered usage prevented him from canonizing liturgical formulae, an activity, we have argued, to be one that occupied much of Yehudai's efforts. And finally we have the impeccable testimony of Ben Baboi, a student of a student of Yehudai, who lived, therefore, about the year 800. He wrote a letter to Palestine admonishing Jews there to heed the wisdom of his departed master Yehudai, who had himself written to Palestine but been ignored. As Ben Baboi puts it,

> It is forbidden to add even one letter to the praise of God, beyond that which our sages instituted . . . and all the more so [it is forbidden] to say *ma'asei merkavah* [matters dealing with the *merkavah*] whether in the congregation or even as an individual.[50]

So Yehudai's natural inclination to oppose a term which he knew to be a matter of local choice, hardly essential to Babylonian talmudic law, and potentially embarrassing because of its negative biblical connotation, was buttressed by the fact that mystical speculation was part and parcel of the poetic movement hailing from Palestine, intent on expanding the liturgy, while Yehudai wanted just the opposite: to regulate and order it.

A century later the same issue perplexed Amram. But by then, as we shall see when we look at the *piyyut*, a compromise on the issue of liturgical poetry had been reached. Both Natronai and Amram had given in to the inevitable and allowed the *piyyut* to flourish within certain structural guidelines. Moreover, the mystical tendency was, by Amram's own admission, a matter generally taken for granted. Everyone admitted that there should be seven terms, not just the original one, and everyone knew that the number was intended to represent the seven heavens.[51] The only question was the way in which people counted to seven, and on this Amram had no preference. He himself, following the Suran precedent laid down by Yehudai, did not say *veyitkales*, but at the same time he made a point of refuting Yehudai's attempt to malign the term, saying there was no error involved in doing it either way.

This kind of permissive remark is not in keeping with Amram as the portrait of him has emerged from our study. His responsa, including the major one, his *Seder* itself, are full of vituperative remarks, and he is generally prone to take a side on issues, and to prohibit the alternative strongly. But what issue was involved here? Not the extension of the basic prayers by poetic insertions. That had already been worked out in the compromise alluded to above. And not mystical tendencies, which, if they existed at all by the middle of the ninth century, may have done so only in literary preferences rather than actual applications of worship techniques. Certainly Amram, like the other Babylonians, accepted the mystical literary genre and had incorporated it in many prayers, the *kaddish* being but one of them. In any event, this was no issue separating Babylonians from Palestinians. So we need not reevaluate our basic hypothesis regarding Amram's anti-Palestinian stand on the basis of his leniency here.

Saadiah, too, whom we may mention in passing at this point, though unsympathetic with the mystics' tendency toward anthropomorphism,[52] saw no need to intervene in what was by now a dead issue, except to go on record as using *veyitkales* by including it in his *Siddur* and remarking that even those who omit it do not regard the word's connotation as being derogatory.[53]

We are still left with Hai, however, whose normal leniency is unaccountably broken by his insistence on the use of *veyitkales*. His position cannot be explained with certainty. But two possible reconstructions may be suggested, neither based on more than circumstantial evidence.

The first possibility is related to Saadiah's desire to include the word. Hai himself says that he considers it to be a term of praise in rabbinic idiom, despite its frequent use to the contrary in the Bible. Hai lived precisely at the apex of Karaite grandeur in Palestine, and, as we shall see, some of the few instances of his taking a hard line against his opponents are related to his desire to counteract Karaite claims. Since the Karaites challenged the Rabbanite tradition with quotations from the Bible, it may be that Hai decided to counter by demanding the use of a word whose negative biblical connotations could be overcome only by the acceptance of the priority of talmudic usage. And this would be in keeping with Saadiah (whose anti-Karaite bias is known), who not only used the word but, like Hai, commented on its propriety. As Saadiah says, even those who do not use it admit there is nothing wrong with it; and as Hai put it, in the second responsum cited above, it is always commendatory in rabbinic idiom and thus fitting.

Another possibility is worth considering however, even though it is tentative in the extreme. One is struck by the forcefulness of Hai's first responsum, as well as by the message contained therein. He favors *yitkales* because of its martial connotation, and wishes to emphasize the glorious war of the Lord which will introduce the messianic era. Now Hai has left us another responsum in which he explored the possibilities of the coming travails of the Messiah.[54] And Ibn Daud, writing in the closing days of Omayyad grandeur in Spain, the late twelfth century, records the curious information that:

Some lawless Jews denounced R. Sherira and R. Hai, and the king of Babylonia imprisoned them, confiscated all their possessions, and left them no source of support whatever. However, R. Sherira did manage to get some aid, although he was at the time approximately one hundred years old, and they were not deposed from the gaonate.[55]

Now scholars are unsure of what to do with this startling information regarding the final years of Sherira and his son, Hai. Lewin cites several opinions, none of them convincing, as he himself admits, and Cohen, who edited Ibn Daud's history, lists others.[56] The most plausible seems to be that Sherira and Hai were suspected of trying to overthrow the established order of the caliphate, and were therefore imprisoned until the charge was refuted through the powerful contacts they had made during their lengthy tenure in high office. Certainly the Abbasid dynasty at the end of the tenth century was not what it had been in its heyday a century and a half before. If indeed it appeared that the colossus of the Arab world was tottering through Fatimid triumphs without and internal scheming within, it is conceivable that Hai, the gaon at the time, might have resurrected Jewish traditions regarding the end of days and seen that promised end of time in the cataclysmic rumblings that threatened to overthrow the greatest power ever known to him. And he may for that reason have been partial to a term which he took to imply the final messianic battle, especially in a prayer which spoke openly of the promise of God's kingdom on earth.

Whatever the reason, and we shall probably never know it for sure, we must admit that this is one example where Hai's usual leniency is not to be found. There will be others. Yet in the main we shall find him and his father still to be essentially permissive, thus upholding our contention that the third period of geonic canonization was one of open-mindedness and compromise.

We have meanwhile, let it be noted, established both Saadiah's continued concern with grammar and language, and Yehudai's opposition to Palestinian poetic embellishments. Our schema of tracing Amram's polemical intent all the way back to Yehudai has been confirmed, as has our picture of Saadiah, the grammarian and biblical stylist. In doing so we have had to introduce the problems attendant on *piyyutim*, so before proceeding with other liturgical services and rubrics which entail *piyyutim* all the more, we should pause and consider the origin of the *piyyutim* and the geonic attitude to them.

4: The *Piyyut*

BEFORE DEALING WITH THE MANY INDIVIDUAL PROBLEMS OF SABBATH AND festival liturgy, it would be well to investigate one basic underlying consideration, the geonic attitude to the *piyyut*. Most of the pertinent texts discuss particular questions regarding specific additions, and have therefore been postponed to later chapters. Here we are interested in arriving at a general understanding of the geonic attitude toward poetic additions in the prayers.

Perhaps the hardest task would be to arrive at an adequate definition of *piyyut*. It is poetry, certainly, but how is it to be distinguished from certain standard prayers which are also couched in poetic form? Fortunately, for our purposes we require no precise definition. We need merely note that sometime before the geonic period, certainly before the coming of Islam, and possibly as early as the tannaitic period itself, poets, particularly in Palestine, were experimenting with highly stylized poetic formations of prayers. These were not the standardized liturgical selections in the usual rabbinic *berakhah* prose, designed to express the basic themes mandated by the time of Rabban Gamaliel, but additions which could be inserted into such standarized prayers so as to enrich them.[1]

Piyyutim, to be sure, were not exclusively a Palestinian product. Scholars have unearthed relatively early poetry by Babylonians as well. But the *piyyut* was born in Palestine; and there it flourished. Not until the tenth or eleventh century do we find evidence of significant poetic creativity elsewhere.[2]

Of course national boundaries did not really exist then, at least not in the sense that we define the term. There were, rather, spiritual spheres of influence, cultural traits that marked one as basically Palestinian or Babylonian: whether one depended on the Babylonian Talmud or the Palestinian; what cycle of readings from the Torah one used; what form of written culture (legal responsum, biblical commentary, etc.) one preferred. Palestinians could live as Palestinians in Egypt, and Babylonians could exist as Babylonians in Palestine. So in deriving the geographical provenance of the *piyyut*, our concern is not so much the particular city a poet inhabited, but the cultural expression he appropriated as his own.

It is in this sense, then, that the *piyyut* must be considered a Palestinian phenomenon, and the *payyetanim*, at least in period 1 of geonic consolidation, Palestinians by spiritual proclivity. Indeed, whatever finds we may have regarding Babylonian *payyetanim*, the truly great synagogue poets of antiquity, whose mark was left indelibly on all future generations, were residents of cities in and around Palestine, and took their cue from Palestinian culture, influenced, no doubt, by Byzantine cultural models. Hymnology and masters of the poetic art, like Romanus, were typical of the high cultural development of the Eastern Church in the sixth century; and that was precisely the period which saw the labors of the greatest Jewish *payyetan*, Eliezer Kalir. Without Kalir and his Palestinian predecessors, Yannai and Yose, the development of the *piyyut* would be sparse indeed, its classical period shrinking to what can hardly be called a period at all.

Only the Palestinian origin of liturgical poetry can explain the fact that despite valiant efforts by men like Saadiah—who had a Palestinian background, note—it is not Babylonian liturgy but Palestinian genizah fragments that are so rich in poetic embellishments. And it is the same assumption alone which can satisfactorily explain the early geonic communications on the subject.

We have already referred to Yehudai and the recollections regarding him in the letter of Ben Baboi.[3] The latter is a strident champion, generally, of Babylonian prerogatives, and specifically of Yehudai, whom he idolizes. In his letter, about the year 800, he mounts a particularly eloquent opposition to *piyyutim*, dismissing unwarranted liturgical additions of any kind. One who says an unnecessary blessing deserves excommunication, in his view, and one who alters the formal structure of a blessing—as would be the case if poetic additions were inserted at random—not only falls short of discharging his obligation but deserves death besides.[4] Ben Baboi cites the Babylonian Talmud to make his point here, even though his quotation is taken out of context, as he himself must have known.[5] One should, he concludes, avoid adding as little as one word of praise to the blessing formula. In the first three and the last three benedictions of the *tefillah* one should add neither petitions nor lore (*'aggadah*) nor matters dealing with the *merkavah* (*ma'aseh merkavah*). As examples of such deviations, Ben Baboi singles out two *piyyutim*: *vayavo' 'amalek* and *'eikhah 'evkeh*.[6] In sum, "One may not say any blessing which is not in the Talmud; it is forbidden to add even one word."[7]

The letter is filled with such diatribes. Rather than list them all, we would do well to concentrate on the general lessons which we can learn regarding the state of liturgical fixity and the credit Yehudai received for achieving it. Yehudai is a paragon of virtue in Ben Baboi's eyes.

> There has not been one like him for years, one whose greatness extended to Scripture, Mishnah, Talmud, Midrash, Tosafot [i.e., Tosefta, considered here as tannaitic additions to the major tannaitic corpus, the Mishnah], rabbinic lore, and practical law. He never said

anything that he had not heard directly from his teacher, and he excelled in holiness, purity, piety, and humility.[8]

For good reasons, Ben Baboi can think of no better way to substantiate his own opinion than to cite Yehudai, though he admits that when the latter himself wrote to the Palestinians regarding "all the commandments which they observe improperly they rejected his opinion, responding, 'custom annuls law.'"[9] Nevertheless, says Ben Baboi, Yehudai should be heeded, since "Yehudai said, 'You have never asked me anything to which I did not respond with an answer that both had talmudic proof and that I had learned as a practical rule of law from my teacher, and he from his teacher.'"[10]

Now Yehudai's claim for authority is very important for our gauging his role in the propagation of Babylonian tradition as universal orthodoxy. Ben Baboi tells us explicitly that Yehudai was embroiled with the Palestinians over *piyyutim* specifically, rules of liturgical propriety generally, as well as a host of other issues, some of which we shall analyze later. This is entirely in keeping with our description of period 1, extending from Amram back to Yehudai. Moreover, we now know why it took so many years of arduous battle to get the Babylonian tradition accepted. The Palestinians were most reticent in accepting Babylonian usages since they considered their own customs to have priority. And now we see from Yehudai's own words that his citation of the Talmud alone would not have gone very far in convincing anyone of the rectitude of his opinion. For that, he must offer yet another guarantee, the assurance that his every utterance has been gleaned through the time-honored method of oral transmission through the generations. Indeed, as we postulated earlier, the Babylonian Talmud itself was not yet worth very much in the eyes of the Jewish world at large. It was still not codified; its dicta not universally applauded. Only the assurance that what it contained was identical to oral transmission from known and accepted authorities could win the day for Yehudai in this very early stage of canonization.

Natronai's stand, almost a century later, is quite different.

> If people say *piyyutim* in the *'avot* and the *gevurot* [the first two blessings of the *tefillah*] on any occasion when the *tefillah* is recited, on any particular holiday, and if the subject matter of the *piyyut* is pertinent to the holiday so that they expand the blessing with rabbinic lore; if, that is, on the Ninth of Av or on Purim they add material in any given blessing whose subject matter is relevant to that blessing [*me'en 'otah berakhah*] or if, on Rosh Hashanah and on Yom Kippur they add words of entreaty and poetry dealing with forgiveness, and on the Ninth of Av matters dealing with the destruction of the Temple, they may do so. The main thing is that in each blessing people should say words tantamount to the blessing's introduction and conclusion, and in the middle they may say words of lore [*'aggadah*] and praise of God. That is fitting. But *bekibbuts geluyot* and *behikabeits betulot*, and similar

things . . . one should not say, and if one says them, we instruct him not to do so.[11]

This is the regnant principle, or compromise, by which the geonim, intent on liturgical fixity, found room for poetic expansion. Natronai allows additions in the first two blessings as long as they are *me'en berakhah*. That is, they must be related to the general topic of the blessing involved. They thus require a fitting introduction and conclusion, and aggadic matter of a harmonious subject matter. He cautions against two *piyyutim* whose contents would not be in harmony.[12]

So real change has developed since Yehudai's outright condemnation of the addition of even one word, and Natronai's acceptance of entire *piyyutim* providing that their subject matter be relevant to the blessing in question and that they lead naturally from the blessing's introduction and back again to its conclusion. Amram simply follows the view of his predecessor, Natronai. He supports the removal of *chazzanim* who change the blessing's formal structure, saying, "If we happen on a place where the *chazzan* says something [structurally incorrect] we remove him."[13] But he gives them the same leeway as Natronai did, allowing *piyyutim* generally, and declaring them to be optional, not obligatory.[14]

The theoretical point which distinguishes Yehudai from Amram is their respective use of the concept *me'en berakhah*. Where this technical phrase appears in tannaitic literature, it has generally been understood to mean "a summary of the blessing." But that translation is based on the philological understanding of liturgical origins. Since the main passage in question refers to Rabban Gamaliel's desire to say eighteen blessings, and Joshua's insistence that *me'en shemoneh 'esreh* will do, scholars have tended to interpret Joshua's recommendation as a summary of the original eighteen mandated by Gamaliel.[15] Actually, Joshua may have meant only that the thematic order laid down by Gamaliel had to be followed; its eighteen topics covered, but not necessarily in eighteen different blessings. So *me'en* has the connotation of similarity in topic. In our case, *me'en berakhah* implies that the validity of a *piyyut* depends on its thematic harmony with the blessing in which it is inserted.

But Yehudai uses the principle negatively. He discusses a common addition to the High Holiday liturgy inserted in the first blessing of the *tefillah*, calling on God to "remember us for life," and he contends against it on the ground that at the very most only that which *me'en berakhah* would be permissible, his examples of the latter being personal petitions in the middle benedictions, or, as he phrases it, petitions "for health in the blessing regarding healing," and such.[16] But this is no concession at all. It is merely a talmudic precedent used to exclude everything else. Nowhere does Ben Baboi even suggest that the interpolations he opposes might possibly be reworked to merit justification under the concept of *me'en berakhah.* For Yehudai this category serves to exclude all but the bare talmudic examples which he quotes.

Both Natronai and Amram, on the other hand, use the concept positively, stretching it to admit regular poetic insertions.[17] And therein lies the legal loophole underlying the geonic compromise with the *piyyut.*[18]

The only potential problem with this solution is a responsum attributed to Amram's Suran successor, Nachshon Gaon (871–879).

> Rav Nachshon wrote that in the academy and wherever our rabbis reside, they alter nothing of the prayers which our rabbis instituted . . . [and they say] no *piyyut* and admit no *chazzan* who knows *piyyutim* to the synagogue. Any congregations where they say *piyyutim* testify of themselves that they are not scholars.[19]

How is one to harmonize Nachshon's opinion with that of his two predecessors, Amram and Natronai? Even if Nachshon were simply of another mind—a highly doubtful possibility, considering the fact that Nachshon would not lightly turn his back on the last eighteen years of highly effective Suran leadership—how could he state that *piyyutim* were not said in Sura? We know from Amram and Natronai that they were.

These considerations raise the possibility of emending the passage in question. This approach to the text can be justified further by the fact that the responsum is first quoted by a very late and not necessarily reliable source.[20] Ginzberg, for example, believing Pumbedita to have opposed *piyyutim* more than Sura, emends "Nachshon" to "Nehemiah" (Pumbedita, 960–968) or "Nathan" (uncle of Sherira).[21]

But Ginzberg's solution depends on his highly tenuous assumption that Sura alone favored *piyyutim.*[22] Now it may be true that the two academies differed from time to time on specific insertions, but there is no reason to doubt that on the whole, both schools accepted the compromise worked out by Natronai. To the extent that *piyyutim* were Palestinian in origin, neither academy took to them willingly; but to the extent that the earlier harsh view of Yehudai was unsuccessful in countering the popular appeal of *piyyutim,* both academies made peace with the situation as well as they could. One must conclude, regarding the passage in question, that its authorship is simply unknown. It cannot be used to support or to reject any theory whatever. Its existence does not vitiate what was said above regarding Natronai and Amram.

If it is Natronai and Amram who come to terms with the *piyyutim,* it is Saadiah who makes the greatest use of them. Probably because of his Palestinian background, he exceeds every other gaon in his regular use of Palestinian poetry,[23] and he offers in addition many similar compositions of his own. Yet even these numerous *piyyutim* constitute a mere fraction of what he was tempted to include. He decided, though, to settle for what he considered the best examples.[24] Even so, he incorporates no fewer than twenty-three *selichot* for Yom Kippur![25]

Saadiah's selectivity is governed by various criteria. He favors the recitation of *tekiyot*, for example, but looks askance at those lacking in stylistic elegance, linguistic precision, and praiseworthy content.[26] Similarly, Saadiah employs *'azharot*, but not those beginning with *'atah hinchalta*, since they do not contain all the commandments by his count, and their language he considers cumbersome.[27] Naturally, his three general criteria discussed above apply here as well.

Geonim after Saadiah have left us with no general responsa on the subject of *piyyutim*, and no prayer books from which detailed analyses of their positions might be deduced. Their communications are isolated statements on the subject of specific inserts from which it is hard to generalize. But they never say they are opposed to *piyyutim* per se, so there is no reason to believe they were. They probably accepted the compromise worked out by their predecessors, and for that very reason did not write their own general treatises on the subject. The *piyyut* was by now an accepted entity. The specific cases which they accepted or rejected will be discussed elsewhere in these pages.

5: Sabbath Liturgy

WE HAVE ALREADY REMARKED THAT THE DAILY SERVICE FORMS A CORE around which Sabbath and holiday liturgical expansions are grafted. Many such expansions are *piyyutim*. Others are changes in the service's thematic structure, designed to reflect the mood of the special day in question.

For our purposes, we need note only a few of the alterations that distinguish the Friday night service from the usual evening liturgy.

1. A *kiddush*, or sanctification prayer, ushers in the day.[1] Technically it is a home prayer introducing the Sabbath-eve meal, but since early amoraic times (at least), it was also recited publicly in the synagogue. A major conflict did arise over a variant version of the home *kiddush* (the *yein 'asis* formula), but we have already discussed this in connection with the Passover *seder*.

2. The daily evening service is introduced with a biblical citation, *vehu' rachum*,[2] emphasizing God's plenteous mercy toward sinners. In Ashkenazic congregations, this is omitted on Friday night; the Sefardic rite retains it.

3. We have already remarked that the daily *shema'* has not one but two blessings after it in the evening. The latter is called *hashkivenu*, and calls on God to protect us while we sleep. Its normal eulogy affirms that God *shomer 'amo yisra'el*, "keeps his people Israel." On Friday the concluding line is changed to *pores sukkat shalom 'alenu*, God "stretches a tabernacle of peace over us."[3]

4. Since late amoraic or early geonic times, the final blessing, *hashkivenu*, was extended by a series of short statements having no internal connection with each other except their common theme of praising God. Tradition explained their compilation as being due to the fact that the *tefillah* of the evening service, technically speaking, is not mandatory. To compensate for its possible omission, there were added these statements which, taken together, contain the name of God eighteen times, equivalent to the eighteen benedictions of the *tefillah* that might have been skipped. We should refer to the prayer by its opening statement, *barukh 'adonai le'olam*, "Blessed be the Lord forever." It is omitted on Friday night.[4]

5. This addition to the *hashkivenu* is itself expanded by a prayer expressing God's ultimate sovereignty and our faith in the eventual arrival of His Kingdom. It is called *yir'u 'eineinu*, "May our eyes behold [the deliverance of the Kingdom]." This too is omitted on Friday night.[5]

6. In place of the extended *hashkivenu* (nos. 4 and 5 above) the Friday evening service inserts the biblical verses Exodus 31:16–17, *veshameru venei yisra'el . . .* , "The children of Israel shall keep the Sabbath . . . throughout their generations as an eternal covenant. . . ."[6]

7. With the final eulogy of the *hashkivenu* changed, the normal extensions omitted, and the biblical *veshameru* inserted, the worshipper proceeds to the *tefillah*. Here too, however, there are alterations. The normal *tefillah* has thirteen intermediate petitionary benedictions. These are dropped on the Sabbath (and holidays), and in their place a special benediction called *kedushat hayom*, "the sanctity of the day," is recited.[7] Like the *kiddush*, said to inaugurate the Sabbath, this blessing too affirms the day's holiness.

8. Following the *tefillah*, what appears to have originally been an alternative to the *tefillah* is recited. In shortened form it synopsizes the *tefillah*'s content, using the words *magen 'avot*, from which its title is derived.[8]

With the exception of the *kiddush*, with which we have already dealt, and the exchange of the middle petitionary blessings in the *tefillah* for a *kedushat hayom*, which we shall discuss in the chapter on holidays, all the other alterations figure prominently in geonic discussions. What makes each issue so hard to follow is that they are all really different aspects of one debate! They intertwine in serpentine fashion so that a full comprehension of the basis for any single topic of discussion demands equal and simultaneous attention to all the others. The underlying concern is life after death, and the punishment meted out to sinners in the personal afterlife.

Our rather protracted discussion of the matter might well begin by citing some medieval commentaries relevant to the Sefardic inclusion of *vehu' rachum* on Friday night, and, conversely, the Ashkenazic omission thereof. No attempt will be made to exhaust the entire multitude of fabulous notions on the subject, but just a limited, though sufficient, sampling of opinion to establish the all-pervasiveness of the belief that sinners would indeed suffer in the afterlife, that certain prayers could be expected to alleviate their anguish, and—eventually—that decisions to say or not to say certain daily prayers—the changes, in other words, that we outlined at the beginning of this chapter— are related to the question of whether such departed sinners still require protection on the Sabbath, or whether, conversely, the Sabbath is sufficient protection in itself. We shall also show that these ideas did not originate in Western Europe, but in the milieu represented by the geonim.[9]

The pioneer liturgist, Isaac Baer, provides an excellent summary of early opinion from which we may begin.[10] He quotes the *Rokeach* (by Eleazer of Worms, 1176–1238) to the effect that we normally say *vehu' rachum* in the evening to make up for the fact that in Temple times there was no *tamid*, or daily sacrifice, at night, and *vehu' rachum* grants us atonement in its place. Rashi (1040–1105) goes further by commenting that sinners are punished in hell (*gehinnom*) between the afternoon and evening services, so we begin the latter by praying for compassion and pardon. Zedekiah ben Abraham concurs. 'Or Zarua', in fact insists—following Eleazer of Worms—that the prayer after *vehu' rachum* be drawn out in its recitation on Saturday night, since sinners then must return to their punishment, and we wish to postpone this cruel fate as long as possible.

For the Sabbath, however, opinions differ. Jacob ben Asher (d. 1340) reasons that no punishment occurs then; hence there is no need for *vehu' rachum*. Eleazer of Worms agrees, and adds that we do not supplicate on the Sabbath. But the Sefardim say *vehu' rachum* anyway because (according to Baer) they follow Amram's precedent. Baer also feels that they rely on Eleazer of Worms's reasoning regarding the absence of a Temple sacrifice.

One can see from the above summary that a good deal of superstition surrounded the legal discussion of *vehu' rachum*. Yet as early as the eleventh and twelfth centuries, there was no precise recollection of exactly what it was that had sparked the original debate. Indeed, the debate preceded that period by hundreds of years and took place halfway across the world. Its genesis was geonic.

The first step for determining the issue for the geonim is to decide what Amram's practice was. As Baer realized, Amram does appear to have *vehu' rachum* on Friday night.[11] But the Oxford manuscript does not have it, and there are reasons for believing that here the Oxford manuscript is correct. As is frequently the case, a look at the Spanish savant David Abudarham (mid-14th cent.) is instructive. We shall call his comment (A). Abudarham says the following.

(A)   [Abraham b. Nathan] Hayarchi [of Lunel, author of the *Manhig*, late 12th–early 13th cent.] wrote that since sinners are punished between the   afternoon   and   the   evening   service . . . we   say   *vehu' rachum*. . . . That is the reason for the Spanish custom of saying it [even] on Sabbaths and holidays.[12]

But still feeling constrained to defend his own custom of saying *vehu' rachum* on Friday nights, Abudarham continues with the *midrash* in *Tanchuma*, *Pinchas* 13.

No one ever stood in Jerusalem in a state of sin. How so? Because the morning sacrifice atones for sins committed at night, and the afternoon sacrifice atones for sins committed during the day.

Now it is to be noticed that the *Tanchuma* passage itself neither mentions *vehu' rachum* nor connects it in any way with the pericope taught. So Abudarham adds a connection by mentioning that *vehu' rachum* makes up for the lack of an evening sacrifice. But this reasoning was already known to Eleazer of Worms, as we saw above, who nevertheless did not permit *vehu' rachum* on the Sabbath. Abudarham's logic is therefore faulty. At the very least, his defense is a weak one. Yet (and this is the point) Abudarham is one of the prime sources for *Seder Rav Amram*. He not only knew the book but seems to have had it by his side, referring to it regularly. Why then, if Amram said *vehu' rachum* on Friday nights, did Abudarham not simply invoke the precedent of his most trusted liturgical authority, and say, "We follow Amram"?

At this point we must consider an anonymous responsum carried in two sources, which we shall label (B).

(B)   In the two academies, since the day has been sanctified [as the Sabbath], it is forbidden to say *vehu' rachum* and [as the eulogy to *hashkivenu*] "who keeps His people Israel."[13]

Note that both academies omitted *vehu' rachum* in this author's time, and that the saying of *vehu' rachum* is connected here with yet another prayer, *hashkivenu*, whose customary eulogy, "who keeps His people Israel," was changed, we will recall, to "who stretches a tabernacle of peace." Both liturgical changes were traced to the same motive, the sanctification of the day. But of what relevance is the day's sanctity? Our author apparently assumes a connection without stating it. I argue that its pertinence is due to a corollary notion, the belief expressed above, that on a holy day accusers of sinners who have died are temporarily silenced, and the sinners need no protection. Since the day has been sanctified, in other words, the dead sinners are now at peace, and need no help from us to ease their burden. Thus one may safely omit both *vehu' rachum* and "who keeps His people"; the former, which would have pardoned their sins, as did the Temple cult of old, and the latter, which assured them each night that despite momentary travail, God protects His people forever.

Amram himself testifies that he—like Sar Shalom before him—does, in fact, omit the eulogy promising protection. We shall call it (C).

(C)   Sar Shalom, also, said that in the academy and in *bet rabbenu* it is not customary to say "who keeps His people Israel" on the eve of Sabbaths and holidays. Rather, instead of "who keeps His people Israel," we conclude [the *hashkivenu*] with "who stretches a tabernacle of peace." And after that we move immediately to the half-*kaddish* [which introduces the *tefillah*; i.e., both parts of the extended *hashkivenu* are skipped] but in other synagogues and places they say "who keeps his people Israel, forever," and *veshameru* . . . but in the other academy [Pumbedita] and all Babylonia they omit *barukh 'adonai le'olam*.[14]

So Amram omitted one of the two items, *shomer 'amo*. Since the anonymous gaon (B) considered this on a par with *vehu' rachum*, it follows that Amram also omitted *vehu' rachum*. And that is why Abudarham (A) could not quote him to the contrary!

Amram says, however, that others do say *shomer 'amo yisra'el*. They also say *veshameru*, a biblical passage which Amram leaves out here again, for similar reasons, as is apparent from *Machzor Vitry* (12th cent.). There, the covenant mentioned by *veshameru* is interpreted as the following: just as we keep the Sabbath, so God keeps us from injury. This represents communication (D).

(D)   "And the children of Israel shall keep the Sabbath . . ." An eteranl cove-
       nant was made with them, that they would not be hurt if they keep it
       properly, and that is what is meant by "a sign between Me and you,"
       that I will protect you. [15]

We have three prayers then, all tied to the same theme, protection from injury, and overlaid with concern for the dead: *vehu' rachum*, *veshameru*, and *shomer 'amo yisra'el*. It was not injury to the living which was at stake—though the geonim were concerned about that too. [16] The real concern was for the dead, whom tradition consigned to punishment, particularly at dusk.

And such concern should not surprise us. That the dead were presumed to suffer in the afterlife is clear from the Talmud (*R.H.* 17a, for example). That Jews worried about how they might best relieve the departed's distress is evident from sources like the *Tanchuma*, which says that "the living redeem the dead," and that it is customary "to mention the dead on the Sabbath so that they do not return to *gehinnom*"; or from the mourners' *kaddish*, which was apparently accepted as an efficacious means by which a son might relieve his father of divine punishment. [17]

Moreover, the sayings and interpretations which posit such suffering, as well as the role of prayer in overcoming it, are carried in authoritative sources, so it cannot be maintained that superstitions may have been rife among the masses but would not have motivated the rabbis. The only question is what a particular authority—in our case, the geonim in question—thought of any particular prayer—in our case, the ones discussed here—and, to be sure, our sources do not tell us that. Were the geonim concerned with relieving the suffering of the dead? Was that concern a factor in their ordering of the prayers? If so, does it explain the curious variety of customs regarding the three prayers under discussion?

In the absence of explicit statements one way or the other, I see no way of answering the first two questions with any degree of certainty. But it is at least as likely that the geonim agreed with the *Babli*, the *Tanchuma*, *Machzor Vitry*, and so on, as that they did not; especially since the later sources, which were familiar with geonic opinion, do not cite them in opposition. And as for the last question—whether, that is, the alternative traditions regarding the three prayers in question are explainable by beliefs connected with the suffering of the deceased—the answer, as we shall see, is positive.

The prayers discussed here were connected, almost universally by western European Jewish lore, with the dead, as the sources cited earlier make clear. *Vehu' rachum* pardoned their sins; *shomer 'amo yisra'el la'ad* promised God's protection; and *veshameru* affirmed the covenant's aid. Amram, holding that the Sabbath itself was sufficient protection, omitted all three. Others in his day said at least two of them, and probably the third. And both academies known to the anonymous author omitted at least two and probably all three. The accompanying table will make this clear.

	vehu' rachum	*veshameru*	*shomer 'amo yisra'el*
Both academies (anonymous): (B):	omit	?	omit
Sar Shalom and Amram (C):	omit	omit	omit
Others known to Sar Shalom and Amram (C):	?	include	include

The Palestinian rite is hard to reconstruct, since our fragments of this part of the service are not purely Palestinian, but a mixture of customs.[18] There is no *vehu' rachum*, but *vehu' rachum* was not said there even in the daily service, so its absence on Friday night implies nothing. The eulogy in question is "who stretches a tabernacle of peace," but extended to include yet another clause, *menachem tsiyon uvoneh berachamav yerushalayim 'amen*, "who has compassion on Zion, and builds Jerusalem in His mercy, Amen."[19] Though this is the *pores* form, it is typically Palestinian, not only because it concludes with *'amen* but also because of the double clause in the eulogy. Both are typical Palestinian traits.[20] True to form, Amram cites Natronai against the double eulogy, but obviously not against its first half, which he used himself.

> Rav Natronai said . . . it is forbidden to say the eulogy, "Blessed be He who stretches a tabernacle of peace over us and over the congregation of His people Israel; who has compassion on Zion and builds Jerusalem," since our sages said [*Ber.* 49a]: "Rabbi said, One may not use dual eulogies."[21]

Veshameru too is lacking in our genizah fragments, and this would accord with (D), above, but the omission may be due to Babylonian influence and not represent a "native" Palestinian trait. So Palestine did not differ from *Seder Rav Amram*, as far as we know, except in its inclusion of a dual eulogy in the *hashkivenu*.[22]

The following reconstruction of the above evidence seems likely.

Even by the time of the talmudic age, the rabbis believed that demons threatened people at night. According to R. Judah, for example, scholars required guarding at nighttime (*Ber.* 54a). This belief led to the adoption of various protective formulas, including, according to R. Isaac, the *shema'* itself, which, if recited upon one's bed, keeps the demons away (*Ber.* 5a). The *hashkivenu*, reserved for nighttime recitation, and including an express entreaty to ward off *satan*, may well have begun as such a protective prayer.

Eventually, however, the focus of these prayers changed. True, they protected, but the people they protected were not the living but the dead, whose suffering might be minimized. Thus it became customary to begin the evening service with *vehu' rachum*, a biblical quotation associated with God's mercy and guardianship. In Babylonia, *hashkivenu* was given a special eulogy promising the same protection to the departed. Some said these prayers on the Sabbath as well, but the majority argued that the Sabbath was adequate defense in its own right.

This debate was current in Amram's day, but no regional issue was involved. The Palestinian custom was in basic accord with Amram's views. So Amram merely stated his custom and that of others. The only polemic was Natronai's responsum, carried in Amram's *Seder* and elsewhere, against the dual eulogy of the Palestinian *hashkivenu*.

Those who recited these pieces on Sabbath eve also added a third prayer, *veshameru*, for the reason intimated by *Machzor Vitry*: that is, it linked protection to the covenant as symbolized by the Sabbath. Israel keeps the covenant and God protects Israel "forever," that is, even after death. Amram, consistent in his denial of the necessity of protection on the Sabbath, omitted *veshameru*, noting only that the others who prayed for such protection said it.

Neither party said *barukh 'adonai le'olam*, the extended *hashkivenu*, that is, which was considered a stand-in for the optional evening *tefillah*, because the Sabbath evening service already contained *magen 'avot*, which fulfilled the same function. *Yir'u 'eineinu*, though originally not part of *barukh 'adonai le'olam*, was also omitted, since the former seemed by now to be just one more paragraph tacked on to the latter, and could be left out, accordingly.

Sometime later, the "others" referred to by Amram changed their view to Amram's, probably under the influence of his *Seder*, so that our anonymous responsum could say that *both* academies omitted *vehu' rachum* and *shomer 'amo yisra'el*.

I have deliberately avoided mentioning Saadiah's view on this subject so as not to confuse an already complicated matter. We can now proceed to Saadiah, who followed his own line of thinking. Though Saadiah did not say *vehu' rachum* or *shomer 'amo yisra'el*, he did say *veshameru*. He also said *yir'u 'eineinu*,[23] unlike all the other geonim, who omitted it along with the rest of *barukh 'adonai le'olam*.

Saadiah's omissions (*vehu' rachum* and *shomer 'amo yisra'el*) might be explained either by his Palestinian past (since in Palestine neither was said) or by his use of Amram as his guide (since Amram, too, had omitted both). But his inclusion of *veshameru* and *yir'u 'eineinu* cannot be so explained. All available evidence points to the fact that Saadiah was the first and only authority, either in Palestine or in Babylonia, to call for these two prayers on Friday night.

A glance at his philosophical work reveals that *veshameru* had unique significance for him. In treatise 3, chapter 7,[24] Saadiah launches a long discussion of the eternality of the biblical commandments. His aim is the refutation of certain people who claim that these are subject to abrogation. Most of the discussion is given over to refuting his opponents' arguments. For his own position, Saadiah quotes but one proof-text, the only one, presumably, which he considered both necessary and sufficient to establish his case: Exodus 31:6, *veshameru...*, with its reference to *ledorotam berit 'olam,* "throughout their generations as an everlasting covenant."[25] The proof was so important for Saadiah that his opponents tried to refute it by twisting the meaning of the word *'olam* to refer to finite time periods long since past, and Saadiah rebuts their interpretations with the observation that *'olam* is here connected with the Sabbath, an institution still in force in Jeremiah's time, and Jeremiah lived after the closing date of the alternative time periods referred to by his opponents.[26]

Saadiah goes on to say that these eternal laws remain in force until the resurrection.[27] No wonder he included both *veshameru* and *yir'u 'eineinu* in his prayer book! He prescribed the former, not for the superstitious reason of guaranteeing God's protection, but because it served as his proof for the perpetuity of Jewish law; and—though he saw no reason to include *barukh 'adonai le'olam,* which had always been excluded on Sabbath eve—he did demand the next paragraph, *yir'u 'eineinu,* which was nothing less that the promise of reward for those who keep the law in its perpetuity, and a reminder of the one and only time when the law might be suspended—when God reigns in Zion at the end of days.

Saadiah is the source for another controversy in the prayers of Sabbath eve. His version of the first of the blessings of the *shema'* includes the following: "Blessed art Thou, Lord our God, who completed His work [*'asher kilah ma'asav*] on the Sabbath day and called it a delight."[28] A parallel version is included in a prayer book published by Assaf, and noted earlier in this chapter.[29] Both prayers represent a clear departure from Amram, who not only leaves out *'asher kilah ma'asav,* but even rails against it in Natronai's name: "In your question you remarked that you are accustomed to say 'who completed his work' on the Sabbath. In our academy we do not say it, neither on the Sabbath nor on holidays or on weekdays...."[30] The phrase is surely Palestinian in origin.[31]

So Natronai and Amram again argue against Palestinian custom, while Saadiah incorporates it. Though this time, too, Saadiah's decision may be just a natural result of his eclecticism, the possibility exists that more is involved. A noticeable difference between the form published by Assaf and Saadiah's recension of the phrase is the inclusion of *vayikra'ehu 'oneg,* "and He called it a delight," which appears only in the latter.[32] This line is based on Isaiah 58:13, "you [Israel] call the Sabbath a delight ['oneg]."[33] Now the concept of *'oneg shabbat,* "Sabbath delight," was a major issue separating Karaites from Rabbanites. The former allowed neither the light of candles nor cohabitation on Friday night, and went so far as to recommend fasting on the Sabbath, this latter practice being absolutely prohibited by Rabbanite law.[34] The rabbis, moreover, had utilized the very same Isaiah text to prove their point, as is evident from *Pesachim* 68b, where it is quoted by Rabbah to defend the *prohibition* against fasting on the Sabbath. In *Baba Metsia* 54a it is argued that food dedicated to the Temple, and therefore forbidden for use by private citizens, may be redeemed and eaten—*only* on the Sabbath—because "You shall call the Sabbath a delight." And *Chullin* 111a cites the same text to justify the making of delicacies for the Sabbath. That the Karaites, who favored fasting on the Sabbath, were aware of the rabbinic interpretation of this text, and its implications regarding *'oneg,* is clear from the words of Hadassi.

> The prophet established another warning, saying "You shall call the Sabbath a delight . . ." His meaning is to delight in prayer and contemplation of Torah. . . . However, fasting, and not rejoicing thereby, and mourning over the desecration of His glory and the desolation of His Temple and city—that is permitted to you.[35]

Saadiah, then, included this Palestinian custom for polemical reasons. We are reminded that when God finished the work of creation, He called the seventh day "a delight" with all the material enjoyments we normally associate with the term. Apparently the ascetic spirit that gripped the Mourners of Zion (*'avelei tsiyon*) was an equally magnetic force for others, many of whom were drawn to the Karaite ideology. Thus, Saadiah even goes out of his way to remind those who use his prayer book on the Sabbath, "About half the day we spend in the synagogue praying and reading from the Torah . . . and the rest of the time we eat and drink."[36]

Our survey of Sabbath-eve liturgical debates has been necessarily detailed and drawn out. But no surprises have emerged from it. Beyond the likelihood that certain evening prayers were symbolically referred to the welfare of the dead, and that this symbolic connection was a decisive influence in the determination of which prayers to say, we have had another chance to observe geonim in the first two periods of the canonical process. Amram's two polemical statements, both going back to Natronai, opposed the practice of concluding a blessing with a dual eulogy, and the recitation of a Sabbath-eve prayer affirming, "He completed His work." We have seen the object of Amram's wrath in both cases to be Palestinian custom.

On the other hand, we saw Saadiah include a rather strange mixture of Sabbath prayers, and explained his selection by recourse to his philosophical work, where he argued against those who maintained that the covenant for which he stood was not eternal. These enemies were surely not Karaites, a fact which underlines the point we have made all along: Saadiah is far too complex an individual to be characterized solely in terms of his position on the Karaite schism. Yet his aversion to Karaism is at least one important key to his liturgical decisions, and this was indicated by his insistence that the Sabbath is a day of enjoyment, and his inclusion in his *Siddur* of a biblical quotation to prove it.

We may turn now to the Sabbath-morning liturgy. Here too the first controversy which we shall have to survey is inordinately complex, with apparently contradictory sources. It involves the insertion of the *shema*, though only part of its first biblical paragraph, in the third benediction of the *tefillah*. [37] Our evidence this time comes from the usually outspoken Ben Baboi. Rather than cite his lengthy remarks, we may be content with summarizing the case he presents.

Ben Baboi maintains that the wayward Palestinians have mistakenly been saying the *shema* in the middle of the *kedushat hashem* (the third benediction of the *tefillah*). Yehudai wrote to them noting that their objectionable practice violated the norms of the sages. Prayers should be said only in the places where traditional authority says they belong. He explains that the Palestinians originally fell into this error because at one time the government forbade the saying of the *shema*; the Jews responded to this edict by reciting it surreptitiously during the *kedushah*, [38] a place where it would never be noticed. Now, however, the Moslems have overthrown the evil regime and its oppressive law as well, so the *shema* has been reinstated in its rightful place. Why, then, should the Palestinians make a permanent practice of an emergency procedure by continuing to say the *shema* in the *kedushah* as well? [39]

Complicating matters, however, is a story by Sar Shalom which sounds remarkably similar, except this time the persecution and its attendant secret *shema* are said to have occurred in Babylonia. Here too, we are told, there was once a persecution which occasioned the banning of the *shema* and its insertion in the *kedushah* of the morning service of the Sabbath liturgy. But Sar Shalom's narrative ends on a much more heroic note than Ben Baboi's. Sar Shalom maintains that when the persecution ceased, the *shema* was rightfully retained, but was moved from the morning service—where the original *shema* was now reinstituted—to the *musaf* (or additional) service unique to Sabbaths and holidays, where there was no *shema'*. It is still recited in *musaf*, says Sar Shalom proudly; and in the *ne'ilah* (or concluding) service of Yom Kippur. Amram's prayer book carries this account, adding that when some worshippers tried to discontinue the emergency measure, Natronai adjured them not to change the custom of the sages, but to continue saying the extra *shema'* as a sign of the miraculous deliverance that had terminated the original persecution.[40]

As if these two conflicting reports were not bad enough, there is still one more statement on the subject, this one attributed to Sherira and/or Hai. It must be cited, however, since the editor of the geonic collection in which it is found has emended it. The italicized English words represent his important emendation.

> Those who say [the *shema'*] in the *musaf* service of the Sabbath, holidays, Rosh Hashanah, and on the intermediary days of festivals, do well. Their practice contains no aspect of forbiddenness or unseemliness or impropriety. In many places in Babylonia *there are* people *who* say it *even in the morning service but* in the academy, and in the schools, and in the synagogues of the rabbis, the custom of saying it has never held, not on Sabbath nor on holidays nor at any other such time.[41]

If, for the moment, we ignore Müller's emendation, we see that Hai knew of the extra *shema'* only at *musaf* of Sabbaths and holidays, as well as the intermediary days of festivals, but not in the morning service; and at the same time he relates that in his academy and the other schools and synagogues, it has never been included in the *tefillah* on any occasion.

It is the fact that Hai's last observation contradicts Amram, Sar Shalom, and Natronai that led Müller to emend Hai's account to read as indicated in the italics, that is, "there are people who say it *even in the morning service but* in the academy . . . [no one ever said it at the morning service]."

Hai is also on record as differing from Amram regarding Yom Kippur. He maintains that in Pumbedita the *shema'* was never said in the Yom Kippur morning or additional (*musaf*) *tefillah*, though possibly (he does not say) it was included at *ne'ilah*.[42] So Hai differs from Amram regarding Yom Kippur too. Amram's Sura included the *shema'* as an insert in the Yom Kippur *tefillah* both for *musaf* and *ne'ilah*.

What are we to make of these contradictory sources? Scholars have offered several opinions.

Jacob Mann accepted Ben Baboi's explanation of religious oppression in Palestine and identified it as the Heraclian legislation of 629.[43] This was prompted, he says, by the fact that the Palestinian Jews had supported the invading Sassanians in 614 and helped them hold the country for fifteen years. When Heraclius, then the Byzantine emperor, finally restored Byzantine control to the area, he punished the native miscreants by banning certain of their prayers which he found offensive: their daily *tefillah*, because its twelfth benediction condemning heretics included Christians; and the *shema'*, whose monotheistic proclamation offended his trinitarian beliefs. On the Sabbath, however, the twelfth benediction (as one of the intermediary petitions) was not said, so the *tefillah* was permitted, and the people secretly inserted their *shema'* within the *kedushah* there. When the conquering Moslems reversed the edict, Yehudai requested the removal of the extra *shema'*, a demand later reiterated by Ben Baboi. As for the Babylonian persecution, Mann dates it to the time of Yezdegerd II (438–457), who—under the influence of the dualistic Zoroastrianism—objected to the statement in the *shema'* of God's unity. As in Palestine, here too the *shema'* was said secretly, but when order prevailed it was transferred to the *musaf* service. Mann wonders, naturally, why Yehudai and Ben Baboi did not object also to the Babylonian custom of saying the *shema'* in the *tefillah*. He concludes that Ben Baboi may actually have done just that, though it is more probable that he allowed the Babylonian insertion to stand since it was said during *musaf*; it was the morning recitation characteristic of the Palestinians that he opposed. As for Hai, Mann surmises that his objection was not to the saying of the *shema'* as such, but only to a word it contains, *pa'amayim*, this being the word by which Hai cites the prayer in his responsum. He thus rejects Müller's emendation. [44]

Ginzberg traces the issue to a difference between Pumbedita and Sura. [45] Sura said the *shema'* in the *tefillah* since it was the home of Rav, a Palestinian, and was therefore influenced by Palestinian practice; at Pumbedita, though, it was not said. So Yehudai and Ben Baboi must be seen as polemicizing against both Palestine and Sura!

Ginzberg also notes that Saadiah mentions the custom of saying *pa'amayim* (= *shema'*) but neither objects to it nor recommends it. [46] The implication is that Saadiah followed the Pumbeditan tradition, a phenomenon which Ginzberg explains by saying that in Egypt, Saadiah's homeland, people did not include the word *pa'amayim* in their version of the *shema'*, as is evidenced by the Maimonidean rite.

It would be very peculiar if Ginzberg were correct. Why would Yehudai polemicize against his own academy? Of course he could have written his letter to Palestine before moving to Sura from Pumbedita, but that would antedate his accession to the gaonate, an unlikely possibility. It is even less likely that Ben Baboi, writing sometime after Yehudai died, came from Pumbedita, since we have no Pumbeditan responsa until Paltoi.

I have already remarked on the improbability of Sura's following Palestine just because of Rav. [47] All the more is this unlikely 382 years after Rav's death, when the persecution is said to have occurred.

Then too, the assumption that Maimonides is representative of the

Egyptian rite in the time of Saadiah is hardly warranted. More likely, Maimonides emulated Saadiah, omitting the word *pa'amayim* because Saadiah had done so.

As for Mann's basic hypothesis, one can do no more than say that if the sources are correct, Mann may be right. But we have no way of validating the sources. Somehow, the picture of authorities watching over the service but being fooled by the transfer of a prayer from here to there is hard to accept. I suspect that the whole concept of religious persecution as a causal factor in changing rituals was a legendary device, habitually used to explain contemporary practices.

But whether or not Mann is correct, it is demonstrable that the Palestinians said the *shema'* in the morning *kedushah*, and that Yehudai and Ben Baboi fought the practice. Thus, once again we find the geonim of period 1 confronting a rival Palestinian tradition.

As for Hai, Müller's emendation seems probable, particularly in the light of two other reports. From the *Tur* we learn: "Rav Sherira wrote that one should not say the *shema'* in the *kedushah* on festivals and the Sabbath, except at *musaf*: not in the morning or afternoon service."[48] So Sherira, though not testifying explicitly that Pumbedita said the *shema'* during the *musaf tefillah*, at least implies that they did, for if they had not, he would have said so. Finally, one should recall the quotation from Rav Amram where Sar Shalom says that not only his academy, but *all of Babylonia*, say the *shema'* at *musaf*.[49]

Again it is noteworthy that Hai does not condemn those who say the *shema'* in the morning. He informs his questioner of the practice that obtains in his academy, but admits that there are exceptions.

The other quotation from Hai regarding the *shema'* on Yom Kippur displays equal magnanimity. Though Hai says that Pumbedita waits until *ne'ilah* to say it, he does not condemn those who also include it at *musaf*.

We may now continue with our last topic regarding the Saturday-morning liturgy, the Sabbath Torah reading. The question which engendered the polemic was why we do not read from the Torah at *musaf*. The following is the response given by Hai.

> Hai was asked why we do not read from the Torah at the *musaf* service each Sabbath. He answered: if you take issue with our predecessors in this, the matter will get out of hand. People will ask why we have abandoned the liturgical recitation of the Ten Commandments, the way they used to read them in the Temple. Someone else will say: why have you stopped reading the story of creation, the way the *ma'amadot* [early lay assemblies] used to do? Someone else will ask why we don't read the Torah every day; or at least, on Mondays and Thursdays, when we do read it, we should read the section dealing with instructions for

performing the daily sacrifice. We are obligated to conduct ourselves according to the mandates laid down by those who were greater than our generations in wisdom and number. And we may not vary.[50]

This is hardly the mild, permissive Hai we are used to seeing. To clarify the reason for his sudden harshness, it will help to list his argument point by point. Hai maintains that (1) to read the Torah at *musaf* would result in a bad precedent; (2) people would wonder why we do not say the Ten Commandments as they used to in the Temple; (3) they would want to read the creation narrative daily, as the *ma'amadot* used to; (4) they would ask why we do not read the Torah every day; and (5) they would be moved to read the section on the daily offering each Monday and Thursday.

Hai was most certainly opposing the Karaites in these remarks. The question itself (1) was probably instigated by the knowledge that the Karaites did read the Torah at *musaf.*[51]

The second item mentioned by Hai, the Ten Commandments, may or may not have been part of the early Karaite liturgy. We cannot say for sure, since both Anan and Kirkisani are silent on the point. The Rabbanites had officially dispensed with the Decalogue out of fear of the "heretics," who might have argued that it alone was God-given.[52] Anan had a similar fear,[53] so probably did not read it, but Anan preceded the Palestinian Karaite age by nearly two centuries and can be no index for the custom of Palestinian Karaites in the days of Hai. The golden age of Karaism known to Hai was a Palestinian phenomenon, and even the Palestinian Rabbanites read the Ten Commandments in those days, despite the earlier decision to the contrary.[54] We also do not know Anan's or Kirkisani's practice regarding the Genesis narrative (3), but we do know that today's Karaite rite incorporates it.[55]

The scriptural instructions regarding the daily offering (5), however, were undoubtedly read by Anan every day.[56] Hai specifies Monday and Thursday, but his responsum was going to Rabbanites, for whom these two days were really the only ones in question, these being the only weekdays when they read from the Torah. Hai does note, however, that people might wonder why we do not read the Torah daily (4), and such a custom did characterize Anan's liturgy.[57]

Not all of the questions need refer to documented Karaite practices in order to show that Hai's stand was motivated by concern about these sectaries. His questioner considered himself a good Rabbanite or he would not have written to Hai in the first place. So some of Hai's rhetoric may be statements of *reductio ad absurdum*, hypothetical extensions of a conceivable *musaf* reading, attempts to show how absurd these implications would be if judged by the rabbinic tradition's standards. The *musaf* reading itself, though, was originally Karaitic, and Hai's correspondent, having heard of it, but perhaps of who it was who practiced it, was reminded by the gaon that the rabbis had good reason to frown on the custom.

Here we see Hai at his strictest. He concludes his response with unusual vigor. "We are obligated to conduct ourselves according to the mandates laid down by those who were greater than our generations in wisdom and number, and we may not vary." Had Hai been consistent in his application of this mishnaic principle,[58] he would not have allowed all the variety which we have seen him do. But here, where the Karaites were involved, he reverted to the type of stringency typical of Ben Baboi or Amram.

Our final example of polemic regarding the Sabbath liturgy is the blessing over the Sabbath lights. The entire ritual has been discussed by Lauterbach.[59] He theorizes that the practice of kindling Sabbath lights arose in antiquity, though not before the Hellenistic period; that the custom was Pharisaic, intended as a polemic against the Sadducees; and that no blessing was known until after the talmudic period. The blessing he considers a polemic against the Karaites. Like the Sadducees before them, the Karaites denied that a light kindled prior to the Sabbath might be allowed to burn on the Sabbath, so Sabbath candles were anathema to them. This Karaite hypothesis is documented by an impressive array of evidence.[60]

Lauterbach does not, however, analyze all the geonic responsa on the subject and, in fact, seems to be aware only of those attributed to Natronai.[61] He cites two almost identical reports in Natronai's name, *Halakhot Gedolot* and *Seder Rav Amram*. Our edition of the latter, however, omits Natronai's name, a curious fact if Natronai was indeed the innovator of the blessing, since Amram does not hesitate to credit his predecessor with a good deal of his prayer book's content. Moreover, the passage in *Halakhot Gedolot* is suspect, if only because it is a later insertion. It would not have been out of keeping with Natronai to have prescribed the blessing, since—as we have seen—it was he who first excommunicated the Karaites, railing against what he thought was their *haggadah*. But the attribution to him cannot be more than a hypothesis. The wording in Lauterbach's two communications, as well as a third which he does not cite, is almost identical.[62]

What we really have, it seems to me, is one responsum, so that either the attribution to Natronai is spurious and ought really to invoke Amram, or Amram quoted Natronai without giving him credit. At any rate, we cannot go far wrong if we attribute the blessing to either Amram or Natronai.[63]

The author, whether Amram or Natronai, faced a serious problem in justifying the benediction. Though the practice of kindling Sabbath lights was ancient, the blessing was not, and some case had to be made for it. The only precedent was the kindling of Chanukah lights, so the wording of that benediction became the model for the Sabbath blessing, with the word "Chanukah" changed to "Sabbath."[64] The Babylonian Talmud had itself discussed the two instances of kindling lights in the same context, and the geonim turned to that discussion to explain their decision to require a blessing for the Sabbath.

Our responsa, therefore, quote homiletical reasons for lights, drawn directly from the Talmud's debate (*Shab.* 23a, 25b, 34a). None of the citations originally referred to an actual Sabbath benediction, though. We are given Samuel's edict (*Shab.* 25b) that "the kindling of Sabbath lights is *chovah,* "an obligation,"[65] and informed (from *Shab.* 34b) that Job 5:24, "You shall know that your tent is in peace . . . ," implies lights. But in the end, as Amram—and the Talmud before him—says:

> If you should object, "Whence do we learn that He commanded us [to kindle lights, a necessary assumption for a blessing affirming *vetsivanu,* 'and he commanded us']," Rav Avya said, from [Deut. 17:11] "You shall not turn aside [from the sentence which they shall show you]." Rav Nachman bar Isaac said, from [Deut. 32:7] "[Remember the days of old, consider the years of many generations;] ask your father and he will tell you, your elders and they will tell you."[66]

But this exegetical proof is clearly weak. The first verse describes the context of Deuteronomy 17:8–9, "If there arise a matter too hard for you in judgment . . . come unto the priests, the Levites, and the judges that shall be in those days." The assumption is that kindling lights is such a matter, and that the rabbinic authorities, as the judges of "those days," would simply recognize the divine mandate, from which "You shall not turn aside." The second reasoning implies that kindling lights is quite ancient, part of the oral transmission of the commandments. So, although no direct scriptural warrant may be found for it, it is still valid as part of what past generations will tell you, if you but ask them.

Both of these arguments are given by Amram in response to one who asks where we know that God commanded Sabbath lights, and he borrows them directly from the Talmud's discussion of Chanukah lights, where the same question, "How do we know God commanded us?" is asked, and these two scriptural responses are offered.

Obviously, the geonim were having a difficult time proving the obligation to say a blessing affirming a divine commandment of kindling Sabbath lights. Hai, as well as Amram, faced the issue. He reiterated Amram's lesson, admitted that the citation of Samuel is not absolute proof, and added a mishnaic reference of his own.

> You asked: Is the essence of the blessing ". . . to kindle the light of Sabbath" custom or law? and if law, where is it written in the Talmud? . . . [The answer is] the blessing for Sabbath light is a law, and even though it is not explicitly spoken of, we have, nevertheless, the fact that Rava said to Abaye [*Shab.* 25b], "I say the lighting of Sabbath candles is an obligation." Also the Mishnah teaches [*Shab.* 2:7], "Three things a man must say, as darkness falls on the Sabbath [Friday night]: Have you tithed? Have you erected the *'eruv* [establishing Sabbath

boundaries]? Have you kindled the lights!" And our Mishnah teaches too [*Shab.* 2:6], "For three sins women die in childbirth: their carelessness regarding the laws of menstruation, the laws of separating the *challah* offering, and the kindling of [Sabbath] light."[67]

At roughly the same time, in North Africa, R. Chananel (990?–1050) was expanding the original proof from Job 5:24, "You shall know that your tent is in peace," by commenting, "Peace can only mean light, for it is written, 'And God saw the light, that it was good.'"[68] Perhaps Saadiah elected the wisest course of all by not even undertaking the task of proving the blessing's merit, but simply stating categorically, "We are obligated to kindle the Sabbath light, and most of us say over it the blessing, '. . . to kindle the Sabbath light.'"[69] As a matter of fact, the issue was not solved by the end of the geonic period. A century later in Provence, some people still said no blessing at all![70] The Tosafists knew of an actual argument against such a blessing, and their outstanding twelfth-century spokesman, Rabbenu Tam, had to resort to the scholastic hairsplitting of characterizing candle lighting as a unique category of obligation in order to justify it.[71]

In sum, though kindling Sabbath lights was indeed an ancient practice, attending it with a blessing did not predate Amram (or Natronai) and was not easily accepted. There was certainly no irrefutable scriptural warrant for the practice; and earlier rabbinic sources were embarrassingly silent. The geonim borrowed freely from what talmudic discussion there was on the subject, and applied the proof for Chanukah blessings to the Sabbath. But even by Saadiah's time, only most people said the blessing that Saadiah preferred— some may have said none at all—and this difference of practice characterized western Europe for several centuries. Those who did say the benediction modeled it after the Chanukah blessing, though the wording varied somewhat, as the manuscripts of *Siddur Saadiah* make plain.[27]

Was there any polemic involved in the invention of this novel benediction? Probably. Authorities who composed prayers as late as Amram rarely couched them in the normative benedictory format. Mandating such a prayer that emphasized the divine commandment to kindle Sabbath lights may indeed reflect the geonic desire to underscore the significance of that practice. Since it was this very custom that was under attack by the Karaites, we may see the benediction as a polemic against the Karaite sect.

On the other hand, anti-Karaite polemic is generally not found until period 2. We saw that Natronai and Amram knew very little about this group, having heard of Anan's *Sefer Hamitsvot* only by hearsay. Yet Natronai knew enough about them to excommunicate them, and their stand on Sabbath lights was particularly notorious;[73] so they may well have known Anan's position on the matter and therefore introduced a blessing with classical structure, affirming the fact that kindling Sabbath lights was a divine commandment. Saadiah, we know, was very much concerned about the Karaites.

He did not polemicize at length in support of the blessing, but he rarely argues anything in detail in his prayer book, and he certainly states the commandment apodictically enough, citing the blessing that most people say.

Hai's case is the most interesting. We remarked above on his tendency to categorize liturgical differences as customs. Yet here we have a very late benediction with no clear legal basis. If anything was a custom, this was. The question put to him—is it custom or law, and if law, whence is it derived—suggests as much. Yet Hai insists in this case that he is dealing with law, and he expands on Amram's argument to prove it. So Hai, living in an age of great Karaite creativity, defended the responsibility of saying the blessing in the face of those who maintained that it was only a custom; and so did his younger North African contemporary, R. Chananel, for similar reasons. It was only the Ashkenazim, a century later, who had no Karaites in their midst, who could afford the luxury of debating whether to use the blessing or not.

6: Festival and Holiday Liturgy

Rosh Hashanah, Yom Kippur, and Fast Days

Rosh Hashanah

A COMPLETE STUDY OF GEONIC CANONIZATION WOULD HAVE TO INCLUDE A close analysis of the many insertions in the *tefillah* mandated by holidays. The most famous of these are the ones particular to services during the High Holiday season, asking God to "Remember us unto life," "Write us in the book of life," and so on.[1] These alterations stem from the geonic age, so are perfectly congenial with our subject. Moreover, the subject transcends these few interjections for the High Holiday liturgy, since in geonic times such insertions were common on other occasions of the year, the Sabbath included.

Unfortunately, the unusual enormity of the subject matter prevents our discussing it here. Whether or not to say such responses, what those responses should be, what rules should govern them, and so on, were questions debated not only during the geonic period, when the custom had its origin, but even years afterward in a dozen different countries and locales. Thus every conceivable geonic communication on the subject was collected, weighed in the balance, and recorded by German, French, Spanish, North African, and Italian authorities, in the hope of vindicating their own customs. While it is always helpful for the researcher to have a wealth of comparative data, in this case the abundance is such as to require far more pages for analysis than could possibly be allotted here. The mere presentation and analysis of the twelve basic relevant responsa would be space-consuming in the extreme, since many are self-contradictory and depend on citation in their original language, with careful linguistic comparison and analysis, merely to decide whether to accept them as valid witnesses, and, if so, whether at least to alter the geonic author in whose name they are given.

Though such an analysis would enhance this work, and even strengthen the basic thesis of a trifold division in the canonic process, each with its own biases and concerns, I will have to forgo the exercise.

We need not pass over the festival liturgy completely, however. There are many other controversies which fall in the scope of our study and can be examined. We turn first to Rosh Hashanah, Yom Kippur, and fast days generally; then, in the next chapter, to the three pilgrimage festivals (Sukkot, Passover, and Shavu'ot), Chanukah, and Purim. At times our discussion of these holidays will overlap, since one of the problems facing the geonim was that the clear-cut distinction between holiday types was by no means obvious to them. Indeed, one of our greatest problems will be to fathom the thinking of rabbis who do not know precisely which Hebrew term (e.g., *mo'ed, yom tov*) applies to a given holiday, and, consequently, what rules of prayer refer to it. We shall see with Rosh Hashanah, for example, that a major debate occurred regarding its essential characteristic and that it was the geonic age which determined the features we now associate with the New Year: *yom hadin* ("day of judgment") and *yom hazikaron* ("day of remembrance").

Our survey may well begin with the Rosh Hashanah service of *Siddur Saadiah*. We have already introduced the term *kedushat hayom* as the intermediary blessing which replaces the thirteen petitions normally found in the central section of the weekly *tefillah*. Our discussion is about a phrase in the Rosh Hashanah *kedushat hayom* which Saadiah cites as *vehanchilenu mo'adei kodshekha*, "Let us inherit your holy festivals." (Since the terms *mo'ed* and *yom tov* will prove crucial later in this chapter, I have systematically translated the former as "festival" and the latter as "holiday.") Saadiah then comments that there are those who mistakenly omit the words cited and say instead *vehanchilenu mishpetei tsidkekha*. This is a mistake, he says, since the words omitted constitute the central concept of the prayer (*'ikar*) while the replacement does not.[2] Now as we shall see shortly, Saadiah, the philosopher and logician, was meticulous about characterizing the yearly cycle properly, insisting that the New Year was not a festival but a holiday, and a unique one at that. Only the three pilgrimage festivals were to be included in the first category of *mo'ed*, "festival." Rosh Hashanah was a *yom tov*, and Yom Kippur was neither, but was wholly distinct, a *tsom*, or "fast day." It is surprising, therefore, to find Saadiah intent on maintaining the word *mo'adei*, the construct plural form of *mo'ed*, in this prayer, especially since, as we shall see, elsewhere he avoids it. I can explain the matter only by presuming that Saadiah considered the phrase one which he was just unable to change, perhaps because he believed it had always been there, perhaps because, structurally, it introduced the eulogy and shared with the eulogy the basic theme of *kedushah*, sanctity of the day. Certainly he disliked the alternative more, for it converted the central theme of the prayer, the day's sanctity, into a plea for the gracious acceptance of God's judgment of sin. And even though he had no quarrel with this concept of Rosh Hashanah, his general criteria outlined above prohibited the mixing of categories. So though his use of *mo'adei* here is inconsistent with decisions we shall later encounter, he was consistent with his second general principle, which we discussed in chapter 1, not to alter basic blessing themes as they had been handed down to him.

Significantly, the opinion of this last great Suran gaon was repeated later by Hai, himself the final luminary of Pumbedita, but with an addition typical of Hai. "If someone does say the alternative," he remarks, "we do not remove him from his position of prayer leader."[3] So Hai is consistent with what we have seen so far. As usual, he expresses his views but forfends against the possibility of his own opinion being used to squelch diversity.

Amram's opinion is difficult to arrive at. His prayer book reads with Saadiah, and contains no reference to any others who alter that custom. On the other hand, two manuscripts of the *Seder* omit the phrase entirely; and Abraham ben Nathan of Lunel (Hayarchi), writing in 1205, claims that his copy of Amram's prayer book said, "Some people conclude on Rosh Hashanah with *vehanchilenu besimchah uvesason kol mishpetei tsidkekha...*" and that Amram saw no error in these words.[4] Hayarchi was a faithful follower of Amram's precedents, and is generally an accurate source for the *Seder*, especially when citing Amram's editorial commentary rather than the wording of prayer texts, since the former occasioned less scribal carelessness in transmission. I suspect, therefore, that Amram did contain the *mo'adei* reference, and that he, like Saadiah, knew of others who did not. The alternative, however, does not seem to be Palestinian as opposed to Babylonian, since it appears as a typical characteristic neither in *Massekhet Soferim* nor in the genizah fragments.[5] So Amram had no reason to oppose it.

It remains now for us to prove that Saadiah was in fact inconsistent in allowing the time-honored phrase, "Let us inherit your holy festivals," in the instance just discussed; or, put another way, to prove that he did categorize Rosh Hashanah as *yom tov*, "holiday," rather than as *mo'ed*, "festival"; and that his remaining comments on related prayers can be explained by just such a logical dichotomy. These prayers are three other sections of the same *kedushat hayom* rubric; one is limited to the *tefillah* in the additional, or *musaf*, service, and the others are not. The former (1) is a plaint that "We are no longer able to ascend, to appear, and to prostrate ourselves before you." The others are (2) a petition (*vehasi'enu*), "Bestow on us, Lord our God the blessings of your festivals"; and (3) (*ya'aleh veyavo'*), "May the remembrance of us ascend... and be seen... before you."

Not much need be said about the theological implications of *vehasi'enu*. It is a perfectly natural petition to be inserted in a prayer celebrating festival sanctity, and merely extends the festival mood by requesting the "life, peace, joy, and gladness" that should accompany such an occasion. Its insertion in the *kedushat hayom* of the festival liturgy therefore occasions no surprise.

Nor is there any cause for astonishment at the insertion of the plaint that we can no longer ascend the Temple Mount and prostrate ourselves there as did people in days of yore. For this is the underlying theology of the *musaf kedushat hayom* in all services. The rabbis held that the various daily services were representations of cultic sacrifices in the Temple. Whether their premise be entirely true or not, they did act as if it were, and added a *musaf*, or additional, worship service to those special days when an additional animal sacrifice would have been called for. So this *musaf* service, more than any other, retained its old symbolic connection with the Temple, and the *kedushat hayom* recited in it regularly harks back to the time of the Temple's destruction, bewailing the fact that the glorious commandments entailed in the actual cult must now be replaced with a pale reflection of them, that is, prayer and the recitation of the sacrificial regulations that would be followed were the Temple still standing.

Both *vehasi'enu* and the plaintive recollection of ancient glory are intricately tied only to the three pilgrimage festivals, when people actually traveled to Jerusalem to fulfill the biblical commandment (Deut 16:14):

> Three times each year your first-born shall appear before the Lord your God in the place which the Lord has chosen, for the Lord your God will bless you in all your produce and all your handiwork, and you shall most certainly rejoice.

And the third portion, *ya'aleh veyavo'*, too, is perfectly appropriate for the festival liturgy. Though we may not ascend Mount Zion to appear in accord with the Deuteronomic injunction, at least the memory of our doing so might reach into heaven, and, as the prayer continues, the recollection of the Temple may also ascend to God so that His people might receive the same blessings they would have merited had they actually made the pilgrimage.

These three elements of the festival *kedushat hayom* must be considered together if we are to find any systematic approach in geonic thinking.

We begin with (1), the *musaf* recollection of appearing at the Temple, and note that Saadiah objects to the phrase, "We are no longer able to ascend, to appear, and to prostrate ourselves before You." This belongs in the festival liturgy, of course, since those were the only occasions when such appearances were called for; so Saadiah includes it there.[6] But for the Rosh Hashanah service he prefers to say, "We are no longer able to offer a sacrifice to you."[7] This certainly seems to imply that Saadiah, again the logician, wanted to maintain the integrity of the three pilgrimage festivals as the *mo'adim*, and no less an authority than Abudarham supports this very contention.[8]

No other gaon mentions this point. Amram's prayer book varies in its reading, depending on the manuscript.[9]

The issue is tied, as we have said, to the debate over saying *vehasi'enu* on Rosh Hashanah. The basic problem still was the determination of the category under which the New Year should be subsumed.[10] Though in the Bible its status was uncertain at best, much less significant than either the pilgrimage festivals or Yom Kippur, by mishnaic times it had emerged as a holiday in its own right, and is called a *yom tov*.[11] Later views, however, began to emphasize the judgmental qualities of the day; it was *yom hadin*, "the day of judgment," not of festivity. It was undoubtedly just such an attitude that was expressed by the emendation "your merciful judgment" which Saadiah ruled as irrelevant to the basic subject matter of *kedushah*, "holiness." Amram, living in the ninth century, had yet to isolate the day's uniqueness and therefore included the festival *vehasi'enu* in his Rosh Hashanah liturgy. But Saadiah is again intent on separating the New Year from the festivals. The New Year is not a *mo'ed*, so whereas he includes *vehasi'enu* in his festival liturgy, he omits it from his Rosh Hashanah prayers. [12]

Again, it is Abudarham who recognizes the rationale, though his source is later than Saadiah and probably only indirectly related to that gaon.

> As for *vehasi'enu* . . . Rabbenu Isaac Halevi of Worms [1000–1070] was accustomed not to say it . . . since the blessing regarding "your festivals" applies only to the three pilgrimage festivals. . . . and for the same reason, one should not say in the *musaf* service, "We are no longer able to go up and to be seen . . ." but instead, "We are no longer able to offer a sacrifice." [13]

So Abudarham bears out the distinction Saadiah was trying to make, possibly even quoting Saadiah with regard to the prayer, "We are no longer able to offer a sacrifice."

Now Abudarham goes further in his comments and mentions a question sent by a German authority, Rabbi Meshullam, to the head of the academy in Jerusalem regarding the same point. The latter answered that he did say *vehasi'enu* on the New Year. According to Abudarham, the same was true of Amram, *Halakhot Gedolot*, and "most of the places in Spain" which had decided, unlike Saadiah, that "Rosh Hashanah is in the general category of 'festival.'" [14] Thus, of all the geonic authorities, Saadiah once again stands alone. Only he decried *'or chadash* since its subject matter was inappropriate to the occasion, and only he prohibited *vehasi'enu* and a recollection of ascending Mount Zion, during the Rosh Hashanah service; these too were inappropriate subjects for the occasion.

Before analyzing further where Saadiah might have derived the notion of making such a separation between Rosh Hashanah and the festivals, one more citation is in order. It is none other than the original responsum from Meshullam to Jerusalem. Meshullam's Palestinian contacts were Elijah Hakohen and Abiathar the *'av bet din*, or vice-president, of the Palestinian academy. [15]

> From Elijah Hakohen, head of the academy of Jerusalem, and his *'av bet din*, R. Abiathar, to R. Moses the son of Meshullam of Mayence: Perish the thought that there should be any argument on the matter! For in the two academies of Palestine and in Nehardea we say *vehasi'enu* on Rosh Hashanah and Yom Kippur. [16]

To be sure, Meshullam confirms Abudarham's information; the prayers involved were said on Rosh Hashanah in Jerusalem, as, for that matter, everywhere else whence Meshullam has any information. If, however, we are seeking a source from which Saadiah derived his own particular notion, Meshullam's responsum is of no help since Saadiah seems all the more to stand alone. Yet our investigation is worth pursuing further because its outcome will shed light on Palestinian custom in the dark years preceding Elijah's successful academy at Jerusalem. And it will indicate how it was that Saadiah could stand so independently on the matter, for in fact he probably had Palestinian precedent behind him.

We may start by assuming (1) that the reason Saadiah eliminated *vehasi'enu* and changed *la'alot veleira'ot*, "to ascend and to appear," to *lehakriv*, "to sacrifice," was in order to preserve the distinctiveness of the pilgrimage festivals; and (2) that Amram here represents the normative Babylonian custom, at least in ninth-century Sura, while Saadiah's practice could derive from Babylonia, Egypt, Palestine, or any other locality from which Saadiah's eclecticism borrowed. General logic as well as Abudarham (above) testify to the veracity of the first assumption, and the general nature of the two prayer books seems to support the second one. Moreover, Amram quotes Yehudai as his precedent, thus indicating that at least one earlier Babylonian gaon felt as Amram did.[17]

So Amram followed Yehudai and Babylonian custom, but where did Saadiah get his idea? If we assume that Elijah is correct when he says that Palestine agreed with Babylonia here, we must assume also that it was only Saadiah's personal preference that led him to depart from both major centers of Jewish custom. This is possible for an individualist like Saadiah, but the fact that some later rites omit *vehasi'enu*, as Saadiah did, might suggest that more than one man's opinion was involved.[18]

Lewin attempts to make sense of the matter by identifying the "Nehardeans" of Elijah's responsum as the Surans but not the Pumbeditans.[19] The custom of omitting *vehasi'enu* could therefore be Pumbeditan, and Saadiah, though a Suran, would have learned it from Pumbedita. But Nedardea generally means Pumbedita elsewhere in the literature,[20] and how strange it is to think that Saadiah would cast aside both his Palestinian past and the tradition of his own academy to follow Pumbedita!

I suggest there is no reason to accept Elijah's account as representative of the Palestinian custom from the beginning. He himself does not say that they *always* recited *vehasi'enu* but only that they say it now. It is true that the genizah fragments are so varied that they neither support nor deny this contention,[21] but *Massekhet Soferim* indicates that *vehasi'enu* was not said on either Rosh Hashanah or Yom Kippur, and *Massekhet Soferim* is not only a reliable index for Palestinian practice, but it, unlike most genizah rituals, is clearly datable about three centuries before Elijah, and two before Saadiah.

> Just as we *mekallesin* [= say a *kedushah*] for Rosh Hashanah and Yom
> Kippur, so we do for the *yamim tovim*. And what is *killusan* [their form
> of *kedushah*]? ... *vehasi'enu*, etc., and the eulogy, "Blessed ... who
> sanctifies His people Israel and the festivals of joy and the times of
> solemn assembly [the last days of festivals]."[22]

Now it is possible that the word *killusan* refers back to all the holidays,
including Rosh Hashanah and Yom Kippur, but the sense of the paragraph
indicates that it more probably refers only to the *yamim tovim*, by which the
author must mean the pilgrimage festivals, or what Saadiah would have called
mo'adim. The phrase *ukheshem she ... kakh mekallesin*, "just as ... so ... ,"
is a bridge from the previous paragraph (19:4), where Rosh Hashanah and
Yom Kippur are discussed alone, to this one, where the festivals are brought
in. The author feels free to refer to the pilgrimage festivals as *yamim tovim*
precisely because Rosh Hashanah and Yom Kippur, to which they are being
compared, are not *yamim tovim* in the author's view, but separate holidays
whose form of *kedushah* (or *killus*) is different. Above all, there is the fact that
the eulogy refers only to the pilgrimage festivals! So the question which this
Soferim passage presupposes is: Do we say a *kedushat hayom* for the pilgrimage festivals too? And if so, how does it differ from that of Rosh Hashanah?
The answer is that the festival *kedushah* has a different eulogy and that it
includes *vehasi'enu*.

It is also noteworthy that Elijah does not quote any early Palestinian
authorities to prove his position. The only proof offered by Elijah is carried in
a parallel recension of the responsum, which adds the following to what was
said above:

> In the Palestinian Talmud, section *haro'eh*, Samuel says, "You must
> say *vehasi'enu*. ..." Similarly I have found in *Halakhot Gedolot* that
> one should say *vehasi'enu* on Rosh Hashanah.[23]

But this citation is far from satisfactory. Samuel did prescribe the saying
of *vehasi'enu*, but he was talking about the New Moon, and certainly not all
of the New Moon liturgy was carried over to the New Year. The noted
authority on the Palestinian Talmud, Baer Ratner, who labored assiduously to
collect variant readings to its passages, found himself unable to understand
how Elijah could presume to argue as he does from this passage, and is forced
to conclude that an earlier reading of the Palestinian Talmud included a
reference to the New Year also.[24] He suggests this emendation even though
all his manuscript variants and all his quotations from medieval authorities
read without such an addition.

It is possible to satisfy Ratner's desire for logical consistency without
emending the Palestinian Talmud, simply by assuming that Elijah was citing
his current custom without reference to earlier practice.

Amram did say *vehasi'enu* since he considered Rosh Hashanah on a par with the pilgrimage festivals, there being no distinction in his mind between a *mo'ed* and a *yom tov*. Both carried a *kedushat hayom* in the *tefillah*, and both were outfitted with *vehasi'enu*, a prayer for the blessing, peace, and prosperity symbolized by such happy occasions. This had been the standard Babylonian custom as far back as Amram's records recalled. It had been attested by Yehudai, whose words were cited by Amram,[25] and later had been inserted in *Halakhot Gedolot*, whence they were known to Elijah and to Abudarham. The early Palestinian custom, however, was to omit *vehasi'enu*, as *Massekhet Soferim* makes clear, a practice continued by Saadiah because of his own predilection for distinguishing a festival from a holiday.

But between Saadiah's death (942) and Elijah's election to the Palestinian gaonate (1062) much had transpired. Even by the time of Saadiah's prayer book, differences in the two countries' customs had been blurred. As the gaonate in Babylonia weakened and that in Palestine became stronger, the type of Babylonian opposition to Palestine characteristic of Amram proved fruitless, even inimical to Rabbanite interests at a time when common problems like the growth of Karaism threatened both Rabbanite communities. So the two rabbinic centers abandoned their rivalry. Communications increased and liturgical differences were blurred even more. Daniel ben Azariah, for example, the Palestinian gaon from 1051 to 1062, was originally a Babylonian![26] How different the situation was only a century and a half earlier when the Palestinian leader, Ben Meir, had challenged Babylonian supremacy, after his ancestors had supplanted Babylonian leadership in Palestine.[27] Yet in this later time, here was a Babylonian who was well received in Palestine and who could work together in harmony with Elijah the Palestinian, who became his *'av*.[28]

That good relations obtained during the time of Elijah can be seen, first, from the fact that he chooses to quote Babylonian custom as well as his own. He also mentions the precedent of *Halakhot Gedolot* without hesitation, and elsewhere he quotes Yehudai by name to establish a halakhic point, an "interesting" phenomenon, in Mann's words, considering the parochialism typical of earlier times.[29]

So by Elijah's day *vehasi'enu* was indeed said in Palestine, but it had been borrowed from Babylonia. When Elijah was asked about the custom by Meshullam (or Moses), he said in effect, "This is what we do here and in Babylon," and added as an afterthought, "Besides, there is a ruling in the Palestinian Talmud . . . and also in *Halakhot Gedolot*." He had no genuine Palestinian precedent because there was none. His real reason for saying *vehasi'enu* was simply that such was his custom; its Babylonian origins were probably completely unknown to him.

We are left still with the third of the three prayers related to Rosh Hashanah's status as *mo'ed* (festival) or *yom tov* (holiday): *ya'aleh veyavo'*. If any doubt still remains regarding the problematic nature of the New Year, it will be dispelled by an analysis of the sources regarding *ya'aleh veyavo'*. We may begin with a difference of opinion between Paltoi and Hai. As background for their disagreement we must keep in mind that (1) the theme of *ya'aleh veyavo'* is the plea that God remember us as if we had actually made the pilgrimage called for in Temple times; and (2) the Rosh Hashanah *musaf* liturgy carries an additional section called *zikhronot* ("remembrance") whereby the precentor calls on God to remember us.

The views of Paltoi and Hai are given in the following communication:

> As for *ya'aleh veyavo'*, R. Paltoi said it was a custom to say it, though if one does not say it, he need not do so, since the precentor refers to remembering in the *zikhronot*. So there are some places where they say it and some places where they do not. But one must say [as part of the *kedushat hashem*] "Lord our God, give us, in love, festivals [*mo'adim*] for rejoicing, etc." But Rav Hai Gaon said, "It is not our custom to say 'Give us, in love, festivals for rejoicing,' but rather, 'Lord our God, give us, in love, this day of remembrance.' [i.e., Rosh Hashanah, *yom hazikaron*]."[30]

Saadiah agrees with Hai while Amram sides with Paltoi.[31] Here both Saadiah and Hai are unwilling to refer to Rosh Hashanah as a *mo'ed*. It is *yom hazikaron* by their day.

Now we saw above that some people wanted to refer to God's righteous judgment in their Rosh Hashanah *kedushat hayom*, and that Saadiah considered the reference out of place. Their desire is indicative of the rising significance in rabbinic circles of seeing the New Year under the guise of *yom hadin*, "day of judgment." We now find another conceptual term, *yom hazikaron*, "day of remembrance," emphasized by Hai. Both terms are compatible, even complementary, from a theological perspective. This was a day of *din*, "judgment," for the world; but ameliorating the divine wrath was *zikaron*, God's "remembrance" of our own meritorious deeds, those of our ancestors, the covenant, the Temple cult which atones, and so on.

It was, in fact, the geonic period which saw these complementary notions coalesce, particularly under the influence of Saadiah and Hai, who remove Rosh Hashanah from the category of *mo'ed* and now reveal it as a particular type of *yom tov*: *yom hadin* and *yom hazikaron*, a day of judgment in which God is asked to remember.

This concept of Rosh Hashanah as *yom hazikaron* is certainly postbiblical. The Bible knows of Rosh Hashanah as being *yom teru'ah* (Num. 29:1), and links it with *zikaron* only in Leviticus 23:24, *zikhron teru'ah*. True the concept of *zikhronot*, "remembrance," is present in the Mishnah's discussion of blowing the shofar and in its discussion of Fast Days.[32] It is thus tannaitic but not limited to the New Year. Even in amoraic times, the day was not referred to regularly as *yom hazikaron*. The phrase itself does not even occur in the Babylonian Talmud, and the Palestinian Talmud notes simply,

> Scripture calls it *yom teru'ah* in one place, and *zikhron teru'ah* in
> another. How can that be? When it falls on a weekday it is *yom teru'ah*,
> when it falls on the Sabbath it is *zikhron teru'ah*.[33]

So the amoraim had yet to free themselves from the linguistic shackles of
biblical terminology.[34]

Whence, then, this accent on the phrase *yom hazikaron* in the liturgy?
It is present in Amram and in Saadiah, with Saadiah emphasizing it.[35] But
from Palestinian sources it is clear that the term had not yet been isolated as a
unique description for the New Year. There were a variety of other terms that
were preferred.[36]

So it would seem that though the idea of *zikaron* is early, Rosh
Hashanah was not designated as the holiday of remembrance above all other
holidays until very late. Numbers 10:9–10 lists all the holidays as times when
remembrance is in order (and Exodus 12:14 marks Passover, not Rosh
Hashanah, as the holiday of remembrance), so the Palestinian conception of
Rosh Hashanah as just another holiday of remembrance is closer to the
biblical prototype. Despite Amram's use of the term *yom hazikaron*, he too is
close to the older conception, since he includes the *mo'adim* in the prayer.
His contemporary, Paltoi, in the above-quoted responsum, was perfectly able
to say that *ya'aleh* was merely a custom and need not be said on Rosh
Hashanah since remembrance is a requirement of *all holidays*, and Rosh
Hashanah receives its remembrance quotient in the *zikhronot*. He, like Amram, wants people to mention the *mo'adim* simultaneously.

But by Saadiah's time *yom hazikaron* is emphasized and detached from
the general category of *mo'adim*. Just as he objected to the *la'alot veleira'ot*
formula and to saying *vehasi'enu* on Rosh Hashanah, so, here, Saadiah
excises references to the *mo'adim*. We do not know what Hai thought of the
first two issues, but he stood with Saadiah in emphasizing *yom hazikaron*.

Now our course has not been easy, but we have finally arrived at our
original goal: a further analysis of Saadiah's reasoning, as reflected in the New
Year liturgy. With one exception, we have seen him eschew the equation of
Rosh Hashanah as a festival like the pilgrimage festivals. It is a holiday,
certainly, but more than that, it is the day of remembrance, a celebration of
the divine compassion implicit in God's taking cognizance of our human
frailties, but also, at the same time, a frightening day of judgment, the
occasion of the Lord's inevitable wrath. Thus Saadiah systematically excised
references and prayers dealing with the pilgrimage festivals, borrowing on one
case (*vehasi'enu*) from his Palestinian experience, elsewhere following the
dictates of his own stubborn will. Amram, living some fifty years before, was
completely impervious to this development, as was Paltoi, living a few decades earlier still. But Hai, living nearly a century after Saadiah, sided with his
philosophically minded predecessor. We have now only to unearth the impetus behind Saadiah's insistence and Hai's acquiescence.

We have already seen how Saadiah's thinking is frequently a reaction to the Karaites, whom he opposed throughout his life. Hai, too, we know, was aware of Karaism, as his responsum on the Torah reading showed, and as we would expect anyway, considering the fact that his gaonate coincided with the Karaite golden age in Palestine. It may be, then, that Saadiah and Hai emphasized the unique character of Rosh Hashanah as *yom hazikaron* because that very view was under attack by the Karaites. Anan and Hadassi think the blowing of trumpets on *each and every holiday* is what *teru'ah* implies.[37] For rabbis after Saadiah, however, the New Year becomes both *yom hadim* and *yom hazikaron*. Our being remembered by God is tied directly to the concept of His judgment, since it is the judgmental feature of the day which necessitates God's recalling both our need for mercy and the deeds of the patriarchs, whose merit may carry over to our account.

In sum, it was during the geonic period that Rosh Hashanah received its characteristic titles, and the theological notions of *yom hadin* and the parallel *yom hazikaron* received their fullest treatment. To some extent this was but the continuation of amoraic theology. With Saadiah and Hai, however, the Karaite challenge to the rabbinic concept produced an immediacy which led to an emphasis and clarification of past rabbinic notions.

Yom Kippur

The most awesome day in the Jewish calendar is certainly Yom Kippur. Rosh Hashanah's newly found status as day of judgment and remembrance is a mere prelude to this day on which Jews fast, pray, and wait for their fate to be determined.

Our study of Yom Kippur differs substantially from the preceding labyrinthine discussion of Rosh Hashanah. There we saw several controversial prayers all interrelated and dependent on one's theological identification of Rosh Hashanah's uniqueness. Here, on the other hand, we are faced with several unrelated debates, which fall together in this chapter merely by virtue of their common provenance, the Yom Kippur liturgy. We shall deal in turn with *kol nidre*, the *vidui*, or confessional, an apparent redundancy in the wording of the *kedushat hayom*, the *'avodah* liturgy unique to Yom Kippur, and the Priestly Benediction for both Yom Kippur and fast days generally.

Yom Kippur eve virtually begins with what is perhaps the most familiar and beloved prayer in the entire liturgy: *kol nidre*.[38] This is a call for God to overlook unkept promises and to annul unfulfilled vows in His final tabulation of human weakness. It is fitting therefore, that this should be a prayer much debated by the geonim.[39]

Kol nidre is discussed in no source preceding them, the earliest possible reference to it being a statement by Yehudai:

> We do not elucidate [*mefarshin*] the talmudic tractate "Vows" [*nedarim*], for we lack the competence to grasp the depth of such matters, all the more so the annulment of vows; it is not customary in the two academies or in all of Babylonia to annul vows.[40]

It is questionable, however, whether Yehudai is actually discussing the prayer *kol nidre* here, or whether this, like so many other responsa, deals with the legal annulment of vows generally, a practice about which earlier rabbinic literature has a great deal to say, none of it connected to the liturgy. Poznanski is probably more correct when he says, "The first [gaon] who mentions it [*kol nidre*] is Natronai bar Hillai in Sura."[41] Natronai repeats Yehudai's information that the subject of vows is not studied,[42] but then adds,

> It is not customary in the academy [another manuscript says, "the two academies"] nor anywhere [else] to annul vows, neither on Rosh Hashanah nor on Yom Kippur. We have heard, however, that in other countries they say *kol nidre*, but we have never heard or seen any record of it from our rabbis.[43]

A complicating consideration is the fact that there are actually two versions of *kol nidre*. One asks God to annul vows made during the past year, and the other refers ahead to vows that may be made in the year to come. It is not clear which of the two Natronai had heard about, but the formula for the past is found in *Seder Rav Amram*, where the practice is denigrated as illicit, and labeled *minhag shetut*, "a nonsensical custom," followed by others.[44] Later Hai bar Nachshon of Sura (885–896)—not to be confused with the more illustrious Hai bar Sherira, whom we have been quoting all along—also proscribes *kol nidre* and testifies, as Natronai had, that in his day neither academy recites it.[45]

There are reports, however, of geonim who permitted the prayer. The first is by Paltoi.

> In a responsum of Rav Paltoi Gaon it is written that our custom and that of *bet rabbenu* of Babylonia is that the precentor says *shehechiyanu* and then *kol nidre* and then *barekhu*.[46]

Since the other gaon to favor *kol nidre* is a Pumbeditan, Hai bar Sherira, and since Paltoi also hailed from Pumbedita, while all the negative opinions so far recorded are by Surans, Ginzberg concludes, "It would appear that this is one of the legal differences between Sura and Pumbedita."[47]

But Paltoi's gaonate lasted from 842 to 857, the latter part of his reign overlapping with Natronai's at Sura. If the report about Paltroi is correct, how could Natronai have said that all Babylonia knew nothing about *kol nidre*? Besides, Amram says distinctly that the prayer prevailed only in "other countries." And Hai bar Nachshon, too, who took office in 885, was adamant about "both academies" omitting it. By Ginzberg's own criteria, in fact, this responsum cannot be by Paltoi, since it cites *bet rabbenu*, which Ginzberg thinks is never mentioned by Pumbeditans.[48] Above all, it should be noted that independent grounds, internal textual evidence, led Poznanski and Mann to assert that Paltoi did not say *kol nidre*.[49] If Paltoi wrote the responsum at all, they maintain, he did so without the phrase "and then *kol nidre*." These instructions, at the end of the line, were appended by a later hand.

Hai bar Sherira, however, not only permitted *kol nidre*, but even included it in his own *siddur*, which unfortunately is no longer extant, but is known to us from medieval references. According to the author of *Shibbolei Haleket*, "Most of the geonim prohibited the saying of *kol nidre*, since nothing but evil could result from it, except Rav Hai Gaon, and thus it is found in his prayer book."[50] True, Hai is elsewhere reported to have opposed *kol nidre*, but his words there leave no doubt that his negative judgment was limited to the formula regarding future vows.[51] The formula for the past, which is the one recorded of his prayer book, he accepted.

Saadiah's position is hard to ascertain. There are reports that he allowed the formula, but with reservations. It was established for the limited purpose of annulling vows made in error by whole congregations, to satisfy the biblical contingency (Lev 4:13), "If the whole congregation of Israel errs." But, says Saadiah, it is certainly not intended for people who go around making vows all year expecting ultimately to be able to annul them.[52] So *kol nidre* is not found in his prayer book. It was not meant for individuals to say as part of their worship, but was to be limited to the unique circumstances mentioned above. In fact he may not even have intended it for Yom Kippur at all, but only as an ad hoc procedure, so limited in its application that it would never actually be carried out.

It is fairly evident that this was no native Babylonian custom. It was probably Palestinian.[53] So again we see Natronai, Amram, and Hai bar Nachshon (also of period 1) opposing a Palestinian innovation; Saadiah goes along with it, though he omits it from his prayer book and limits its applicability. And Hai is the first gaon to include it for regular recitation, probably out of respect for the beloved custom's integrity.[54] *Kol nidre* alone illustrates our hypothesis of the three periods of liturgical canonization and their respective characteristics.

Regardless of how beloved *kol nidre* became to later generations, it was hardly an essential feature of the geonic Yom Kippur liturgy. Far more essential was the confession of sins, or *vidui*.[55]

The *vidui* did not always have the connotation of confessing one's sins. A prominant usage of the word in the Mishnah, for example, regards the bringing of the second tithe to Jerusalem and making a *vidui* to the priest there,[56] and it is quite clear from what the pilgrim says that he is confessing no sin, but affirming his proper conformance to the Torah. The *vidui* is positive, celebrative, here; and it is intoned to remind God that He too has a covenantal obligation to fulfill. On the other hand, the term also appears with negative connotations, that is to say, the other side of the same coin: admitting one's failings under the term of the covenant. After 70, when Temple-based rituals disappeared, the positive *vidui* ceased, and by amoraic times it was *vidui* as confession of sin that became predominant. A variety of such confessions are recorded of the amoraim.[57]

As with so many other prayers, the wording of the confession varied widely, though there was general agreement on the prayer's placement within the Yom Kippur liturgy. Individuals were to confess privately after their *tefillah*.[58] The precentor, or *sheliach tsibbur*, whose role it was to represent the congregation before God, was entrusted with the task of repeating the *tefillah* for those who could not say it themselves. He also, therefore, came to repeat the confessional on behalf of the same people, doing so as part of his repetition of the *tefillah*. Customarily, he inserted it during the middle or fourth blessing (the *kedushat hayom*) of this holiday *tefillah*.

The unanticipated factor that this careful structure did not take into consideration was the tannaitic practice of saying a private confession even before Yom Kippur began, preferably at the dinner table of the last meal eaten before the fast set in (T. *Yoma* 4[5]:14). Since the confession was still without formal set wording, this custom occasioned no difficulty even for the unlettered average Jewish householder. By the geonic time, though, the confessional had become a prescribed set of fixed words, and many people assumed that it was this specific prayer, rather than the original ad hoc formulation that was required of them at dinner time. So our responsa deal with the knotty problem of people who know they should confess at dinner but feel unequal to the task; the people suggest that the precentors say the confession for them during the afternoon *tefillah* preceding dinner, but the precentors wonder just exactly how that can be done, particularly since the normal rubric for such a practice would be the *kedushat hayom*, which is absent in the *tefillah* in question. The matter is interesting from the perspective of the process of harmonizing legal requirements with changing times. The responsa also show us the degree to which simple beginnings become grandiose liturgical events, weighted down with lengthy prescribed texts and a maze of detailed regulations. And they give us interesting pictures of Jewish life in geonic times: unsophisticated average worshippers, prayer in the vernacular, and a gaon (Sherira) who insists that confessions cannot be mere formalities.

We begin with the end of a responsum whose first part is lost to us.

As for your second question regarding a confession by the precentor at the eve of Yom Kippur [he means the afternoon service which comes at the end of the day before Yom Kippur, Yom Kippur officially beginning with the evening service following], we have no such custom; nor have we ever heard of it, i.e., the precentor approaching the ark [then] and confessing. But if the precentor wants to expand the blessing, "He is compassionate and great in pardoning" [i.e., the sixth blessing of the *tefillah*, which deals with the pardoning of sins] into a sort of confession, he should not be stopped.[59]

If only we had the first part of the responsum! But at least the part we have can be satisfactorily dealt with, since a comparison with parallel texts shows this to have been written by Hai.[60] So it is Hai who opposed the custom of having an extra reader's confession at the afternoon service before Yom Kippur. But he compromises with popular will. He allows the reader to expand *selach lanu*, the pertinent *tefillah* blessing,[61] into "a sort of confession" (*devarim kegon vidui*); if he does that, "he should not be stopped."

But Hai's responsum is not as clear-cut as it seems, because of his curious contention that he has never heard of this extra confession; in point of fact, his father, Sherira, had addressed himself to the very same practice, so Hai must have known of it.

From R. Sherira: You request information regarding the permissibility of the precentor at the afternoon service before Yom Kippur saying a confession after the *tefillah*, in order to exempt the unlearned, since there are many members of the congregation who are unknowledgeable yet have a responsibility to fulfill. [Sherira identifies what responsibility is meant later in his answer.] How are they to acquit themselves? If the precentor may make a confession, where should he say it, since some of the earlier geonim said he should recite it in *selach lanu?*

Answer: Regarding the confession of Yom Kippur, the sages certainly said: Where should it be recited? [The individual worshipper should say it] after his *tefillah*, and the precentor should say it in the middle of [his repetition of] the *tefillah*. Those earlier geonim advised you well when they said, regarding your question, that he should say it [the extra confession] in *selach lanu*, since, thematically, it resembles [the confession] more than all the other blessings; but he should make it clear, publicly, that what he is adding is a Yom Kippur confession, so that it will not be mixed up with the *tefillah*. Now [the tradition] says only that the precentor should say [the confession] in the middle [of the *tefillah*] only for the morning, additional [*musaf*] afternoon and concluding [*neʿilah*] services [of Yom Kippur itself], but as for the afternoon *tefillah* preceding Yom Kippur, regarding which they said, "A person should confess before dinner, and if he fails to do so, he should do it [as an individual] after his *tefillah*"—we have never heard in all of Babylonia that a precentor recites a confession in the *tefillah* preceding Yom Kippur! As for your saying that you require just that, you should announce to the congregation in language they all understand that they are all obligated to make confession before their creator before they eat the final meal that precedes Yom Kippur. The easiness with which one may make confession should be explained to them, so that every single person will rise and confess with full comprehension in a language which he understands. [62]

Sherira's answer clarifies the issue, providing an honest portrait of people in his day. He refers to the *Tosefta* (*Yoma* 4 [5]:14), with its instructions to say a confession before eating supper on Yom Kippur eve. Some interpreted this to imply an obligation to institutionalize a formal confession at the afternoon service, for the sake of those who felt too ignorant to recite the prescribed prayer themselves. We know from Amram, in fact, that the afternoon service was deliberately held before supper (rather than at sunset after supper, just immediately before the evening service), probably for this very reason. The people then went home, with their "supper confession" already made for them by the precentor during the afternoon service. Then they ate supper, and returned for the Yom Kippur evening service. [63] Naturally, people wondered where to say the extra confession, no easy question to answer because it was normally inserted in the reader's repetition of the *kedushat hayom*. But that blessing occurred only on holidays, not the day before, so it was absent from the afternoon *tefillah* in question! Amram solved the problem by placing his afternoon confession after the *tefillah*, [64] since even though the precentor was saying it, it was really just a stand-in for the missing confession of the individual, and that is where the individual's confession would have been.

Generally, though, the rabbinic tradition had distinguished the precentor as "representative of the congregation" (*sheliach tsibbur*) and kept his role distinct from people who might lead prayers in other capacities. From the very earliest of times the terminology referring to him differed from that defining other such functionaries. [65] As the service grew in bulk, the *sheliach tsibbur* came to fulfill other roles too, so that the original definition of his role was absorbed by his new tasks. Still there remained a distinction between the original role and the new ones. Technically, he was the congregational spokesman before God only during the *tefillah*, which he said aloud (after his own personal recitation) on behalf of those who could not say it. But his representation function was limited to that prayer. That is why individuals could confess after the *tefillah*, but he could confess for them only during it. Amram's decision to place the precentor's confession after the *tefillah* was, therefore, a break with tradition occasioned only by the fact that the normal place within the *tefillah* where it would have been situated (the *kedushat hayom*) was simply not part of the ordinary weekday afternoon *tefillah*, even though it happened to be the one preceding Yom Kippur.

Sherira and Hai were, therefore, astounded to find that a questioner even considered a reader's recitation of the confession after the *tefillah*'s

conclusion. So they adopted another strategem. They allowed the extra confession, but only in the middle of the *tefillah,* and since its normal location
there, the *kedushat hayom,* was missing, they selected the most logical alternative, its sixth blessing, whose theme is for pardon, *selach lanu* ("pardon
us . . .").[66] The questioner was aware of earlier geonim who had already
suggested that very solution, so Sherira's suggestion was not uniquely his
own.[67]

We have here an interesting side-effect of the canonization process. The
amoraim still considered the confession before supper to be a private matter.
But the people began to interpret it as a formal confession with fixed wording,
an interpretation whose acceptance could only be hastened by Amram's inclusion of a full reader's confession in his prayer book. Sherira, however,
fought this notion. While allowing this confession, he asserted, nonetheless,
that the people were not thereby released from their own private, personal
confession, to be said in any language they understood.

Sherira's accent on spontaneity with all the individual differences
therein entailed is perfectly congruent with what we have seen of him so
far—and of Hai, his son. Their gaonate was marked by a desire to accept local
liturgical preferences rather than to insist on one solitary acceptable form of
worship. Amram's stand, too, is in character. Unlike Hai and Sherira, his
liturgical decisions tended to limit alternatives. It follows that he would fix the
character of the extra *vidui,* taking it out of the hands of the individual and
standardizing its recitation in the role of the precentor.

Another problem which vexed the geonim was whether to conclude the *vidui*
with a eulogy. The root of the controversy is the same *Tosefta* passage that
discussed the private confession at dinner.[68] The apparent meaning of the
passage is that R. Meir demanded a eulogy after the confession, while the
sages made it optional. This difference of opinion continued well into geonic
times and beyond, so that some worshippers probably never added a eulogy,
some said it in every confession, and others concluded this way only at the
concluding *ne'ilah* service.[69]

Because of confusion arising from their understanding of the *Tosefta,* as
well as the variety of geonic precedent, Amram and Saadiah take opposing
sides on the issue, and tell us what the regnant eulogy was.

> According to Saadiah, some people add a eulogy to it [the confession],
> "Blessed art Thou, the forgiving God" [*ha'el hasalchan*], but this is a
> mistake since this is no place for a blessing![70]

Heinemann sees Saadiah's ruling as another example of his general criteria,
the first one, in this case, by which Saadiah would not compromise the
essential structure of the blessings taken individually, or the structural rules of
a series of blessings considered together. Saadiah must have believed that the

addition of a eulogy would convert the confession into an independent blessing, thus creating an unwarranted extra benediction in the *tefillah*. [71] Amram, however, allows the reader—though not the individual—to recite the eulogy. But the location of his comment indicates that he considers this appropriate only at *ne'ilah*. [72] Amram made this decision because he thought the Babylonian Talmud favored a eulogy by the precentor during *ne'ilah*, and—as he does elsewhere—he supported its ruling. Saadiah, for whom logic and structure played more significant roles than Babylonian textual precedent, disallowed the eulogy.

A relatively minor matter deals with the *kedushat hayom*, the blessing containing the reader's repetition of the confessional. Though apparently a trivial problem in itself, this issue bears important evidence regarding Saadiah. *Siddur Saadiah*'s version of the *kedushat hayom* reads, *umibal'adekha 'ein lanu melekh ki 'atah hu' mochel vesolei'ach*, "Other than You we have no king, for it is You who forgive." To this reading Saadiah appended a cautionary remark, "It is forbidden to say 'other than you' [*'ela' 'atah*], and anyone saying it makes a mistake by such an addition."[73] Obviously there is no theological issue here. Nor is Saadiah fighting sectaries of any kind. He is just being gramatically precise. "Other than you" (*'ela' 'atah*), coming in the same line as "Except for you" (*umibal'adekha*), would be redundant, so Saadiah excises it. This concern for syntactical precision in the prayers is, as we have already seen, typical of Saadiah.

The unique day of Yom Kippur retains many vestiges of the Temple cult. The confession, which we have already surveyed, originated there, but it was only part of a far more elaborate ceremony that consumed the whole day, its preparations having been begun a full week earlier. The highlight of the day's ritual consisted of the slaughter of a bullock, in which the priest's every action was carefully choreographed.[74] This sacrifice, known as the *'avodah*, or "cultic service," of the priest, was clearly not something easily forgotten. Even an ordinary day's activities in the Temple were such as to make an eyewitness, Ben Sira, exclaim:

> How glorious he was when the people gathered round him
> as he came out of the inner sanctuary!
> Like the morning star among the clouds,
> like the moon when it is full;
> like the sun shining on the Temple of the Most High,
> and like the rainbow gleaming in glorious clouds;
> like roses in the days of the first fruits,
> like lilies by a spring of water,
> like a green shoot of Lebanon on a summer day;
> like fire and incense in the censor,
> like a vessel of hammered gold.[75]

And Yom Kippur was no ordinary day! The Yom Kippur proceedings contained many memorable gestures: priestly oblations and clothing changes from gold, to linen, to white, and back to gold again;[76] a scapegoat driven to its death over a precipice;[77] circumambulation of the large altar in the courtyard; and the sprinkling of blood on its four corner bases and on the curtain separating the courtyard from the inner chambers which were enclosed beyond ordinary Israelites' vision.[78] And above all, perhaps, the High Priest's entrance into the innermost of those chambers, the Holy of Holies. There he surrounded himself with clouds of incense and uttered a short prayer. Then he emerged before the hushed crowds massed in the courtyard. The drama can be appreciated by attending to the Mishnah's simple admission that he hastened to emerge "lest he terrify the Israelites" by a more protracted absence.[79]

Even after the Temple was destroyed, this annual cultic highlight was not easily forgotten. Initial reminiscences were preserved in tannaitic literature, and steadily romanticized with legendary and mythic embellishments. *Payyetanim* of the classical period virtually enshrined the memorable scene with poetic renditions of its every moment, illustrious portraits of the High Priest officiating in his glorious finery. More than a few such *piyyutim* circulated until, eventually, some were conflated into an independent liturgical rubric which was inserted in the additional (*musaf*) service of the Day of Atonement, and entitled the *'avodah*.[80]

But the decision to place the *'avodah* in the *musaf* service was an issue into geonic times. *Musaf* had been preferred since that was when the original Temple *'avodah* had occurred. The liturgical *'avodah* was a conscious emulation of the cultic one. This reasoning is repeated by Natronai, Amram, and Saadiah,[81] the last mentioned using his typical terminology to indicate that the recital of the *'avodah* elsewhere would be a thematic misplacement.[82] With so many authorities reiterating the impropriety of saying an *'avodah* elsewhere, we would not be surprised to find that an alternative placing of this rubric was common. Far from dealing with a theoretical issue, the geonim from Natronai to Saadiah were trying unsuccessfully to limit the *'avodah* to one service.

An anonymous gaon who also fought the practice tells us more precisely what others did: they recited an *'avodah* not only in the additional service but also in the morning and afternoon.[83] Their *piyyutim* varied with each service. In the morning they said *'atah konanta*, in the additional service, *'azkir selah*, and in the afternoon, *'asaper gedulot*.

Our recognition of this continuous opposition by the geonim, at least since Natronai, makes the following responsum by Hai most significant, because he takes an entirely different attitude to the problem. Since it illustrates the leniency which we claim as his hallmark, I include it here in some detail.

Rabbenu Hai said: As for your writing that your custom is to say an 'avodah on Yom Kippur in the morning and the additional services, and that you discovered that Rav Amram said the 'avodah belongs only in the additional service, like the *piyyutim* dealing with the blowing of the *shofar* on Rosh Hashanah, know that basically what Rav Amram said is correct. At that time the practice of saying an 'avodah other than at the additional service was known neither in Nehardea [Pumbedita] nor at Sura; just as we do not recite the scriptural verses pertaining to the sacrifices appropriate to Sabbaths, holidays, festivals, and New Moons except at the additional service [of those days]. But in Baghdad, since they love the 'avodah, they used to say it at the morning service too. Rav Hai Gaon ben Rav David, who was [then] a *dayyan* [lit. judge] in Baghdad for many years before becoming gaon, could not sway them from their custom. He was the first of the geonim to take up residence in Baghdad. He came to terms with them regarding their custom, and the geonim in Baghdad after him also decided not to speak out against it. So you too need not change your age-old custom.[84]

We can now deduce a great deal more about period 3. Predictably, Hai bar Sherira gives his correspondents the right to place the 'avodah where they wish, again resorting to his usual categorization of liturgical variety in terms of "customs" which may rightfully vary and have their own authenticity derived from their own unique histories reaching back into the past.

But until now we have seen only Hai and Sherira take this position. This is undoubtedly because Sura's closing in 944, and the consequent weakening of the gaonate that ensued, resulted in fewer responsa being issued until the time of Sherira. It was only then that the gaonate was restored to its luster and the volume of responsa increased to what it had been in earlier times.[85] The weakening of the gaonate certainly went all the way back to Saadiah's time, and was acerbated later by internal rivalries that closed Sura and left Pumbedita stunned for almost half a century. Only the forcefulness of Saadiah's own personality and his prodigious literary output made his gaonate stand out from what was otherwise a slowly deteriorating situation throughout Babylonia.

Our responsum allows us to fill in some historical background between Saadiah and Sherira. Hai bar David of Pumbedita (890–898) had been a *dayyan* in Baghdad and later became gaon. In essence, he was more than a judge there; he was the liaison between the commercial hub of the empire and his academy. The appointment of such *dayyanim* to other cities, many of them thousands of miles from the academies, is what made the whole geonic enterprise possible. The *dayyanim* collected taxes, sent responsa, and returned from time to time to *kallot*, postgraduate study sessions, where they could strengthen their ties with their alma mater and add to the training necessary to represent the geonim properly in the local towns and villages.

That Hai was assigned to the signally important city of Baghdad indicates his high personal qualifications, and it is no wonder that he ultimately succeeded to the gaonate itself. He then took the drastic move of trying to halt the ebbing fortunes of Pumbedita by relocating the academy in Baghdad, and there it remained through successive geonim. It may have been this very decision by Hai that saved his academy from closure as economic conditions forced Sura to close its doors. When Sura was reopened in 988, it too was reopened there.

Now Baghdad, perhaps the largest Jewish community in Babylonia, must certainly have followed geonic mandates to some extent. But at least with regard to the *'avodah*, Jews there followed their own procedure: they recited it more than once on Yom Kippur. And the geonim, following Hai, "decided not to speak out against it." The original language of the responsum *hu' gilgal 'imahem* makes it difficult to establish Hai's precise response. The verb *gilgal* means "to rotate, to roll," but also "to put up with," so I have translated the source as "[Hai] came to terms" with their deviant practice. If this be true, and if that attitude characterized Hai ben David, we may now antedate period 3, with its hallmarks of lenience, modesty, and acceptance of liturgical diversity, to the last decade of the ninth century, at least. If period 1, that of geonic assertiveness, marked most clearly by Amram (858–871), extended at all beyond him—and it probably did include at least the gaonate of Nachshon (871–879)—then we are really dealing chronologically with two periods not three, the first being an age in which the geonim, particularly at Sura, where power was located then, tried desperately to harmonize prayer diversity; the second, beginning almost immediately afterward, but personified most clearly by Sherira and his son Hai, at the end of the tenth century, when the geonim, now especially at Pumbedita, to where power had been transferred, recognized the folly of a harsh approach and began accepting local differences in custom. So Saadiah was not a "period" but a single individual, who attended to his own specific problems in his own characteristic way. We shall continue calling him a period, however, since the problems to which he addressed himself were typical of his lifetime and represent a unique historical perspective.

Our portrait of the geonic period is becoming more and more complete. We must still, however, continue citing other related evidence before we can finalize our position and explain the full historical background for the geonic attitude toward canonization of the synagogue service.

The final controversy regarding Yom Kippur prayers deals with the Priestly Benediction, which we have already had occasion to discuss in terms of its daily inclusion in the *tefillah*.[86] Its use on fast days such as Yom Kippur is recorded in the Mishnah,[87] where it is prescribed four times each fast day, including the afternoon service. The Babylonian Talmud provides an entire gamut of possible interpretations of this mishnah.[88]

At issue is the remarkable notion that the priests doing the blessing might be drunk on certain occasions, and should be prohibited from blessing the people in such a state. The evening service had never been in question, since no daily sacrifice was offered then anyway and thus the benediction had never occurred then. But it had been part of the morning and afternoon offerings of ordinary days, and on fast days in the additional (*musaf*) and concluding (*ne'ilah*) services, since additional Temple sacrifices had been the norm at those times.

So the tannaitic discussion carried by the Talmud discusses these four occasions: morning, additional, afternoon, and concluding services. It had already been determined that priestly inebriation was common enough in the late afternoon to annul such a blessing in the normal synagogue service. But what should be the custom on Yom Kippur, a fast day, when it might safely be presumed that the priests had not imbibed anything and could not be drunk?

To this question, R. Meir answers that the blessing belongs both at the afternoon service and at the concluding service held shortly afterward, just before dark. Judah, diametrically opposed to Meir, holds that we ought to be consistent with the rule for ordinary days, limiting the blessing to the morning. Hence there should be no blessing at either the afternoon or the concluding service, even though this is a fast and drunkenness is no real concern. Yose forms the compromise position. Like Judah, he generalizes to all afternoon services, thus forbidding the blessing then, even on a fast day; but like Meir, he allows it in the concluding service, since it is unique to fast days and there is thus no daily concluding service from which to generalize. Yose's compromise position emerges as the law, but only theoretically. In practice the Talmud notes that they say it in the afternoon service anyhow, and rationalize their practice by observing that the blessing is recited near the end of the service. It is, therefore, like the concluding service which follows.

With such talmudic inconclusiveness, it is no wonder that the debate continued into geonic times. An anonymous responsum, for example, rules that on fast days other than Yom Kippur we say the blessing at the afternoon service since there is no concluding service. (Though originally part of all fast days, it had been limited by now to Yom Kippur.) On Yom Kippur, however, when we have a concluding service and can postpone the blessing to it, we do so.[89] Amram reiterates this position, adding that both academies follow the rule.[90]

A pair of related responsa published by Müller are more difficult to explain. "Thus said Rav Mattathias Gaon: the law is [or was] in the Temple [*bamikdash*] to have a Priestly Benediction."[91] Müller wonders why a gaon would bother informing people of a law that had been irrelevant since the Temple's destruction, so he decides to emend *mikdash*, "temple," to *minchah*, "afternoon service." He thus has Mattathias Gaon addressing himself to a live issue in geonic times and urging a Priestly Benediction for the afternoon service of Yom Kippur. This is obviously in contradistinction to Amram and the anonymous gaon mentioned above, and it differs also from an opinion attributed to Kohen Tsedek which is identical in wording to Mattathias' responsum except (1) the gaon is Kohen Tsedek, not Mattathias; (2) the word *mikdash* reads *minchah*; and (3) instead of *yesh bah* "there is [a Priestly Benediction]" we find *'ein bah*, "there should not be," or "there is not [a Priestly Benediction]."[92]

Now Müller had assembled data on differences in customs between Palestine and Babylonia, and published them ten years earlier in a well-known classic referred to earlier: *Chilluf Minhagim bein Bavel Ve'eretz Yisra'el*. Drawing on this study, Müller explains that Palestine said the blessing at the afternoon service while Babylon did not. Thus he has Mattathias (Pumbedita, 860–869) confirming what he thinks is the Babylonian practice, and Kohen Tsedek deviating, but for no apparent reason. Lewin accepts Müller's theory but says Kohen Tsedek may be the Pumbeditan gaon (926–936), not the Suran (838–848). Thus he has two Pumbeditans opposing the standard Babylonian interpretation, and he explains Kohen Tsedek's allowing the blessing by stating (with no documentary substantiation), "The Surans followed Palestinian custom in many matters."[93]

But Müller's emendation cannot be correct, at least not if we accept the trustworthiness of Amram's observations. Amram said expressly that both academies omitted the benediction at the afternoon service in his day, and Mattathias was Amram's contemporary! Moreover, Müller misunderstood his own source, *Chilluf Minhagim*, which relates,

> The Babylonians say the Priestly Benediction three times [i.e., morning, additional, and concluding services] on Yom Kippur, while the Palestinians [say it] four times: morning, additional, afternoon, and concluding services.[94]

So despite Müller's theory, we see that it was the Babylonians who omitted the Priestly Benediction at the afternoon service, thus following the theoretical conclusion of the Babylonian Talmud, and it was the Palestinians who added the fourth recitation at the afternoon service. Thus Amram, the anonymous gaon, and Kohen Tsedek (regardless of which academy he came from) all follow Babylonian custom, as we would expect, and only Mattathias is a problem; but his view is problematic only because Müller emended his words in the first place. As his communication stands, he is talking about what was done *bamikdash*, "at the Temple," and is not even addressing the problem of what to do *baminchah*, "at the afternoon service." Unfortunately, the quotation preserved for us is so short that we have no certain knowledge of the question he was answering at the time. Since letters to geonim frequently request interpretations of the past rather than instructions for the present, it is likely that Mattathias' correspondent asked for a description of the ancient Temple ritual and he told them that they used to have a Priestly Blessing there. There are certainly no grounds for assuming Mattathias himself to have favored a Priestly Benediction at the afternoon service, especially since we have Amram's testimony that he did not.

Again, we should note that Amram supported the Babylonian practice against the Palestinian. An anonymous gaon and one of the Kohen Tsedeks who occupied the gaonate agreed.

Fast Days

Since we have dealt with the major fast day, Yom Kippur, we might well append here the single relevant controversy regarding fast days generally. Such days were exceedingly common in the geonic period, and became even more so later—the sixteenth-century law code, the *Shulchan ʿArukh*, lists no fewer than twenty-five![95] But even by geonic times Jews understood rabbinic law to demand four major fasts (based on Zechariah 8:19), as well as others. Moreover, community fasts could be declared in times of distress.

A genre of *piyyut* known as a *selichah* (from the root *slch* = "to pardon") had been developed for fast days, and the responsum which concerns us is an explanation of where such *selichot* should be recited. It also cites part of a prayer which evokes the gaon's ire. The source is *Seder Rav Amram*, quoting Sar Shalom.

> Thus said Sar Shalom Gaon. You asked about people who say *selichot* after ʿoseh shalom [a eulogy for the final *tefillah* blessing] and whether it is permissible to do so. We have never seen or heard of people doing so. Also in the conclusion of the *selichot* [you mention] he [the *chazzan*] says, "May no sin or iniquity foil our prayer, for You are a good and forgiving God. Blessed be He who forgives abundantly" [*barukh hamarbeh lislo-ach*]. You should not do so, and the custom of the two academies is [to say *selichot*] only in "... He who is merciful and forgives abundantly."[96]

Apparently, Sar Shalom's correspondents said the entire *tefillah*, ending it, as usual, with the *birkat shalom*. Then, probably on the analogy of the individual confessional, they said various *selichot* beseeching God not to let their sins inhibit their prayer's potency. They concluded with a eulogy drawn from the sixth benediction, whose theme, appropriately, is forgiveness.

Sar Shalom objected first to the placing of *selichot* after *birkat shalom*. He thinks they should be inserted in the sixth benediction itself. He also opposes the concluding words of his respondents, "May no sin or iniquity foil our prayer, for You are a good and forgiving God." He gives no reason for his opposition to this line.

Based upon what we have said so far, we would expect Sar Shalom to stand with Amram, a prominent representative of period 1, when the single

Babylonian practice of Sura was being pitted against Palestinian alternatives. And it can be demonstrated that this most surely is the case. The proof lies in the direct citations of the question which he quotes in his answer. They include the phrases *ʿoseh shalom* and *hamarbeh lislo-ach*. Now neither of these are Babylonian eulogies. The Babylonian parallels are *hamevarekh ʾet ʿamo yisraʾel bashalom*, "who blesses His people Israel with peace," and *chanun hamarbeh lislo-ach*, "who is merciful and forgives abundantly." But they *are* Palestinian![97] The gaon mentions them only in the process of quoting the question to which he is about to give an answer. The questioner lived someplace where Palestinian precedent had made inroads, and Sar Shalom repudiated it.

The probability for the Palestinian origin of the words condemned by Sar Shalom increases when we note that Saadiah has them. For fast days he says: "In the midst of the sixth blessing one may say 'Pardon us, our Father, for we have sinned . . .' and when he finishes, he says, 'May no sin or iniquity foil our prayer. Blessed art Thou, Lord, who forgives abundantly.'"[98] Saadiah is, however, against saying this after the *tefillah*, noting expressly that it must be said in the sixth blessing, whose theme is *selichah*, "forgiveness." As with his objection to the eulogy *haʾel hasalchan*, "the forgiving God," so, here, he is concerned lest an extra blessing be framed, for he knows very well from his Palestinian past that it was customary to conclude the *selichot* with a eulogy, just as Sar Shalom's correspondent indicated.

True to form, Sar Shalom and Amram oppose Palestinian custom, and Saadiah incorporates it, changing only that which opposes his basic principles.

7: Festival and Holiday Liturgy

Pilgrimage Festivals, Chanukah, and Purim

WE HAVE NOW SURVEYED THE GEONIC ARGUMENTATION REGARDING THE *yamin nora'im*, or Days of Awe: Rosh Hashanah and Yom Kippur. And in our study of the latter we have included fast days generally. We have yet to examine the remaining special days in the calendar, the daily liturgy that precedes the *shema'* and its blessings, and the life-cycle ceremonies. In this chapter we shall turn to the first of these three topics, thus completing our survey of holiday liturgy: specifically, the *shelosh regalim*, or pilgrimage festivals (Sukkot, Passover, Shavu'ot), Chanukah, and Purim.

Fortunately, the background for this chapter has already been laid. Most of the discussion regarding the pilgrimage festivals relates either to the *haggadah*, to which we devoted an earlier chapter, or to the constituents of the *kedushat hayom*, such as *vehasi'enu* and *ya'aleh veyavo'*, which we discussed in relation to Rosh Hashanah.

So the analyses in this chapter can be shortened considerably. Except for one or two major debates regarding Passover which were deliberately postponed for independent consideration here, we shall find ourselves dealing primarily with relatively uncomplicated issues, on which one or two easily understandable opinions can be cited and explained in terms of our trifold periodization of the geonic era.

Sukkot

Though much legal debate can be found on matters related to Sukkot, particularly the details of building a *sukkah*, there is remarkably little controversy about liturgy. The only actual polemic comes from Hai and deals with a type of *piyyut* very common in his time. We have already mentioned the specialized *piyyutim* for the fast days (*selichot*); we now encounter a similar phenomenon for Sukkot. Since Sukkot has always borne the underlying theme of deliverance, these poems were known technically as *hosha'not*, a word derived from the root *ysh'*, "to save." They frequently carry a refrain patterned after Psalm 118:25: *hosha'na'*, or *hoshi'ah na'*. These poems were recited while circumambulating the synagogue (*hakafot*), carrying the four species (*lulav* and *'etrog*), either after the *hallel* (Pss. 113–18) or after the *musaf* service.[1] *Siddur Saadiah* carries a separate prayer beginning *hosha'na'* to be said in place of the *hallel* by an individual who cannot recite the latter because of the absence of a quorum. For a quorum Saadiah has the precentor call out loudly, *hosha'na'*, followed by a like congregational response, and then the actual *hosha'not*.[2] This practice was still in use in Sherira's day, and the precentor's call was so loud that Sherira banned it on the Sabbath lest it confuse children, who might want to carry a *lulav* and inadvertently would break the Sabbath laws of carrying.[3] At issue is the desirability of adding a eulogy to the *hosha'na'* refrain of the poem, thus converting it into a blessing.

> Rav Hai said that if a precentor finishes *hosha'na'*, and then says "Blessed art Thou, Lord, a saving God" [*barukh . . . ha'el hamoshia'*], he makes a mistake, and it is better to silence him, since he says a super- fluous blessing which the sages ordained only to be said along with the reading of the [Purim] *megillah* [the Book of Esther, read from a scroll on the evening and morning of Purim].[4]

So according to Hai, though the disrupted eulogy is theologically inof- fensive, it should be limited to its proper occasion, Purim. The sages to whom he refers are the amoraim who discuss the blessing in a talmudic debate. Indeed, according to Rava, this blessing is the preferred form for Purim. Rav Sheshet is said to have preferred another formula (*barukh . . . hanifra' leyis- ra'el mikol tsareihem*), and Rav Papa concludes the discussion by suggesting that the two blessings be merged into one.[5] The combined form is none other than a dual eulogy, the sole example of the Babylonian Talmud abandoning its own dictum against such hybrid blessing conclusions. Both Amram and Saadiah use it for the *megillah* reading, in the dual form recommended by Rav Papa.[6] But neither prayer book displays the blessing at *hosha'na'*.

Hai's extreme opinion of those who do say the blessing at Sukkot is out of keeping with his opinions so far surveyed; this time, he apparently goes so far as to advocate silencing the miscreants. So this responsum warrants careful scrutiny.

The citation is from a relatively late source (1205), *Hamanhig*, written by Abraham ben Nathan of Lunel, better known as Hayarchi. His method was to travel widely, observing the variety of customs then extant and com- menting on them from the viewpoint of geonic traditions. His book is there- fore both a source for the practices of his day in southern France, the Rhine- land, and Spain, and a synopsis of geonic opinion from a somewhat earlier time. There exists also a similar compendium by Isaac ibn Giyyat (1038– 1089), a Spaniard who headed the academy of Lucena and later became a prominent personage in Cordova. Only a fragment of his monumental work has survived, retitled (ever since its first publication in 1861/62) *Sha'arei Simchah.* Ibn Giyyat's method was not unlike Hayarchi's, though it seems to lack the latter's polemical tone. Ibn Giyyat would assemble many related geonic responsa, summarize them one at a time, and then relate his own custom and the degree to which it accorded with the geonic opinions under discussion.

Now Ibn Giyyat gives an alternative version of the same responsum by Hai. Its content, in fact, is identical, but not its wording, and the difference in words is significant.

> Rabbenu Hai said, as for what you report, that the precentor recites a eulogy after he finishes saying *hoshi'ah na'*, saying "Blessed art Thou a saving God, *leitah* ["that is not to be found," or "it is wrong"], and it is a blessing which is not necessary; and there are people designated by the sages [*chakhamim*] who silence them [such precentors].[7]

Now a comparison of the *Manhig* and the *Sha'arei Simchah* on the few sections relating to Sukkot worship shows that the subjects are discussed in exactly the same order. Both books give a variety of geonic quotations about several related issues, and then add comments by other authorities up to their own time. But the fact that the *Manhig* follows the exact order of *Sha'arei Simchah*, coupled with our knowledge that the author of the *Manhig* traveled extensively, suggests that he came across a copy of Ibn Giyyat's book and used it. That means that the earlier, and probably truer, version of Hai's responsum is the one carried in *Sha'arei Simchah.*

We have already noted that the *Manhig* has a bias in favor of polemical language. Moreover, the *Manhig* is a small book, a synopsis, really, for people who cannot avail themselves of fuller, more discursive discussions on liturgical and related matters. So the author customarily summarized the lengthier versions of his original sources, but maintained and even added to their polemical tone. This seems to be precisely what Hayarchi did to Ibn Giyyat's citation of Hai's responsum, except that in the process he confused Hai's original words with those of Ibn Giyyat.

Thus, what the *Manhig* assumed to be a complete answer by Hai is actually only partly by him and partly by Ibn Giyyat. Hai ends his remarks by saying *leitah*, "[the eulogy] is not found [in the Talmud?]" or "should not be found [in the Sukkot liturgy according to the Talmud?]," and that "it is a blessing that is unnecessary." It is Ibn Giyyat who then added that the *chakhamim*, or worthies, of his Spanish town—the *chakham* was a Jewish official unique to Spain—have posted representatives whose job it is to remove precentors from their tasks if they are found saying the eulogy. Such action is perfectly in keeping with what we know about Spanish Jewish autocracy of the time.

But the *Manhig*, its author from southern France, misquotes Ibn

Giyyat. He thinks that the decision to remove erring precentors is Hai's recommendation. Moreover, he makes the general language of the responsum more vitriolic than it really is. According to Ibn Giyyat, Hai said of the eulogy in this rubric, *leitah*, "It is not to be found [in the Talmud!]." The *Manhig* says *to'eh*, "[Such a precentor] errs." Then, summarizing Ibn Giyyat's remark that people in Spain are removed from their post for the error, the *Manhig* proclaims, "It is better to silence him."

In sum, we do have a responsum from Hai banning the use of a eulogy that, talmudically, belongs to Purim, not Sukkot, but—contrary to the *Manhig*'s faulty reading of Ibn Giyyat—we do not have any indication that Hai urged disciplinary action against a wayward precentor.

I have already remarked that this eulogy in this place is known neither to Amram nor to Saadiah. It is also not to be found in any Palestinian fragments known to us or to the Karaites. Hai was dealing with a variant rabbinic practice, probably in Spain where he communicated frequently. His words, even without Ibn Giyyat's addition, are rather strong, but so were his remarks about the *minhag bara'ei*, the heretical custom of the Passover *seder*. So we have no way of knowing how he finished his responsum, whether by making an exception to his general lenience here, or by telling the people that local custom was acceptable to him, or just by stating the facts regarding the eulogy's misplacement and allowing his correspondents to do what they wished about it. I suspect that their question was whether the eulogy was ever found in the Talmud as part of the Sukkot liturgy, to which Hai answered, *leitah*, "It is not," and therefore it is "a blessing which is not necessary." But I doubt, based on what we have seen so far, that he urged his Spanish correspondents to abolish their custom. He certainly does not do that elsewhere under similar circumstances.

Passover

Our first chapter dealt exclusively with geonic debates regarding matters pertinent to the Passover *haggadah*. Rather than include every single subject of interest there, however, we limited our remarks to a few specific matters which provided a clear picture of the three geonic subperiods that constitute the major hypothesis of this book. In succeeding chapters we continued surveying other liturgical debates, attempting to fill in the outlines of the picture provided in chapter 1. We may now return to some subsidiary matters related to the Passover *seder*. Though their inclusion at the outset of this book might have marred the clarity of the overall perspective intended at that point in the argument, they can be handled here with relative ease. And they provide no deviation from the normative geonic perspectives so far discovered.

The first case involves the recitation of the Egyptian *Hallel* (Pss. 113–18) during the *seder*. These psalms formed part of the cultic worship during Temple times; according to the Mishnah, the Levites chanted them while the Paschal Lamb was being slaughtered.[8] This took place on the afternoon preceding the *seder*, and the pilgrims then took the slaughtered animal away for consumption at the *seder* that evening. The *hallel* was again recited during the *seder* itself.[9] Since the arrangement of the psalms during the *seder* is discussed by the Hillelites and the Shammaites, whose existence coincided with the period between the beginning of the present era and the year 70, we may see this *hallel* as constituting part of the earliest stratum of the *seder* festivities, predating the destruction of the Temple and its aftermath, the period in which a relatively unstructured liturgy for the evening was expanded into the complex ritual we know today.

So the recitation of the psalms themselves was not at issue in geonic times. But a question was raised regarding the propriety of introducing them with a blessing. To complicate matters, it must be noted that at least two different forms of the blessing were known. The first praised God for commanding us *ligmor*, "to complete," the *hallel*, and the other praised Him for commanding us *likro*', "to recite" it.[10] Thus geonic opposition may imply antagonism to a blessing per se or just to one of the two forms.

The compendium of geonic responsa *Sha'arei Teshuvah* quotes both Amram and Tsemach against the *ligmor* formula. Their opposition is grounded in the fact that the *hallel* psalms are not recited all together as a single unit but are interrupted in the middle by the *seder* meal; and to say that God has commanded us "to complete the *hallel*," but then to recite only part of it immediately afterward, would be inconsistent with the general rabbinic assumption that one says a blessing affirming a commandment and then immediately fulfills the commandment.[11] The same source cites Hai's opposition also, though for a different reason. He acknowledges his awareness of his predecessors' argument, but then adds an objection of his own. "At the *seder* we say the *hallel*," he notes, "not as a recitation, but as a song."[12]

Now Amram and Tsemach are easily accounted for. The inclusion of an introductory blessing was a Palestinian custom, as we can see from *Massekhet Soferim* 20:7, which calls the practice *mitsvah min hamuvchar*, "most desirable."[13] So Tsemach and Amram are in keeping with their usual custom of opposing Palestinian practice. Hai's opposition, too, may be comprehensible if he is reporting his own academy's practice, but one wonders why he felt compelled to invent his own reasoning, especially since he admits knowing the considerations of Amram and Tsemach. Moreover, the reasoning he invents is odd, to say the least. In the Mishnah's report of the Levitical paradigm of the *hallel* recitation, the verb used is *kara*', "recite" (*Pes.* 5:7). Similarly the *Tosefta* (*Pes.* 10:6–8), discussing the *seder* itself, always uses the verb *kara*'. Why, then, should Hai insist that the *hallel* is *shirah*, "a song," not *keri'ah*, "a recitation"?

Before hazarding an answer to this question we must turn to another consideration, the *seder*'s inclusion of Psalm 136, known as *hallel hagadol*, "the Great *Hallel*," and the practice of drinking a fifth cup of wine.

The normal *seder* ritual contains four cups of wine. Yet, as is well known, *Pesachim* 118a originally portrayed R. Tarfon as holding: "At the fifth cup, one completes the [Egyptian] *Hallel* and says the Great *Hallel*." I say "originally," since our printed text of the Talmud incorrectly substitutes the word "fourth" for "fifth"; R. Tarfon's practice, though current in some circles well into the Middle Ages, was not the normative custom, and scribes, unaware of the fifth cup or unwilling to accept it, "corrected" the text to correspond to their own experience.

Now R. Tarfon's additional activities included not only this fifth cup; he accompanied it with a recitation of the Great *Hallel*. Only those who drank the fifth cup said the Great *Hallel*. Moreover, though we now identify this *Hallel* with Psalm 136, we cannot be sure that was what R. Tarfon meant by the term. In the Babylonian Talmud's discussion of the matter,[14] R. Judah does indeed say it is Psalm 136, but Judah's is not the only answer. R. Yochanan (a first-generation amora) and R. Acha bar Jacob (a third-generation amora) give different opinions. The Babylonian Talmud, then, no longer knows what the Great *Hallel* is, and is unable even to fathom why it is called that. The participants in the debate feel constrained to adduce several homiletical reasons for the name. In the Palestinian Talmud the whole discussion is conspicuously absent.

Thus neither the Great *Hallel* nor the fifth cup accompanying it received official sanction. To be sure, eventually the former was disassociated from the latter, so that by medieval times Psalm 136 was generally said as it is today, that is, without a fifth cup of wine.[15] But throughout the geonic age they were still inseparably connected, and the Great *Hallel* was no more an obligatory part of the *haggadah* than was the fifth cup which it accompanied. Both were at best optional and still viewed as dependent upon each other.

Amram leaves no doubt about this: "If one wishes to drink a cup after the four cups, one may do so, and, holding the cup, say the Great *Hallel* over it."[16] The fifth cup for him is indeed optional, as is Psalm 136. If a fifth cup is not drunk, Psalm 136 is not said. Saadiah too comments, "One who wishes to add a fifth cup should say [Ps. 136] 'Give thanks unto the Lord' over it."[17] And the same position is documented for Moses, Sar Shalom, and Kohen Tsedek.[18]

But Hai takes a remarkably different position in a responsum quoted by Ibn Giyyat and the *Tur*.

Rabbenu Hai was asked: We find that Rav Saadiah said that if one wants to drink a fifth cup, he should say the Great *Hallel* over it and postpone the recitation of *yehallelukha* until after it. [I.e., *yehallelukha* is the blessing of song said after the *hallel*. Without Ps. 136 it would follow the Egyptian *Hallel*. Saadiah advises his correspondent, who says Ps. 136, to wait until the Great *Hallel* is said before concluding with this blessing.] But now, some students have come and claimed that ... we should say *yehallelukha* after the [Egyptian *Hallel*] ... and then drink a fifth cup saying the Great *Hallel* over it, and then say *nishmat kol chai* [i.e., another version of the Blessing of Song, attested to in *Pes.* 118a]. Hai responded: such is indeed Rav Saadiah's opinion, and your custom is a good one. As for us, our custom is not to have a fifth cup at all. But regarding those students who say a blessing [of Song] after the [Egyptian] *Hallel*, and after the Great *Hallel*, the opinion of Rav Saadiah and yourselves carries greater weight than theirs. [19]

The question here involves the fifth cup, the Great *Hallel*, and the Blessing of Song. The original Blessing of Song of the Mishnah (*Pes.* 10:7) was just what its name implies: the blessing said over the portion of song, that is, the Egyptian *Hallel*, the only compulsory song which the mishnaic account knows. But those who had a fifth cup and added Psalm 136 wondered whether to say the blessing in its normal place or to postpone it until after the added psalm. Both Amram and Saadiah do advise postponing it under such circumstances, and Hai's correspondents did so, following Saadiah. But they complain of dissidents who—unlike Saadiah, who treated the Egyptian *Hallel* as the real song and Psalm 136 as an optional addendum thereto—imply that both the Egyptian *Hallel* and the Great *Hallel* are songs in their own right. Each is to get one of the versions of the blessing found in the Talmud, *yehallelukha* after the former (following R. Judah), and *nishmat* after the latter (following R. Yochanan). [20]

Hai responds by affirming the questioner's understanding of Saadiah. He says that he, Hai, never partakes of the fifth cup, so for him the dilemma never arises. But for those who do have the problem, Saadiah's (and the questioner's) solution is better than that of the dissidents. The parallel text in Ibn Giyyat is somewhat corrupt, but not contradictory to the *Tur*. It adds, however, that the custom recommended by Saadiah is practiced in *kspyh*, a place which the editor, Bamberger, identifies as the biblical Casiphia (Ezra 8:17). Hai's final answer, then, is to reaffirm Saadiah's position, granting people the option of a fifth cup and the Great *Hallel*, but urging the postponement of the Blessing of Song until that *hallel* is concluded. He is typically lenient here, since he himself has no fifth cup and attendant extra *hallel*, yet he allows others to do so if they wish. [21]

Now we can return to our original problem, the blessing which introduces the *hallel*. Amram and Tsemach, it will be recalled, argued against such an introduction, since the *hallel* is interrupted by the meal, and a blessing recalling the obligation to conclude it should not be said before what in effect is only part of it. Thus, Amram opposed Palestinian precedent in favor of a Babylonian talmudic legal principle. Hai acknowledged that reasoning, but added another: the *hallel* is a song not a recitation. We can explain

Hai's added note by two facts: (1) he, unlike Amram, knew of the second version of the blessing mentioned above, that which read *likro'*, "to read," rather than *ligmor*, "to complete"; and (2) Hai never said the Great *Hallel*, and thus said his Blessing of Song after the Egyptian *Hallel*. So he had to view the·latter as song, not recitation.

Amram, in other words, intent on opposing Palestinian custom, especially as it contravened Babylonian notions of legality, banned a blessing affirming the *hallel*'s completion. This was probably the regnant form of the blessing at the time, possibly the only one Amram knew. But by Hai's time one could argue that the alternative form of the blessing, affirming only the commandment "to recite" the *hallel*, not "to complete" it, would still be fitting. Hai's problem with that was the fact that he said the Blessing of Song after the *hallel* and had to view its psalms as song, not recitation. So for him even a blessing affirming a command "to recite" the *hallel* was inapplicable.

We may still ask, however, whether Hai, in decrying the blessing, also intended to proscribe it. If so, he would here be displaying a strictness typical of Amram but not in keeping with the other decisions we have seen him make. The answer to this question depends on how one reads Hai's responsum. The report in *Sha'arei Teshuvah*, the source quoted above, concludes: "Thus it is taught in our Mishnah, *and it is thus customary in all Israel, so if someone tries to say the blessing we silence him*" (emphasis added).[22] If this report be correct, Hai is certainly far from lenient here.

But the prevailing custom of silencing dissenters referred to in the last phrase is reminiscent not of geonic practice in Hai's time, but, as with the case of the Sukkot controversy above, of Spain. Could it be that here too we have a conflated report in which the gaon's original words are conjoined to a later addendum reflecting Spanish execution of liturgical decisions?

Indeed a comparison of variant versions attests to this being the case. The *Sha'arei Teshuvah* version is copied verbatim from Ibn Giyyat's *Sha'arei Simchah*,[23] the very same source in which the similar statement regarding the Sukkot controversy was found. On the other hand, *Sefer Ha'eshkol* carries the same responsum, but omits the italicized words after "Thus it is taught in our Mishnah."[24] Its author then continues in his own words to interpret Hai's opinion, but that interpretation nowhere includes the admonition, "It is thus customary in all Israel, so if someone tries to say the blessing, we silence him." If Hai had actually urged repressive measures, *Sefer Ha'eshkol* would surely have included his advice, since its author sided with Hai and wished to enforce his ruling. So the harsh conclusion, "We silence [dissenters]," must, once again, be from Ibn Giyyat, not from Hai.

Thus, Hai himself did not say a blessing and may even have advised others not to. But he did not say that he in Baghdad, or anyone else, did or ought to silence those who disagreed with him. We have now found two cases where an apparent statement by Hai implying actual action against miscreants was in fact only Spanish Jewry's enforcement of a ruling by Hai. As usual we do not even know in either case just what the original question to Hai was. He may, for example, have been asked why he did what he did, with no implication of instructing others regarding alternatives.

In sum, we have traversed a complicated path only to arrive at further confirmation of our original position. Amram still opposed Palestinian custom. Hai still explained his own practice, but refrained from advising the enforcement of his ruling on others.

We have reserved three more controversies regarding the Passover *seder* for discussion in this chapter. They require no elaborate discussion, and two, at least, serve to underscore Amram's anti-Palestinian bias.

We shall shortly deal with a debate regarding the wording of the holiday insertion known as *'al hanissim*. The extra reading is customarily introduced for Chanukah and Purim as a means to recall and celebrate the deliverance of Jews from enemies in the past. A form of this same liturgical selection was apparently interpolated into the *haggadah* of some Jews in geonic times, for the obvious reason that Passover, too, commemorates God's deliverance of His people—the paradigmatic act of divine intervention into history, the exodus from Egypt.

But Amram takes issue with this practice:

> One need not say *she'asah nissim la'avotenu*, during the *kiddush* [*'al hakos*]. Why not? Since [later, in the introduction to the *hallel*] one must say "[We are obligated to praise . . .] Him, who wrought all these wonders for us," and there one must mention enslavement and bondage, miracle and redemption; so one need not mention [the same things] here [i.e., during the *kiddush*]. If a person does mention them twice, he takes God's name in vain [*motsi' shem shamayim levatalah*]. On Chanukah and on Purim, we say it . . . since then there is no *kiddush* no *haggadah*, and no [recounting of] the chain of miracles as there is on Passover. This is the custom of the two academies.[25]

For Amram, the whole *seder* recounts the miracle; to commemorate it with a special blessing would be superfluous. Such a benediction should be reserved for Chanukah and Purim, where no other commemorative event is the norm.

Amram opposes Palestinian custom here.[26] The *kiddush* of Goldschmidt's major genizah fragment reads, "for on it [Passover] the Lord our God wrought miracles [*'asah nissim*] and mighty acts for those who loved Him; wonders in the presence of His beloved."[27] Saadiah endorses the Palestinian custom with his own poetic form of *'al hanissim* in the *kiddush*.[28]

So Amram opposes Palestinian custom; Saadiah incorporates it. Both geonim are consistent with their decisions elsewhere.

The blessing preceding each of the four cups of wine was also an issue, albeit a rather straightforward one. Ibn Giyyat quotes Amram, Natronai, and Kohen Tsedek as demanding a separate blessing for each cup.[29] Kohen Tsedek is also quoted in *Geonica*, where additional information is given. We are told there that both academies say a blessing before each cup.[30]

The custom of drinking at least the second cup without a blessing has been traced to Palestine.[31] So again Amram and Natronai oppose the Palestinians, this time accompanied by Kohen Tsedek, probably the Suran by that name (838–848), who lived in period 1 and is likely to have had his name included along with other like-minded Suran worthies from the same period: Natronai and Amram.

Our final Passover controversy is a deviation in the *kiddush* fought by Natronai and Amram. Our normal version praises God *'asher bachar banu . . . veromemanu*, "who chose us . . . and exalted us." Some people apparently took the occasion of Passover to substitute a *lamed* for the *vav* preceding the final word *romemanu*, thus praising God because "He chose us . . . to exalt us." No doubt these people had in mind the chronological time-frame of the Passover holiday, since it was then, long ago, that the redemptive chain of events began, the Jewish people being chosen in the depths of their servitude and later being exalted through exodus and eventual entry to the promised land.[32]

But Natronai and Amram are uninterested in such reasoning. They relate that

> People from Kairouan came to us and said that on Passover eve they say, "He chose us to exalt us [*bachar banu leromemanu*]." They are in error [*ta'ut hu' beyadam*] since all the festivals have the same *kiddush*, even though each one has its own event [which it commemorates].[33]

I have been unable to find this variant in any known genizah fragment. Presumably it was a local custom in Kairouan, and perhaps elsewhere in North Africa. When Natronai heard about it, he condemned it roundly as *ta'ut*, "error," a common term of approbrium found in the responsa of period 1. Unlike many such cases, this one cannot be traced directly to Palestinian practice. But the rigidity of this gaon's insistence that there be one, and only one, proper *kiddush* for all the festivals typifies the early attempt to provide a single authoritative liturgical canon.

Chanukah and Purim

Chanukah and Purim are minor holidays in the Jewish year. Yet they do occasion some changes in the liturgy, the most significant for our purposes being the insertion of the section already mentioned, *'al hanissim*. It is added to the penultimate blessing of the *tefillah*, (the *hoda'ah*, or Blessing of Thanks), and represents a recollection of the miracle from which the holiday in question evolved, the story of Esther (in the case of Purim), and the Hasmonean victory over Antiochus IV Epiphanes (in the case of Chanukah).[34] We first encountered this prayer in our discussion of the *tefillah*. There the question was whether to insert a petition for future redemption into this recollection of past miracle. Here we deal with a relatively minor grammatical point regarding the *'al hanissim* insertion itself.

We have no firm evidence to pinpoint the exact date at which the prayer in question was composed, but it would seem to be post-talmudic. True, the Babylonian Talmud says of Chanukah, "They [the Hasmoneans] established holidays for praise and thanksgiving,"[35] and Rashi interprets the last phrase to imply, "saying *'al hanissim* in the *hoda'ah*." But Rashi reads his own practice back to talmudic times. The injunction referred originally to the recitation of the Egyptian *Hallel*, a daily addition to the morning service during the eight days of Chanukah. The first explicit mention of the prayer *'al hanissim* in our sources is *Massekhet Soferim*,[36] which we have already seen to be a Palestinian work reflective of early geonic times. We are instructed to insert the prayer both in the *hoda'ah* and in the second of the four blessings that constitute the Grace after meals.

Even centuries after the composition of *Massekhet Soferim*, it was not clear precisely where within the *hoda'ah* the insertion was to be placed. Abudarham (14th-cent. Spain) reports that some placed it with the words *shebekhol 'et 'erev vavoker vetsohorayim*, "At all times, evening, morning, and noon," while others postponed it until *me'olam kivinu lakh*, "We have always hoped for You."[37] A responsum incorrectly attributed to Yehudai, but actually reflecting a Palestinian decision and deriving from the Palestinian work *Sefer Hama'asim*, gives yet another location. "In the *tefillah*, when one says *lo' histarta panekha mimenu*, 'You have not hidden your countenance from us,' one should mention *'al hanissim*.'"[38] The line from the *hoda'ah* cited here is interesting because it is found in neither Babylonian nor Palestinian fragments of the prayer as far they are known to us, and must represent yet another version of the blessing no longer extant.

The insertion itself notes among other things that the Assyrians attempted "to make the Jews forget the Torah." In the standard Ashkenazi wording, the verb appears in the *hiphil: lehashkicham toratekha*. The Sefardi parallel utilizes the *pi'el: leshakhechem*. In either case, the syntax of the sentence requires that the next word be a direct object. In this context, Abudarham recalls Saadiah's objection to the practice in some communities of prefacing that word with the preposition *mem*, thus converting it into an indirect object.[39] He says that Saadiah based his reasoning on Jeremiah 23:27, *lehashkiach 'et 'ami shemi*, and this may be so, since Saadiah is quick to cite grammatical paradigms from the Bible. But Abudarham himself liked to quote biblical precedent just as much as Saadiah, and rarely says anything without finding some scriptural warrant. So the proof-text may be his.

In any event, the error probably occurred accidently since the preceding word, *leshakhechem*, ends with a *mem*, and could easily have been attached to the following *toratekha* as well. Grammatically, however, it is incorrect, and Saadiah, whether for scriptural reasons or just for grammatical purity, had it removed. Again we see Saadiah displaying his sense for grammatical nicety and linguistic perfection, as well, possibly, as his reliance on biblical paradigm.

Summary

In this chapter we have looked at discussions of Sukkot, Passover, and the minor festivals of Purim and Chanukah. We have seen how geonic communication was seized on in Spain to the point where those who deviated from geonic decisions were silenced by community officials. Our sources mistook such action for Babylonian custom, and attributed it to Hai. In fact, however, Hai maintained his usual flexibility regarding alternative customs, allowing the fifth cup and Great *Hallel*, for example, even though he never included them in his own *seder*. Amram was again shown to be championing Babylonian talmudic legality and his native liturgical tradition against Palestinian practice. And Saadiah, as usual, displayed his own unique concern for language.

We may now turn to the introductory prayers that form the beginning of the daily service.

8: Preliminary Morning Service

THOUGH THE CONGREGATION IS OFFICIALLY CALLED TO PRAYER ONLY AT THE *shema‹* and its blessings, today's service contains considerable additional prior material. This is generally classified into two separate sections: the *pesukei dezimrah* (lit. Verses of Song), and the *birkhot hashachar* (Morning Blessings).

The *pesukei dezimrah*, also called *zemirot*, immediately precede the call to prayer and consist of psalms as well as (nowadays) other biblical and nonbiblical readings.[1] The entire section is introduced by one blessing and concluded by a second, the latter being a *birkat hashir*, or Blessing of Song,[2] the same blessing type we have already encountered in the Passover *haggadah*. There too it followed psalms, either the Egyptian, or the Great, *Hallel*. The psalms which form the core of the morning *pesukei dezimrah* are also called a *hallel* but are differentiated from the other two by their own qualifying modifier: *hallel shebekhol yom*, or "Daily *Hallel*." *Hallel*, then, is a generic term implying psalms of praise, there being three of them in total, each concluded by a Blessing of Song.

The recitation of such morning psalms is apparently an optional custom dating at least from the second century.[3] The tanna Yose ben Halafta is reported to have said, "May my lot be among those who complete a *hallel* every day," and the Babylonian Talmud identifies this *hallel* as the *pesukei dezimrah*.[4] Yet there is no way of knowing exactly what psalms either the tanna or the amoraic commentator had in mind by these terms. Elbogen identified them as the six psalms that make up the core of our contemporary rubric, Psalms 145–50,[5] apparently depending on a report in *Massekhet Soferim* which referred to "the six daily psalms," and misquoted Yose as saying, "May my lot be among those who pray these six psalms daily."[6] Elbogen is in good company in this identification, since Isaac Alfasi made the same claim by commenting on the Talmud's use of the term *pesukei dezimrah:* "And what are they? From 'A song of praise by David' [Ps. 145:1] to 'Let every living thing that hath breath praise the Lord' [Ps. 150:6]."[7]

But there is no reason to believe that either Alfasi, in the tenth century, or Elbogen, in the twentieth, knew exactly what the amoraim meant by *pesukei dezimrah*, nor that the amoraim knew what psalms Yose ben Halafta had in mind when he used the word *hallel*. In fact, neither party may have intended any specific set of psalms at all. A precise delineation of mandatory readings had yet to evolve, as Rashi himself seems to have recognized. Though by his time our six psalms were clearly a widespread custom in France,[8] Rashi's commentary to the relevant talmudic passage identifies Yose's psalms as Psalm 148 and Psalm 150 alone.[9]

It is no great surprise, therefore, to find wide-ranging variety in this rubric during geonic times, ranging from the recitation of thirty-one psalms in their entirety (Pss. 120–50), to random collections of verses drawn from different psalms and strung together for the occasion.[10] Amram has our customary six selections, and Saadiah, unaccountably, includes five of the six, omitting Psalm 146.[11]

But even before the *pesukei dezimrah*, there is another large section of devotional material, known as *birkhot hashachar*.[12] This was the last general rubric of the daily service to be codified,[13] and contains extensive material of both ancient and medieval vintage. Originally the entire section was much smaller, being composed of blessings to be recited upon awakening in the morning, and both biblical and rabbinic passages intended for study.

This is not "public" liturgy at all, then, though Amram included it in his comprehensive listing of mandatory prayers. In doing so he was actually citing a prior and independent responsum of his predecessor, Natronai, and his apparent decision to include the rubric in public worship was debated by authorities until at least the thirteenth century.

What we have then, in sum, are two distinct rubrics sharing the characteristic of being treated historically as somewhat loose entities which might easily be rearranged, with material added or subtracted. The geonic responsa reflecting controversial wording, then, are relatively few.

The practice of saying blessings each morning is recorded in both Talmuds. The Palestinian parallels the Babylonian, but with a difference in one of the blessings.[14] According to the former, one is to thank God for not creating him a *bor*, an "ignoramus," because of the *Tosefta* statement, "An ignoramus cannot be God-fearing."[15] The Babylonian Talmud records the same blessing, but adds a significant incident.

> Rav Acha bar Jacob heard his son saying, "[Blessed art Thou] . . . who has not made me an ignoramus.'" He said to him, "Must you go so far?" The son answered, "What, then, should I say?" [Rav Acha] replied, ". . . who has not made me a servant." But [it may be objected,] that would be equivalent to saying, ". . . who has not made me a woman" [another blessing which is said, so that the suggested "servant" formula would be redundant. But the objection can be dismissed by noting] a servant is on a lower status [than a woman, so the two formulas are not identical].[16]

Thus the Babylonian Talmud rejects the "ignoramus," or *bor*, formula in favor of one containing the word *'eved*, "servant."[17]

Both blessings are surely much older than the talmudic discussions of them, and it is difficult to know the extent to which the differing talmudic accounts reflect already crystallized geographic preferences throughout Babylonia or Palestine. On the other hand, once certain blessing forms were recorded and thus preserved in the Talmuds, at the expense of others which were not, we can surmise that at least some Palestinians, faithful to their own Talmud, would prefer their talmudic version, and the same would be so of Babylonians. Unfortunately, the genizah fragments, whence actual Palestinian custom can be deduced, do not carry either of the blessings in question. (This absence, of course, reflects the fact that the morning blessings were still considered private home liturgy.) But surely we can at least surmise that some Palestinian Jews followed their own native Talmud's instructions faithfully.

And, given Amram's dependence on the *Babli*, it is certainly no surprise to find him discussing the blessing quoting the account of Rav Acha and his son, and declaring the *bor* formula illegal.[18] In this he is consistent with his other stands, supporting Babylonian talmudic precedent over Palestinian custom.

The only other related geonic comment is attributed to Hai, but the fragmentary nature of the extant version prohibits a definitive reconstruction of his opinion. We are told simply: "Rav Hai, may he rest in peace, [cited?] the Palestinian Talmud, in *Berakhot*, that a man must say daily... '... who has not made me an ignoramus'; since an ignoramus cannot be God-fearing."[19]

We cannot say from this what Hai's personal preference was. Yet his citation of the *Yerushalmi* is itself significant. As Ginzberg notes, it is very rare to find a gaon quoting the Palestinian Talmud as precedent for law. "Most of the geonim never used the *Yerushalmi* at all, and those who did use it did so... by accident." He holds that "not one geonic responsum before Saadiah mentions the *Yerushalmi*," and "even Saadiah never quotes the *Yerushalmi* in his *halakhic* books." True, Amram's *Seder* does contain *Yerushalmi* quotations, but these are limited to the stuff of folklore, *'aggadah*. Moreover, some of these citations are later additions, and others may have been used by Amram without his realizing their Palestinian origin.[20]

Now we have already seen the Babylonia of Hai's day to have been in contact with Hai's Palestinian counterpart, Elijah.[21] By Hai's time Palestinian Rabbanites had emerged with their own authoritative leader, also known as a gaon. The enmity between the two communities had subsided as both strove to adjust to a new world where the young Jewish communities in western Europe were becoming virtually independent of both Palestine and Babylonia. And from within, both Jewish centers of antiquity found themselves equally threatened by the Karaites, who were by now enjoying their golden age in Palestine.

So Hai's citation of the Palestinian Talmud and the correspondence between the Babylonian and Palestinian leaders, both called "gaon," mirror the general situation which we have called period 3. Amram's firm championing of Babylonian custom has given way to cooperative endeavor and cultural interchange between Palestine and Babylonia, and Hai's general leniency provides him ample opportunity to find merit in Palestinian custom and precedent.

Another issue in the morning blessings was whether to say a benediction after removing the phylacteries, or *tefillin*. An anonymous responsum, which Lewin attributes to Paltoi, reports that the Babylonian academies do not say a certain blessing ending with the words *lishmor chukav*, "to keep His ordinances," at that time. Whether Paltoi actually interdicted the practice or merely commented on the fact that the usage was not Babylonian is uncertain. He says merely that "In the academies"—that is, both Sura and Pumbedita—"it is not our custom to say a blessing after donning *tefillin*."[22] Elsewhere, Hai concurs, but adds this significant comment: "Our rabbis are not accustomed to do so in Babylonia, but if an individual wants to do so ['*i nicha*' *leih*] he may."[23] From Hai's perspective, then, this benediction is not part of the Babylonian custom, but one may say it anyway if he wishes.

Fortunately, the Talmud itself reveals the blessing's origin. *Berakhot* 44b and *Niddah* 51b both record it as the practice of *benei ma'arava'*, the Westerners, that is, Palestine. The Palestinian Talmud cites the same custom.[24] This, therefore, is a Palestinian practice dating at least from the amoraic period. Babylonian Jews ignored it from the very beginning. Paltoi so informed his questioner, possibly intimating that the practice should be avoided, possibly not. Hai reiterated the fact that the Babylonians did not say this blessing, but made sure to allow it anyway if the individual liked it. So we see again an overt expression of Hai's leniency, in this case regarding a definite Palestinian custom. The criterion of '*i nicha*' *leih*, "if one finds [an alternative] appealing," could not be a more apt statement of Hai's general perspective. He frequently allows the people to follow those customs which they personally enjoy.

Thirdly, mention must be made of the morning recital of the Song of the Sea (*shirat hayam*), Exodus 15:1–18, a custom first cited by Natronai.[25] He says that it was never recited in the major academies of Sura and Pumbedita, nor in *bet rabbenu*. But he knows of other places where it is said on the Sabbath and on holidays, a practice to which the academies take no objection. The gaon does not identify these "other places," but he seems to be giving an eyewitness account, so it is probable that he means various congregations in Babylonia. Saadiah, too, testifies that some say it and some do not, though—unlike Natronai—Saadiah adds that it is a nice custom, even though no obligation pertains thereto.[26] Jacob ben Asher correctly understood the geonim to have been of different minds on the matter.[27]

The use of the *shirah*, or "song," as a liturgical element originated in Palestine. This does not mean that all Palestinian services incorporated it. As with other liturgical matters, practices varied, so that even by Maimonides' time (1135–1204) there were differing opinions as to which reading ought to compose the *shirah*.[28] So *shirah* as a technical term in the sources can be misleading. Even Anan uses the word, denoting by it the daily psalm.[29] But despite continued variety and difference, the liturgical use of *shirat hayam* had begun in Palestinian circles.

Yet by Natronai's time it had long been said in Babylonia too, and thus had ceased being purely Palestinian in character. Natronai was probably unaware of the custom's place of origin. Since it was not part of the rite of either major academy, he did not recommend it. Since it was said in some Babylonian synagogues, though, he did not condemn it either. Saadiah, having spent much of his life in Palestine, admitted that it was a matter of choice, but went further than the purely Babylon-oriented Natronai and advised it as a nice custom.

We now turn to a rather complex issue regarding the recitation of the preliminary prayers after, rather than before, the formal call to prayer. Natronai was apparently asked whether people coming to synagogue too late for the *zemirot* can make them up after the *tefillah*. Natronai refers to a prior statement on the matter by Moses Gaon. One ought not to say them after the *tefillah*: "There is something unseemly about the practice." The complete omission of psalms of praise is preferable to their recitation after petition.[30]

Unfortunately, this rather straightforward opinion by Moses is complicated by another report, this one attributed to Yehudai. Yehudai is asked whether one who says *pesukei dezimrah* after the *tefillah* must first say a blessing, and he replies in the negative, since such a person would already have recited the *shema'*, so would have fulfilled his obligation through the saying of *'ahavah rabbah*, the Torah Blessing which precedes the *shema'*.[31]

This very question to Yehudai is problematic, since one wonders what blessing the questioner had in mind, and why the saying of the *tefillah* would have any bearing on his responsibility to recite it. Since Yehudai responds in terms of *'ahavah rabbah*, it is apparent that he understood the question to have been concerned with a form of the *birkat hatorah*, a Torah Blessing, but such an interpretation hardly clarifies matters, since *birkat hatorah* was never demanded for psalms in the first place. Yehudai's answer seems dependent on his recollection of the discussion of *birkat hatorah* in *Berakhot* 11b, but the issue there is studying Torah, not saying psalms. The Palestinian Talmud's parallel is *Berakhot* 1:5 (3c), but there, too, there is no hint of *'ahavah rabbah* serving as a substitute for a Torah Blessing to be said over psalms. *'Ahavah rabbah* is a blessing over Torah, and it is said before the *shema'* because the *shema'* is Toraitic. Nowhere in either Talmud is there any indication that it—or any parallel blessing such as *ha'arev na'*[32]—is said before psalms; or that the previous recital of such a blessing exempts the individual from saying whatever introductory blessing there may have been before the psalms, such as *barukh she'amar*.[33] Musafiya, the editor of the responsa collection containing Yehudai's enigmatic words, tries to shed light on the matter by referring us to the thirteenth-century work *'Or Zarua'*, where a long discussion of Torah study and its accompanying blessings occurs.[34] But here too, these blessings are discussed with reference to studying Torah, as is the case elsewhere in the literature, such as *Tosafot* to *Berakhot* 11b.[35]

Musafiya's responsum ought therefore to be emended. Frequently, the whole service prior to the official call to prayer is spoken of as if it were one unit. In the above-quoted passage from *'Or Zarua'*, for example, Rashi's practice is described in the following words:

> When he arose early in the morning to study Torah, he would say the Torah Blessings [i.e., only the Torah Blessings, not the rest of the Morning Blessings that by now were part of the public service] and then when he went to the synagogue to say [the rest of the morning] blessings and the Verses of Song [*berakhoth upesukei dezimrah*] he would say a blessing over the Torah again.

The question to Yehudai, therefore, was probably about someone who said some blessings *and* the Verses of Song after his *tefillah*. In all likelihood, the blessings corresponded to some form of our Morning Blessings. Since readings from the Torah, written and oral, were included, a Torah Blessing was called for as well.

So our case is that of a man who says his *shema'* and *tefillah*, and then wants to make up the Morning Blessings and preliminary psalms. Presumably, a goodly number of such people were those who simply woke up too late to say the early prayers. Since by the time they arrived at services the congregation was already up to the *shema'*, they wanted to make up the first two elements of the morning liturgy later, at their own convenience.

But there is an alternative possibility. The situation may be tied to the practice of an ancient group known to the tannaim as the *vatikin*. They were scrupulously pious and used to finish the *shema'* exactly at sunrise and then say the *tefillah*, so as to recite the *shema'* at its earliest possible time and still connect the *ge'ulah* directly to the *tefillah*,[36] this latter goal being demanded by the tannaitic insistence that nothing interrupt the flow from the *shema'* and its blessings to the *tefillah*. That people still used the instance of the *vatikin* to justify their own practice is evident from Amram, who polemicizes against the use of such a precedent. "As for the *vatikin*, that is not common, and not everyone can act with the intention of the *vatikin*."[37]

Now Amram, it should be noted, included this reference to the *vatikin* in the context of one who says his *shema* late rather than early, despite the fact that with the *vatikin* it was the other way around. Consequently, if Amram is referring to a custom in his own day, he may have in mind people who do their business before coming to pray, and thus arrive too late to say things in their proper order and time. Such people may have argued from the case of the *vatikin*, who also said things out of order, albeit for other motives. Amram answers their argument by objecting that (1) the *vatikin* are a rarity and (2) not everyone has the right to compare himself to such holy men.

Now, Amram's opposition may have been tied to more than just the issue of the *shema* in its proper time. We have already seen how the Palestinians tended to argue against Babylonian decisions on the basis of *minhag mevatel lehalakhah* [sic], "custom annuls law";[38] and *Massekhet Soferim*, another excellent index of the relations that existed between Babylonia and Palestine in the time we are discussing, links this very justification directly to the *vatikin!*

> Law is not set until it has become a custom. When they [the Palestinian amoraim] said that custom annuls law, they meant a custom of the *vatikin* but [one who includes in that category] a custom for which there is no scriptural warrant, errs in his judgment.[39]

The following reconstruction, then, seems warranted. Yehudai lived in the eighth century, when neither the Morning Blessings nor the Verses of Song were fixed liturgical entities. He therefore saw nothing wrong with people beginning their prayers with the *shema* and the *tefillah*, and then saying some blessings, studying, and reciting some psalms. Sixty-eight years later, Moses Gaon was confronted with the same practice, but by now the gaonate itself was more established, and its move toward fixing the liturgy more pronounced. Moses ruled against the custom, going so far as actually to prohibit latecomers from making up those sections of the service which they had missed. His success was limited, and Natronai had to repeat his admonition some twenty-five years later. Amram too saw fit to include Moses' words, both for their own sake and because they bore on the subject of the *vatikin*, a topic which itself evoked Amram's hostility because it was used to justify local customs in the face of geonic instructions.

Just as the choice of psalms was not determined in geonic times, so too the blessings before and after them varied.[40] Amram opposes the eulogy in which God is described as *mehullal berov hatishbachot*, "lauded with much praise"; one should say instead, *melekh mehullal batishbachot*, "King, lauded with praise."[41] It is difficult to know why Amram opposes the additional word *rov* ("much") or, for that matter, exactly what blessing he is talking about. On the face of it, Amram seems to be discussing the blessing which introduces the morning psalms, not the *birkat hashir* (Blessing of Song), which concludes them. And, indeed, the phrase he recommends is part of the introductory blessing in our rite today.[42] The matter is more complicated than this, however.

First, with regard to his reasoning, Amram draws, as usual, on the Babylonian Talmud. Though this source nowhere objects to the specific eulogy in question, it does oppose another formula containing the word *rov*: *rov hahoda'ot*, "greatly to be thanked."[43] The discussion relates that Yochanan concludes his prayer with *rov hahoda'ot* while Rava demurs, preferring *'el hahoda'ot*, "God [deserving] of thanks." It is this discussion that Amram cites to support his argument against the parallel liturgical construction *rov hatishbachot*. What he fails to mention, however, is the Talmud's conclusion: Rav Papa's compromise, "We may say of both of them—God [deserving] of thanks, and greatly to be thanked."

Amram was apparently so opposed to *rov hatishbachot* that he was willing to quote an irrelevant talmudic discussion to start with, and to omit the Talmud's own conclusion besides. This leads us, then, to suspect a motive beyond a desire for legal probity in Amram's proscription of the *rov* eulogy, and one would suspect, based on previous instances of his ire, that Palestinian alternatives were being countered.

But now we return to the problem of identifying the blessing in question. Amram, it will be recalled, is plainly discussing the introductory blessing, not the concluding one. And we have yet to uncover a genizah fragment with this eulogy in the introductory benediction. On the other hand, there are several fragments which include it in *yehallelukha*,[44] the concluding Blessing of Song in Palestine, equivalent to our *yishtabach*.[45] The response prohibited by Amram, then, may well have been the concluding formula for *yehallelukha* = *yishtabach*. Either this phrase was also used in the introductory benediction in Amram's time—a distinct possibility, considering the looseness of this liturgical rubric then—or Amram mistakenly believed that it was said there. Whatever the case, it seems once again to be a Palestinian practice that Amram opposed.

9: Life-Cycle and
Grace after Meals

HAVING SURVEYED THE CALENDRICALLY BASED LITURGY, WE COME FINALLY
to occasional devotions, that is, the large and diverse corpus of prayers reserved for moments of personal significance in the lives of individuals and
groups. Jewish history knows many such prayers, and it may be that of all the
areas of potential liturgical research, it is this realm of occasional liturgy,
which has received the least attention, that offers the most promise. It is here,
after all, that one discerns echoes of lives from the Jewish past as well as events
that forced themselves on the attention of whole communities. Prayers of the
former type include those composed as blessings for one's children, and
personal worship habits linked to activities like entering the synagogue, suffering nightmares, or returning safely from a dangerous journey. The latter
category includes communal memories of massacres or of earthquakes, coro-
nations of new monarchs, and centennial celebrations. Jewish history is writ
large in these prayers, as are the personalities of the people who composed
them.

Though most of these occasional prayers never passed beyond the stage
of personal or communal idiosyncrasy, some of them made claims on
worldwide Jewry and were thus the object of the canonization process. Such is
the case with the many occasional blessings discussed at length in tannaitic
and amoraic sources, for example. To be sure, not every rabbi's favorite
blessing became normative; in fact, even the selection of occasions at which
blessings were deemed desirable was not easily or universally arrived at. But by
the end of the amoraic period, the determination of certain events and the
fundamental structure of blessings that should mark them had been de-
lineated. In many cases even the preferred wording had achieved relatively
common consensus. These prayers were now a part of the public liturgy no
less than daily, Sabbath, or festival worship, and attracted the same degree of
geonic discussion as well.[1]

Life-cycle ceremonies and the Grace after meals (*birkat hamazon*) stand
out as exceptionally significant rubrics in this regard. Though both categories
have changed since geonic times—as has the liturgy generally—their essential

nature was mandated by the geonim and included prominently in geonic responsa and prayer books.

The *birkat hamazon* is one of the oldest staples of Jewish liturgy, antedating the tannaitic period and probably originating in the milieu of fellowship meals.[2] Because of its early origins, it does not comply with the full gamut of structural regulations enforced by later rabbinic legislation, but the structure, in general, is sufficiently clear as to be easily subdivided for purposes of discussion. It begins with an invitation to join in the Grace (the *zimun*) and then continues with four blessings: a blessing over food (*'al hamazon*), one over the land of Israel (*'al ha'arets*), another over Jerusalem (*'al yerushalayim*), and a final benediction praising God, "who is good and does good" (*hatov vehametiv*).[3]

The life-cycle liturgy, similarly, is easily divisible into discrete ceremonies, each with its own unique structure and ritual order. Some ceremonies current today, notably the rite of passage marking male puberty, *bar mitsvah*, are medieval, and in some aspects even modern, in the elaborate form which has become our standard practice, so they postdate the geonic time-frames of this study. Thus, in the case of *bar mitsvah*, for example, sources up to and including the geonic period display a concern for the criteria which determine when a boy becomes a man, legally responsible for fulfilling the dictates of Jewish law, but almost no discussion of the ceremony itself, since it was so brief as to almost be undeserving of the name "ceremony." In other cases the opposite is true; that is, there existed geonic rituals which received considerable discussion but which fell into desuetude afterward. Such, for example, is the *birkat betulim*, a blessing said by a bridegroom after his wedding night, celebrating his marriage to a virgin.[4] Since the first category of ritual was eventually canonized, but not by the geonim, while the latter was not canonized at all, neither has been included in the discussions in this chapter.

We are left, then, with those life-cycle events canonized by the geonim and still practiced today. These are: circumcision (*berit milah*), redemption of the first-born male child (*pidyon haben*), the dual marriage ceremony (*kiddushin*, known also as *'erusin*, and *nissu'in*), and various aspects of the funeral ritual which I have classed generally under the rubric of mourning (*'avelut*). The grace after meals (*birkat hamazon*) is a prominent feature of both the marriage and the mourning rites, and, for reasons which will become apparent later, is best discussed in connection with them.

Circumcision

The liturgy accompanying the circumcision, or *berit milah*, ritual has grown considerably through the ages,[5] but its essence is tannaitic in origin.[6] This core consists of three blessings, one recited by the father of the child, and the other two by the circumciser, or *mohel*. The former is cited in the *Tosefta* as "Blessed art Thou . . . who has commanded us to admit him [the child] to the covenant of Abraham our father." The latter two are: (1) "Blessed art Thou . . . who has commanded us concerning circumcision"; and (2) "Blessed art Thou . . . who has sanctified the beloved [child] from the womb, engraving a statutory mark on his skin, and sealing his offspring with a sign of the holy covenant. For the sake of this reward, therefore, our living God, our Portion, our Rock, has commanded [us] [or: command us!] to save the beloved of our flesh from destruction. Blessed is He who makes a covenant."

It can readily be seen that the beginning of the second sentence of the last blessing, "For the sake of this reward," is not an essential continuation of the first sentence. The blessing reads quite adequately with the first sentence; then the latter part of the second, "Therefore our living God . . ."; and the final eulogy affirming the covenant which circumcision signifies. Indeed the manuscripts of the *Tosefta* itself do not agree on the inclusion of the extra clause. The Erfurt manuscript adds it, as does the Babylonian Talmud. [7] But the Palestinian Talmud cites the *baraita'* without the addition. The wisdom of including this supplementary clause is debated by the geonim.

Two other problems are raised as well. The first is the understanding of the word *tsvh*, "to command." Should it be read as *tsavei*, an imperative, or *tsivah*, the third-person singular perfect, descriptive of God's commanding Israel in the past? The other debate does not deal with wording but is of interest to us nonetheless. Normally, a blessing is recited prior to the act which it sanctifies. In the case of *milah*, however, there were those who suggested delaying the father's blessing until the conclusion of the actual operation, since there was a possibility that the operation would fail, and the blessing, if recited prematurely, would be in vain (*berakhah levatalah*). All three of these issues—the additional second line, the reading of *tsvh*, and the placing of the father's benediction—can be discussed together.

We have already seen the extent to which Amram, the inheritor and guardian of the Babylonian tradition, was dependent on the *Babli* for his precedents. So here he simply repeats its text, including, therefore, the additional clause. He does not specify whether to read *tsivah* or *tsavei*. He does, however, introduce a polemical remark by citing a prior responsum from Sar Shalom, to the effect that (1) the father's blessing should follow the act of circumcision lest the operation prove unsuccessful, and (2) "one should neither change nor add to 'who has sanctified the beloved [child] from the womb . . .' since that is our reading in the Talmud." [8]

We have seen, likewise, that Saadiah was not firmly wed to Babylonian precedent. He opts frequently for Palestinian tradition, and here we find just such a decision. Following the *Yerushalmi*, he omits the addition. He solves the semantic ambiguity of *tsvh* by avoiding it entirely, paraphrasing the verb with *yehei chelkenu lehatsil*, "May it be our lot to save. . . ." The intent of his emendation, however, indicates a petition for the future, not a description of the past, and suggests that Saadiah would have preferred the imperative, *tsavei*. The father's blessing follows the operation, as in Amram's prayer book.[9]

Besides being quoted by Amram, Sar Shalom's opinion is recorded independently in a responsum to some people who include the addition and say *tsivah* (the perfect). They have heard that in the academy of Sura the additional phrase is omitted, and also that one should say *tsavei* (the imperative).[10] As Amram was later to indicate, Sar Shalom responded by advising the community to follow precisely "as is written in the Talmud," thus including the extra phrase. But in his citation of the prayer, he gives the version of the disputed word *tsvh* that Saadiah later employed; that is, he avoids the word and substitutes "May it be our lot to save. . . ." But he claims this is the Talmud's own reading!

Regarding the disputed word *tsvh*, therefore, we must conclude that even though we now say *tsivah* (perfect), the original reading was *tsavei* (imperative), as the plain sense of the *Tosefta* allows.[11] This petition was carried in at least two forms, either *tsavei*, "command," or *yehei chelkenu*, "May it be our lot." The *lema'an* addition, "For the sake of this reward," is a sort of modifying clause with petitions, and found its way into the *Babli*, whence it influenced one manuscript of the *Tosefta*.

But by Sar Shalom's time *tsavei* had become *tsivah* to many people. His correspondents were completely unaware of the *yehei chelkenu* formula. They had changed *tsavei* to *tsivah*, and had heard that *lema'an* was not said in the academy. So they inquired about the proper wording, only to be told that *lema'an* was said, and that the petitionary formula was *yehei chelkenu*, not a form of *tsvh* at all. Now Amram quotes Sar Shalom, so he must have known Sar Shalom's talmudic reading. But Amram has *tsvh*. Since both Sar Shalom and Saadiah read *yehei chelkenu*, Amram's *tsvh lehatsil* may be a later editing of his original text. Moreover, Amram's reiteration of Sar Shalom's prohibition against changing or adding to the wording may refer explicitly to a desire not to change the *yehei* formula to *tsavei*, lest it be read incorrectly as *tsivah*. Saadiah, too, preferred the unambiguous reading, *yehei*, but he omitted *lema'an*, knowing that Palestinian sources did not have it.

Hai's opinion is also recorded for us: "We have heard that Rabbenu Hai was asked whether the word is *tsivah* or *tsavei*, and he answered: *tsivah*, not *tsavei*."[12] Elsewhere he contradicts both Amram and Sar Shalom by holding, "There is no need to worry whether [the father's benediction] be before or after the operation."[13] His preference for the past, *tsivah*, is linked to another responsum where he is asked what *yedid*, "the beloved," refers to. He replies that *yedid* is Jacob.[14] It was this legendary identification which led him to prefer the perfect. God had sanctified Jacob, the progenitor of the Jewish people, and *tsivah*, "commanded" him to perform the covenantal act of *milah*. Whether he actually insisted on this reading we do not know, since the *'Ittur*, from which the quotation is taken, gives only a paraphrase of a fraction of Hai's original words. He may simply have been answering a question about the talmudic recension, quoting his text, which had already been altered to read *tsvh* rather than *yehei chelkenu*; so he may have allowed an alternative reading, the imperative, to be used by those who wished. We have seen him decide matters with such latitude frequently enough, after all. Moreover, from Hai's responsum about the timing of the father's blessing, we can see that he did not really care when it was said, though he must have done it one way or the other himself; so he may have been equally amenable to variations in wording as well. [15]

At any rate, with respect to the blessing's timing, we see Hai with his usual openness. And, in general, we find Saadiah still freely utilizing Palestinian precedent. Amram and Sar Shalom, too, conform to the pattern seen previously. Both depend exclusively on the Babylonian Talmud, and stipulate, specifically, that its reading be maintained without any alteration.

Redemption of the First-Born

If Saadiah's own unique form of stringency is not apparent in the ritual of *berit milah*, it is readily visible in *pidyon haben*, the next ceremony of our investigation. [16] The ritual itself is derived from the Bible, [17] and involves the symbolic buying back of the first-born from God through a ritual payment to the priest. [18] The problem to which Saadiah addresses himself is a blessing said by the priest upon receipt of the redemption money. Saadiah condemns it roundly, complaining that people who use it are innovating incorrectly; the words distort the basic ritual; the priest has no right whatever to say the benediction. [19]

Though Saadiah mentions only the first few words of the blessing in question, we are fortunate in having it entirely preserved in a responsum of Hai's. Hai knows it is irregular, but rather than forbid it, he labels it the custom of specially zealous people (*zerizim*).

> When those who are particularly zealous redeem the first-born of the womb, they bring a cup of wine and a myrtle branch saying [over them] "... Creator of the fruit of the vine" and "... Creator of spice trees." After that the priest says, "Blessed art Thou, Lord our God, King of the universe, who sanctifies the fetus inside his mother. From the tenth day onward, He apportions 248 bodily parts, and after that breathes a soul into him, as it says [Gen. 2:7]: 'He breathed a living soul into his nostrils, and the man became a living being.' He dresses him with skin

and intertwines him with bones and sinews, as it is written [Job 10:11]: 'You have clothed me with skin and intertwined me with bones and sinews.' Through the miracle of his wonders He feeds him with food and drink, honey and milk, to make him rejoice, and summons his angels to watch over him in his mother's innards, as it is written [Job 10:12]: 'You granted me life and favor. . . .' "[20]

So Saadiah objected on one of his usual grounds: the benediction was not *'ikar*, related essentially to the ritual in which it was placed. It explores the miracle of human birth, not the redemption of the first-born.[21] Hai, on the other hand, shows his usual lenient temperament. He again classifies differences in liturgical practice as customs and identifies the custom with one group or other—in this case, those Jews whom he knows to be particularly zealous. As usual, too, he refrains from judging variant customs negatively. His respondent is told neither to follow the practice nor to avoid it. He is informed only of what the custom is and who does it; and the decision to follow it or not is left to the correspondent's discretion.

Marriage

The Jewish marriage ceremony consists of two distinct parts.[22] The first of these, known as *kiddushin* or *'erusin*, is generally translated "betrothal," though it has almost nothing in common with what we generally mean by that English word. *Kiddushin* is actually the legal state of marriage, except that the couple, originally, did not yet live together. Their separation was based not so much on moral reasoning but economic; having declared themselves wed by the *kiddushin* ceremony, the bride was to return to her father's home, where he continued his financial obligation to care for her, while her husband worked to save sufficient funds to assume the financial burden of family responsibility. Thus some months passed before the couple began living together. At this point there took place the second half of the wedding ceremony, *nissu'in*. It was known also as *chuppah*, the word now used to designate the bridal canopy, but originally, perhaps, the bridal chamber in which sexual consummation of the marriage occurred. Of the two parts, the first was incomparably more significant, since it was then that the marital state was established, and after which, for example, full divorce proceedings were required if the couple wished legally to separate. Both ceremonies are still part of the wedding ritual, but now they are held at one and the same time. They are easily differentiated, however, since separate blessings constitute each.

The blessing for *kiddushin* is carried in the Babylonian Talmud. To simplify the discussion, two key Hebrew words are left untranslated: *kiddushin* and *chuppah*

What blessing should one say? Rabin bar Rav Ada and Rabbah bar Rav Ada both said in the name of Rav Judah: "Blessed art Thou, Lord our God, King of the universe, who has sanctified us by His commandments, and commanded us regarding illicit relationships, forbidding to us those who are betrothed and allowing us those who are married [*hanesu'ot*] by means of *chuppah* and *kiddushin*." Rav Acha the son of Rava concluded it in the name of Rav Judah: "Blessed art Thou, Lord, who sanctifies Israel by *chuppah* and *kiddushin*."[23]

It can be seen that both the body of the blessing and its eulogy include the phrase '*al yedei chuppah vekiddushin*, "by *chuppah* and *kiddushin*." In the former, the phrase modifies the noun *hanesu'ot*, "those who are married"; in the latter, it modifies the verb *mekaddesh* "sanctifies." So the blessing defines full marriage as consisting of *chuppah* and *kiddushin*, while the eulogy praises God for sanctifying Israel by the same means.

As we would expect, our editions of Amram simply quote the printed text of the *Babli*.[24] Saadiah, however, omits the eulogy's repetition of the phrase "by *chuppah* and *kiddushin*," and concludes simply with, "who sanctifies Israel."[25]

Hai has also left us a responsum on the subject. From it we learn first that his Talmud text read without the word *hanesu'ot*, "those who are married," and secondly, that he assigned the modifying clause "by *chuppah* and *kiddushin*" to the body of the blessing alone (as Saadiah had done). Though he has no quarrel with those who insert *hanesu'ot*, he attacks the repetition of the '*al yedei* phrase in the eulogy. He argues that (1) the *Talmud* does not have it, (2) neither academy has ever said it, and (3) the addition is objectionable in its own right. In Hai's words:

> You wrote asking what the eulogy for the '*erusin* blessing is, [adding that] some people conclude it with "who sanctifies Israel" alone, while others conclude with "who sanctifies Israel by *chuppah* and *kiddushin*." Is it fitting to do so or not?

> The answer: the eulogy is an explicit talmudic statement. "Rav Acha the son of Rava concluded it in the name of Rav Judah: 'Blessed art Thou who sanctifies Israel.'" This is how we have said the eulogy from the time of the earliest sages until now. Your addition is a diminution since the sanctity of Israel is not dependent on such things. It would be [fitting] for you to return to the *halakhah* and to our custom, by means of general consensus.[26]

We should handle each of Hai's points in order. He says first that the Talmud does not have the expanded eulogy. Others would have argued differently, however, since well into the Middle Ages talmudic texts differed in this regard. Nachmanides (1194–1270), Rabbenu Nissim Gerondi (mid-14th cent.), and the Meiri (1249–1306) are all aware of that fact.[27] Meiri even tries to explain the clause of the "mistaken" insertion, saying that, technically speaking, the eulogy without the qualification "by *chuppah* and *kiddushin*" would not refer back to the benediction properly, so the phrase was added consciously to make the eulogy fit better.[28]

This is possible, of course, but two other explanations seem equally likely. It may simply be a scribal error. Having written the phrase in the blessing proper, three lines up, a scribe mistakenly wrote it again in the eulogy. Alternatively, it may even be a post facto alteration in the talmudic text to make the talmudic source reflect the way the blessing was being said by then. If the latter be true, the talmudic emendation may be very late indeed, after Hai, who did not have it.

So we have here, at the very least, a case of variant readings. Hai defended his version and denounced a blessing based on what he saw as the incorrect one.

But Hai states also that neither academy has ever said the eulogy with this addition; and we have indeed seen that Saadiah, at any rate, omitted it. *Seder Rav Amram*, on the other hand, displays it, both in our printed text and, more significantly, in the version known to Abudarham.[29] Assaf opines that the Surans said the phrase in the eulogy until Saadiah, and then changed their practice under Saadiah's influence. Hai must, then, have mistakenly inferred that Sura had *never* said it.[30] So we may have a case of Saadiah and Hai deliberately omitting the phrase in the eulogy, with Hai believing, correctly or not, that it was never said. And that brings us to Hai's third point, his claim that the additional clause is unseemly in its own right.

Hai certainly maintains this third point strongly enough. With fine irony he describes the addition as a diminution and calls on his correspondents to return to the way of the true *halakhah*. Since Hai abandons his usual leniency in this case, even resorting to a statement of *halakhah* rather than *minhag*, we ought to look more closely at his reasoning.

The Hebrew clause he uses is crucial to our appreciation of his position. The addition is a diminution, he says, since *'ein kedush[at] yisra'el teluyah bekhakh*. Now this could mean many things. The second word is actually written in its apocopated form *kdsh'*, indicating it is short for something else, probably *kedushat*. That is how the printed text of Rabbenu Nissim Gerondi's commentary renders it. If so, it could mean "sanctity" in English parlance, and Hai could be making a theological point: i.e., that Israel's sanctity is not *teluyah*, "dependent," *bekhakh*, "thusly." Ginzberg seems to imply that he thinks this is what Hai intends.[31]

But theological consideration of Israel's general sanctity is not a usual conceptual model for the rabbis. They thought in legal, not theological, terms. Granted, the *halakhah* may sometimes have theological relevance, but it is the legal bases that one must confront before drawing theological implications. So the word *kdsh'* probably refers to something more concrete. Though it is probably not an apocopated form of the word *kiddushin* itself, in all likelihood it does mean *kedush(at) yisra'el* as the specific "sanctified" state effected by *kiddushin*. *Kiddushin* is, after all, the legal context of the benediction. So the legal, rather than the theological, question would be, why Hai thought the addition of "by means of *chuppah* and *kiddushin*" misrepresented the sanctified state that resulted from the legal act of *kiddushin*. And the answer to that question is obvious. Of the two acts, *chuppah* and *kiddushin*, only the latter was necessary to bring about this specific state of *kedushah*. By *kedushat yisra'el*, in this context, Hai is thinking of the first of the two marital rituals, the one by which a man "betroths" a woman and is now legally married to her, even though they do not yet live together. This is the state of separateness of *kedushah* which the blessing marks. Granted that the body of the blessing contains the same otherwise objectionable phrase, but there it modifies the noun *hanesu'ot*, i.e., those who have already passed through the second stage of the marriage ceremony. So there the phrase is in place.[32] But to mention *chuppah* as a sine qua non along with *kiddushin* in the act of setting people apart as betrothed, sanctified one to the other, would do grave violence to the rabbinic conception of marriage. It would, at the very least, imply that both marital ceremonies need be undergone before legal marriage occurs. This would alter rabbinic law drastically, implying, for example, that full divorce proceedings would no longer be required to nullify the bond of the first stage alone. And this assumption Hai fought.

Now Hai may have taken a harsh stand under any circumstances to protect the rabbinic concept of *kiddushin* as full marriage. But in Hai's day particularly, the issue required clarification. The identification of *kiddushin* as marriage in full was denied by Karaite *halakhah*. Of course the theoretical equivalence of Hebrew *kiddushin* and English "marriage" is not discussed in the sources, but related legal issues are, and they make the difference between Rabbanites and Karaites plain indeed. At issue, basically, is the question of whether divorce proceedings are required for a legal separation after *kiddushin* but before consummation of the marriage by means of *chuppah*. Certainly, rabbinic opinion was unanimous that it was. And Karaite sources indicate clearly that in the opinion of Anan, Benjamin Nahawendi, and the later Hadassi, at least, it was not.[33] Legal marriage for Karaites was incomplete without consummation, so that betrothal could be broken off with only financial indemnity resulting. In fact, the very term *kiddushim* was used by the Karaites for the final marriage ceremony, not the betrothal.[34]

So Hai's strong stand becomes clear. The fact that his Talmud did not carry the eulogy would probably not in itself have resulted in his cry for the people to return to the *halakhah* and the custom of the academies. He rarely cites *halakhah* elsewhere, and treats the customs of others with respect regardless of talmudic precedent. Similarly, in other instances where he hears of people doing something contrary to what the two academies do, he does not invoke his second criterion, Babylonian custom. Only his third reason makes sense, then, and we can well understand why. The addition in the eulogy was objectionable in its own right because it made the marital bond of sanctity dependent on both *kiddushin* and *chuppah*. As Hai puts it, *'ein kedush[at] yisra'el teluyah bekhakh.* The accent should be on the word *bekhakh.* That is, *kedushat yisra'el* is not dependent *in that way.* It depends only on *kiddushin,* not on *chuppah* as well.

So here we have Hai once again coming to terms with the Karaites. We note, too, that the other gaon who took Hai's position was Saadiah, whose antipathy to Karaism has been noted all along. Amram, living before the Karaites established themselves as any real threat, and probably unaware of Karaite *halakhah* on the question—recall, he had never even seen *Sefer Hamitsvot*—retained the extra clause in the eulogy without concern.

The liturgy for the second half of the marriage ritual, *nissu'in,* consists of seven blessings found originally in the Babylonian Talmud.[35] The eulogies of the last two blessings are almost identical. The first reads, *mesameiach chatan vekalah,* "Blessed art Thou who make the bridegroom happy *and* the bride." The second says, *mesameiach chatan 'im hakalah,* "Blessed art Thou who make the bridegroom happy *with* the bride."

These two final eulogies were variable throughout the geonic period. Amram concluded both benedictions with the identical words, "Bridegroom *and* bride," and appended, as support for his decision, Sar Shalom's edict regarding the penultimate blessing: "The practice in both academies, and in every place, is to conclude it with '. . . who make the bridegroom happy *and* the bride.'"[36] While there is no explicit warning here against any specific alteration, this sort of language from Sar Shalom, Natronai, or Amram frequently implies some particular polemic, and such is the case, as we shall see. But before identifying the object of the polemic, we must turn to two other geonim who have left us records of their practice: Saadiah and Sherira.

Saadiah concludes the last blessing as Amram does, but he ends the one before it with *mesameiach 'amo birushalayim,* "who make His people happy in Jerusalem"; or, according to other manuscripts, *mesameiach 'amo uvoneh yerushalayim,* "who make His people happy and build Jerusalem."[37]

Now Sherira is asked what the ending of the last blessing should be. The questioner says he uses *mesameiach 'amo uvoneh yerushalayim,* the same dual eulogy employed by Saadiah for the second-to-last benediction. The questioner reasons that it seems foolish to repeat the same eulogy twice, and that is why he has chosen this alternative for the second one. Sherira answers that his custom is to conclude first *mesameiach . . . ve . . . ,* and then *mesameiach . . . 'im. . . .* Thus the two are not entirely identical: the first one says "and," while the second says "with." But the questioner's custom is fine too, since Saadiah set the precedent for it.[38]

We know very little about the Palestinian wording here. Beyond the fact that the Palestinians used three blessings instead of seven, we are unable to say very much that is definite about their practice.[39] But the variant custom represented by Sherira's correspondent seems Palestinian. Its eulogy is a dual one, and Saadiah incorporated it. It is also reminiscent of the Palestinian eulogy for *hashkivenu*.[40]

So the polemic mentioned above by Amram and Sar Shalom may again be directed against the Palestinians. Saadiah adopted the variant, and Sherira, though following Babylonian precedent, allowed his correspondent to continue the usage to which he was accustomed. The three periods into which we have subdivided the geonic era are all represented here, each in its own characteristic fashion.

Grace after Meals

Since the discussion of the blessings involved in mourning (*'avelut*) revolves to a great extent about the ritual of the *birkat hamazon*, or the Grace after meals, our discussion of *'avelut* must be preceded by a consideration of the controversies involved in *birkat hamazon*. The *birkat hamazon* is composed, we may recall, of four blessings. The introduction to these blessings is the *zimun*.[41] There then follow: *birkat hazan*,[42] *birkat ha'arets*,[43] *birkat yerushalayim*,[44] and *hatov vehametiv*.[45] Geonic debate can be found on the subject of the *zimum* and *birkat yerushalayim*.

Regarding the *zimun*, the Mishnah itself gives several customs which vary according to the number of people present.[46] There was also a difference of opinion on the phrasing of God's name. The *Babli* formulation of the Mishnah reads *nevarekh 'eloheinu*, "Let us praise God"; but the same text in the *Yerushalmi* says *nevarekh le'loheinu*, "Let us give praise to God." This textual difference between Babylonia and Palestine remained a matter of note even as late as the twelfth and thirteenth centuries.[47]

Amram tells us not to say *le'loheinu*, "to God," on grammatical grounds.

> One is not required to say *le'loheinu*. Why? Because Scripture says, "Sing unto the Lord" [*l'adonai*]; "acclaim greatness to the Lord" [*l'adonai*]; "chant unto the Lord" [*l'adonai*]. All are with a *lamed*. But in blessings we find it written, "So David blessed the Lord" [*'adonai*]. We do not find a blessing with a *lamed*, and that is *halakhah*.[48]

Saadiah, however, has *le'loheinu*. Though in his discussion of the Mishnah, he cautions against following Yose's advice to alter the blessing according to the number present—apparently this was still an issue—he is silent on the possibility of saying *'eloheinu* without the *lamed*.[49]

Amram was supporting the Babylonian tradition of *'eloheinu*. Aware of the *Yerushalmi*-based convention—probably still current in Palestine—of saying *le'loheinu*, he admonished against it. Saadiah, conversant with Palestinian practice from personal experience—he probably learned the Mishnah there—recorded *le'loheinu* without comment. That Amram's grammatical reasoning was simply an excuse used to justify his own tradition is evident from the fact that Saadiah, the grammarian par excellence, who stops again and again in his prayer book to make grammatical corrections, allows *le'loheinu*.

Secondly, we find a controversy over *birkat yerushalayim*. Regarding the eulogy, Amram quotes Natronai against the addition of *bimherah veyameinu*, "quickly and in our days," after *'amen*.[50] Saadiah too lacks it, but differs from Amram in that he does not actively oppose it.[51] The only putative Babylonian source with it is *Halakhot Ketsuvot*, published by Horowitz in *Toratan Shel Rishonim*.[52] But we have already seen that this work is not by Yehudai, and not even Babylonian. Rather, it is Palestinian, part of *Sefer Hama'asim*.[53] Moreover, the assumption that *'amen bimherah veyameinu* is Palestinian is in harmony with the genizah texts at our disposal. Mann's fragments 18, 19, and 20 all have variants of *'amen bimherah veyameinu*.[54] So, too, does Finkelstein's version.[55]

Again, the inevitable conclusion is that Natronai and his successor, Amram, opposed Palestinian practice.

Mourning Customs

The pregeonic mourning customs are lost in antiquity. We have only hints at what they were. M. *Megillah*, according to the *Babli* 23b, mentions something known as *birkat 'avelim*, "the Blessing for Mourners," and another practice called *tanchumei 'avelim*, "Comforting of Mourners." The parallel *Yerushalmi* text omits the latter, but elsewhere, in *Pesachim* 8:8 (36b), it cites a *baraita'* dealing with both customs. They are mentioned throughout our two Talmuds in other places also.

But what were these practices? We simply do not know, since even by amoraic times the terms were sufficiently unclear as to require interpretation. The Palestinian amoraim explain: "By the Blessing for Mourners we mean what people say in the synagogue. By the Comforting of Mourners we mean what people say in the rows. [People attending a funeral formed two rows between which the mourners passed.]"[56] On the other hand, the *Babli* assumes the *birkat 'avelim* to be something said *birechovah*, "in the town square," not the synagogue.[57]

As Lieberman understands it,[58] the tannaitic custom was to say *tan-*

chumei 'avelim, the Comforting of Mourners, in rows at the cemetery. Thereafter the *birkat 'avelim*, or Blessing for Mourners, was said, either in synagogues or in the open. The former location is represented by the *Yerushalmi*, while the *Babli* knows of the latter. In Palestine the blessing was invariably repeated in the mourner's house for two days. In Babylonia the repetition was determined by the presence or absence of new guests in the house of mourning during a seven-day mourning period.

The custom was certainly fluid in tannaitic times. *Tosefta Berakhot* 3:23 knows of at least three variations: saying one, two, or three blessings as part of *birkat 'avelim*. The four blessings on *Ketubot* 8b, associated with the Palestinian amora Resh Lakish, are only ad hoc creations, from which we can infer that there were no hard-and-fast liturgical blessings by the early amoraic period. But whatever custom one followed, the blessings were said on an additional occasion beyond that referred to above. They were also integrated with the Grace after meals in the mourner's home.

The *Tosefta* notes that one who follows the custom of saying three blessings should:

> Include the first one in *techiyat hametim* and conclude it with *mechayei hametim*, "who revives the dead"; the second, in *tanchumei 'avelim* and conclude it with *menachem 'amo be'iro*, "who comforts His people in his city"; the third, in *gemilut chasadim*, to which there is no concluding eulogy.[59]

Lieberman argues that *techiyat hametim*, *tanchumei 'avelim*, and *gemilut chasadim* were names given to the parts of the Grace in mourners' homes. The first was the introductory *zimun* plus *birkat hazan*, to which the words *menachem 'avelim* were added; thus giving us the introduction, *barukh menachem 'avelim 'al hamazon she'akhalnu mishelo*, "Blessed be He who comforts mourners, for His food which we have eaten."[60] This Palestinian form of grace is found in *Sefer Hama'asim* and in the later Karaite rite of Hadassi.[61]

The second term, *tanchumei 'avelim*, Lieberman understands to be *birkat yerushalayim*, which began with *nachem 'adonai 'eloheinu 'et 'avelei tsion*, "Lord our God, comfort the mourners of Zion," and concluded with *menachem 'amo be'iro*, "who comforts His people in His city." Though we have no record of this in our Palestinian sources, it is worth noting that it parallels the *birkat chatanim*, or Blessing for Bridegrooms, which ended with *mesameiach 'amo be'iro* (or *birushalayim*) or *uvoneh yerushalayim*.[62] The *birkat 'avelim* formulas were probably of similar format.

Finally, *gemilut chasadim* is to be identified as *hatov vehametiv*, the last benediction to be added to the Grace, for which there is no eulogy (following the instructions of *Tosefta Berakhot* 1:7).[63]

Now these ancient customs survived better in Palestine, the land of their birth, than in Babylonia. As we have seen, various forms of these blessings are to be found in Palestinian sources, and *Massekhet Soferim* still knows of *birkat 'avelim* being said in the synagogue.[64]

We can now turn to the Babylonian geonic sources and see how these customs are reflected there. A responsum attributed to Natronai interprets *birkat 'avelim* as *birkat rechovah*, "The blessing in the town square," and *tanchumei 'avelim* as visiting mourners and comforting them, as Mar Zutra did to Rav Ashi (*Ber.* 46b). But Natronai writes of the former, "Nowadays the custom has disappeared";[65] it was no longer practiced in his day. Natronai is asked elsewhere, too, about what appears to be an equivalent of *birkat 'avelim*, and he says that he has never heard of it, it is not talmudic, and neither academy says it.[66] Similarly, Hai remarks that the *birkat rechovah* is not practiced in Babylonia.[67] Paltoi, too, in a responsum to be discussed below, says that the *birkat rechovah* disappeared long ago. Thus Natronai, Paltoi, and Hai testify independently that whatever the custom of *birkat 'avelim* may once have been, they know absolutely nothing about it in their day.

But as we noted, these customs had ceased only in Babylonia. Hence we have responsa which strike out against remnants of them elsewhere.

To begin with, Paltoi is against the inclusion of the phrase *menachem lev 'avelim*, "Who comforts the heart of mourners." This is part of the Palestinian *zimun*.[68] Paltoi calls it *ta'ut* "a mistake," and warns, "People should never say anything except 'Let us praise Him whose food we have eaten' or 'Let us praise the Lord whose food we have eaten.'"[69] It was only, in the Grace, however, where Paltoi objected to the insertion of this formula. Elsewhere he allows the equivalent blessing to be said over wine in the mourner's house.[70] It too concludes, *barukh . . . menachem lev 'avelim*, so Paltoi's objection to the same phrase when inserted in the Grace cannot be explained by theological antipathy to its content. It must be based on other considerations. Paltoi's gaonate in Pumbedita fell in period 1. He was a contemporary of Natronai and Sar Shalom. He objected, therefore, because of the bias of his period. The Grace was a common prayer which he wanted fixed, so he objected to a Palestinian insertion. When used as an informal and uncanonical statement in the mourner's home, he had no objection. But the Grace, like all other regular liturgical staples, was not to be tampered with.

Saadiah's attitude toward these insertions is typically eclectic. He certainly took the Palestinian customs seriously. He allows *menachem 'avelim uvoneh yerushalayim* as the eulogy of *birkat yerushalayim*. But he may be against adding to *nevarekh le'loheinu she'achalnu mishelo*.[71] Hence he allows one Palestinian custom—*menachem 'avelim*—and repudiates another—*nevarekh menachem 'avelim* within the *zimun*. This latter prohibition may be based on the fact that such a form of the *zimun* was common among *'avelei tsion* and Karaites, as noted above.

Amram's opinion is difficult to arrive at. The very end of the *seder* purports to have *birkat 'avelim* and *birkat hazimun la'avelim*. [72] But these are manifestly later additions to the text. After all, both Natronai (Amram's predecessor) and Paltoi (who died the year before Amram took office) said not only that Babylonia did not have a *birkat 'avelim* but that this very blessing quoted by Amram was unknown to them. Moreover, it is unlikely that Amram would incorporate *nevarekh menachem 'avelim she'achalnu mishelo* considering the fact that Paltoi rails so fervently against it. And would he have *barukh . . . menachem 'avelim uvoneh yerushalayim*, a dual eulogy, considering the stand he takes elsewhere?[73] That Amram had some form of *birkat hamazon* for mourners is probable, but our text is certainly not the original.

To sum up, we find Paltoi opposing any changes in the Grace after meals other than those common to Babylonia. The ones he mentions are Palestinian, and are traceable to ancient practices rooted in the *Tosefta*. Saadiah alternates in his opinion of his native customs, and Amram's opinion is lost to us.

10: Miscellaneous Debates and Liturgical Alternatives

WE ARE ALMOST READY TO HAZARD A HISTORICAL EXPLANATION FOR THE triparite periodization of the geonic canonization process. Before doing so, however, we should recall the methodology set forth in the introduction. Manifestly, not every responsum dealing with worship could or should be included in a controlled study. So we limited our selection to those responsa directed toward alternative liturgical formulations, our assumption being that canonization imples limitation of alternatives, and, hence, that the attitude of the various geonim toward those alternatives would indicate their position regarding canonization.

Once these specific data were collected, the trifold division of opinion became clear, and a further decision was required: how should the data be presented? All editorial comment could, for example, have been left until the end, or liturgical issues could have been set down without regard to the arbitrary chapter headings used to organize them. But for the sake of clarity, it seemed prudent to eschew both these possibilities. So we began with a study of the *haggadah*, that being a particularly rich resource of responsa, which, moreover, revealed starkly the basic thesis of this book, and then, throughout the succeeding chapters, we regularly interspersed interpretive remarks with the raw data, building and reinforcing that very thesis.

But human beings, even geonim, are not automatons, whose every decision derives with mechanistic precision from the same set of axioms. So despite the overwhelming evidence of a basic perspective guiding policy in each period, there are exceptions to the rule. Where those exceptions were contrary to the general perspective—as, for example, Hai Gaon's strong stand against a *musaf* reading from the Torah, contrasted with his lenience elsewhere—we have included the data in the relevant chapter, and tried wherever possible to posit some rationale behind the apparent reversal of policy. But where the exceptions were of neutral value—where, that is, a gaon's discussion seemed unrelated to his basic criteria, neither confirming nor opposing his usual standpoint—we have postponed the discussion rather than break the continuity of the argument within each chapter.

Yet such neutral responsa demand inclusion if only because their "neutrality" is a subjective judgment derived purely by editorial decision. Others may find them not neutral at all, but directly relevant to the general hypothesis so far advanced. So they have been collected and set down here. Our task in this chapter, then, is to survey miscellaneous liturgical debates which seem to be unrelated to the usual guiding policy of the geonim in each of three periods. This will also afford us an opportunity to include further discussions of the variety which once characterized Jewish liturgy but is now lost to us.

Birkhot Hashachar

The first such "neutral" case is a blessing taken from the *birkhot hashachar*: "Blessed art Thou, Lord our God, King of the universe, who has formed man wisely, creating apertures and ducts [*nekavim nekavim chalulim chalulim*] within him."[1] The problematic element was the word which I have rendered as "ducts," *chalulim*. Natronai's famous responsum on the hundred daily benedictions reads *chalalim*, not *chalulim* as we have it.[2] *Seder Rav Amram* reads *chalulim*,[3] but this is probably a later emendation, since he subscribed to Natronai's list, and the prayer text of his *Seder* is notoriously corrupt. Saadiah calls for *chalalim*.[4]

The possibility exists, of course, that we have here only a minor scribal deviation. *Chalalim* may simply be *chalulim* written without the full medial *vav*. The geonim themselves may have been unaware of the two readings. Yet later commentators thought that the difference was a substantive one, and their point of view deserves some investigation.

The *Tur*[5] argues strenuously for *chalulim*, since the numerical equivalent of *chalulim chalulim*—the word appears twice in the blessing—is 248, a number equal to the parts of the human body, by rabbinic computation. Joseph Caro's commentary *Bet Yosef* notes that Rashi still reads *chalalim*, though in the end Caro supports the *Tur*. He reasons that *chalal* is simply an empty cavity which, by its very nature of being pure emptiness, cannot be created. Only that which surrounds the *chalal* is amenable to creation. *Chalulim*, however, refers to limbs, of which creation can be predicated. Note *'alef* to the *Bet Yosef* passage infers another reason; *chalalim*, we are told, means "corpses," hardly what one wishes to thank God for. This same thought had been expressed by Joseph ben Moses Beghi, a sixteenth-century Byzantine Karaite, who mocked the Rabbanites of his day for still saying *chalalim*.[6] Abudarham raises yet another objection; for grammatical reasons he prefers the plural *chillim*.[7]

The genesis of the controversy may go back to variant talmudic readings. The blessing as it is found in *Berakhot* 60b does in fact read *chalalim*, but *Massoret Hashas* notes that both Isaac Alfasi (1013–1103) and Rabbenu Asher ben Yechiel (1250?–1328) read *chalulim* in their talmudic texts. Baer noticed, moreover, that even our current editions of the *Babli* read *chalulim* in a parallel passage on *Berakhot* 24b.[8] The *Yerushalmi* has neither word, since the blessing ends there with the word *bechokhmah*, "wisely."[9]

The difference between *chalalim* and *chalulim* is an old one, then, going back at least as far as geonic times. Both terms were still in use in Natronai's day. But, as part of the responsa process, the geonim had to choose one form or the other to include in their epistles abroad. Their preference depended on their grammatical standpoint. Natronai and Saadiah read *chalal* as a noun = "cavity"; plural—*chalalim*. Others, however, treated the word verbally, rendering it as a passive participle, *chalul* = "hollowed out"; plural—*chalulim*. Though *chalalim* was not immediately eliminated from the ritual—as mentioned above, Rashi used it, and so, too, do the Yemenites to this day—the double entendre of the word and/or the *gematria*, the arithmetical equivalent of its alternative, influenced our usage to become *chalulim*; even though *chalalim* remained the accepted text of the *locus classicus*.

Birkhot Hatorah

Extensive and fascinating discussion exists regarding early alternative *birkhot hatorah*, the blessings recited prior to Torah study. We have already seen the considerable debate which raged over the choice between *'ahavah rabbah* and *'ahavat 'olam*, the Torah Blessing which precedes the *shema'*; and we have referred to Torah Blessings said earlier in the morning, upon rising, before studying Torah privately.[10] Similar blessings are said before and after being called to the Torah.[11] The *birkat hatorah*, as a specific type of blessing, is ubiquitous in Jewish liturgy, as one would expect of a religious tradition which so emphasizes Torah study as the vehicle for ongoing revelation.

It is the first instance, however, that preceding the *shema'*, for which we have the most overwhelming evidence of alternative blessing versions. The relative paucity of evidence for the other instances is readily understandable. The early morning benedictions are part of the *birkhot hashachar*, the last section of the service to be canonized, and therefore not included in most prayer manuals until later in the Middle Ages; while the blessings recited upon being called to the Torah were generally assumed to be common knowledge, so that to this day they are often omitted from printed prayer books. The blessing before the *shema'*, however, was an essential part of the very rubric which attracted the most attention in the canonization process. At any rate, whatever the reason for the sufficiency of evidence, the evidence is surely there, and we know now that our usual two forms, *'ahavah rabbah* and '*ahavat* '*olam*, far from exhausted the multitude of alternative forms then in use. Moreover, unlike Saadiah's variant, which at least approximated our formulations, some of the others bear almost no resemblance to our current ritual.

The most interesting such alternative, perhaps, is simply a citation of Psalm 119:12: "Blessed art Thou, Lord, teach me Thy statutes [*lamdeni chukekha*]." It is debated repeatedly by medieval European commentators to the Talmud's discussion of Torah blessings (*Ber.* 11b). Rashi, for example, says, "Our proper [talmudic] reading is, 'Blessed art Thou, Lord, who teaches Torah to His people Israel.' We do not read [*la' garsinan*] 'Teach me your statutes.'"[12] The fact that the commentators react against this version, using the technical term *garsinan*, indicates that some Talmud texts had that reading in their day.[13] It was probably recited, therefore, as late as the Tosafists. In earlier times it had also been part of the ritual, with at least one group, the *merkavah* mystics, reserving it for special use, saying it to get perfect knowledge of Torah.[14] Though no early Karaites quote it, they may well have included it in their prayers, since it is biblical. Hadassi certainly uses it repeatedly.[15]

Ratner traces this blessing back as far as the Palestinian Talmud, claiming it to have been an original reading there, an example of '*omer berakhah pasuk*, "making a blessing out of a biblical verse." His claim, however, has been refuted by Ginzberg.[16] Strangely enough, there are no geonic responsa which discuss this alternative, either for or against it. It follows, then, that although the geonim tried to fix the liturgy, they did not combat all the variants. Nor could they. The criteria which determined the responses they did oppose are developed in this thesis. Though the geonim phrase their criteria in legal language, they go beyond the law, since the adoption of these halakhic positions as points on which to make a stand was determined by nonlegal considerations. Some variants, like *lamdeni chukekha*, never became points of contention, not because they were the essence of halakhic propriety—the Ashkenazim were later to find much that was wrong with them—but because there were no extrahalakhic considerations which demanded they be singled out for attack. *Lamdeni chukekha* was probably long in general use by many groups. It attracted negative connotations only after the geonic age, when later generations began studying talmudic rules to grasp their theoretical ultimate consequences, without any necessary regard for polemic against particular groups. Just as they could exhaust endless pages in discussions of the rules of long and short benedictions, so, too, they proved capable of turning to other talmudic regulations, unfolding their ramifications for prayer. They included the *Yerushalmi*'s mandates as well as the *Babli*'s in their thinking, and applied the former's opposition to converting a biblical verse into a blessing to the latter's discussion of Torah Blessings. Thus, they polemicized against *lamdeni chukekha*, calling it a petition (of David's), not a blessing, and even emending the Babylonian Talmud where its citation as a blessing seemed inconceivable.

Nor is *lamdeni chukekha* the sole alternative which failed to attract geonic ire. Another is a well-known blessing with which the Palestinians introduced their *shemaʿ*. Mann reports that it is to be found in three of his manuscripts: numbers 3, 8, and 17. The fragments of Assaf and Schechter also display it.[17] Though the texts differ somewhat, their basic wording is the following:

> Blessed art Thou, Lord our God, King of the universe, who has sanctified us by His commandments, and commanded us regarding the commandment of reciting the *shemaʿ*; wholeheartedly [*bilevav shalem*] to declare Him King, and willingly [*belev tov uvenefesh chafetsah*] to declare Him One. Amen.

This introduction appears in both the morning and evening services prior to the *yotser*, as well as before the bedtime *shemaʿ*.[18]

Ginzberg argued that it began as a bedtime replacement for the normal blessings of the *shemaʿ*, to be said whenever an individual had completed the evening service immediately after the afternoon service but before night had actually settled in.[19] Since this circumstance necessitated another recital of the *shemaʿ* with its accompanying blessings after nightfall, our short benediction came to be used instead of the usual lengthy ones. The custom spread from this instance to the two daily services in which the *shemaʿ* is to be found, but again intended only for special cases, such as an individual's arriving late for services and having time to say the *shemaʿ* itself, but not the blessings around it. Thus, it was placed before the *barekhu*, that is, the formal call to prayer, and meant only for unique occasions. Ginzberg goes even further and speculates that *ʾel melekh neʾeman* (the introduction to an individual's recitation of the *shemaʿ* when no quorum is present) is a shortening of this blessing with the probably original wording of *ʾel melekh neʾeman namlikhekha bilevav shalem uvenefesh chafetsah*, "God, faithful King, let us declare You King wholeheartedly and willingly."[20] The intense opposition to the blessing resulted in the replacement of the formal benedictory reference to *shem* (God's name) and *malkhut* (His Kingship) with the informal words *ʾel* and *melekh*, respectively.

The latter hypothesis was disproved by Abraham Schechter in his observation that his Turin manuscript contained both *ʾel melekh neʾeman* and the blessing, side by side.[21] Hence the former could not be seen as an outgrowth of the latter.

In Mann's opinion, Ginzberg's scheme reversed the true order of development.[22] Mann thought the blessing began as a part of the daily service and only then spread to the bedtime recital of the *shemaʿ*. In the public service it would not have been said before *barekhu* because *barekhu* was a rarity in Palestine, where other introductory formulas, such as *barekhi nafshi 'et 'adonai*, "Bless the Lord, O my soul" (Ps. 103:1 and elsewhere), were preferred. Mann stopped short of taking the next step and suggesting that the blessing was an actual alternative to the *barekhu = barekhi nafshi* introductions. This logical conclusion was drawn, however, by Jonathan Rosenbaum,[23] on the grounds that wherever the blessing occurs no other call to prayer is to be found. So Palestinian prayers alternated with typical elasticity between *barekhu*—which may have been the rarest formulation, having been borrowed from the Babylonians—*barekhi nafshi*, the benediction in question, and probably other introductions to the general *shema'* rubric as well.

The geonim do not mention this blessing-introduction explicitly. Though later literature does contain references to it,[24] its authors do not quote geonic opinion. But they do show us that the Palestinian custom in question did not cease with the end of the geonic period. It spread and was discussed as a contemporary phenomenon in later European Jewish centers. This issue is particularly important for us because it demonstrates the fact that the Palestinian rite was not limited to Palestine, but was known and utilized as far away as Spain. I argue that the considerable anti-Palestinian polemic which we have seen in *Seder Rav Amram* can be understood as a reaction to Palestinian customs which had spread elsewhere. Amram dispatched his prayer book as a responsum to Spain, or at least the Spanish March,[25] and was aware of the liturgical deviations from the Babylonian norm which were used there. Though he may not have recognized the Palestinian origin of all these variants, the variants themselves were a source of irritation to him, and they were Palestinian in origin.

The Palestinian penchant for novelty in the Torah Blessings is so striking that at least a few other known formulas should be cited here. Though again geonic opposition did not extend to them all, they are included as further evidence of the basic difference of opinion between Babylonian and Palestinian leaders regarding liturgical canonization. As Heinemann notes,[26] canonization was a Babylonian preoccupation, not Palestinian. Palestine, after all, had no central authority of the stature of the Babylonian geonim until period 3, represented by Hai in Babylonia and his counterpart, Elijah, in Palestine. No wonder, then, it was Palestinian license which most stood in the way of the canonization attempts by geonim in period 1.

As Torah Blessings for early morning private study, Rabbenu Asher (1250?–1328) mentions several versions still current in his day.[27] These probably were formulated much earlier, and were thus in use during the geonic period. Assaf uncovered a unique Torah Blessing in the genizah. "Blessed art Thou . . . who chose the flocks of His sheep, and informed them of the ways of His will. Blessed art Thou, Lord, Giver of Torah."[28]

Finally, we should note the poetic version discovered by Mann in his pioneer investigation of the genizah:

> Our God took up a vine from Egypt.
> He displaced nations, and He planted it,
> Nurturing it with Sinai's waters,
> With flowing streams from Horeb.
> Blessed art Thou, Lord, who love Israel. [29]

Though the geonim do not condemn any of these alternatives, the last is attacked in a later responsum, possibly by Alfasi (1013–1103), who knew of people utilizing it instead of the 'ahavah rabbah or 'ahavat 'olam. [30]

In sum, the analysis of Torah Blessings alone indicates that the creativity of the Palestinians knew no bounds. Their alternatives were legion and were known years later in North Africa, Germany, France, and Spain. Geonim from Yehudai to Amram polemicized against only a few of them, those which, for one reason or another, were brought to their attention.

Blessing over the Shofar

Another case of what probably is a neutral issue is the wording of the blessing before blowing the *shofar*. [31] The question was whether to bless God for commanding us *lishmoa'*, "to hear" it, or *litkoa'*, "to blow" it. Several anonymous responsa call for the former. [32] A note in *Machzor Vitry* records Yehudai in favor of the latter, even though Rabbenu Asher quotes him to the contrary. [33] Amram has *lishmoa'*, a fact known to Mordecai and Ibn Giyyat. The latter had heard the opposite and assumed it to be a scribal error. [34] Hai feels strongly enough about *lishmoa'* to say: "One says *lishmoa'* . . . and this is a widespread *halakhah* throughout Israel, which should not be varied. In the two academies people do not say *litkoa'* but *lishmoa'*." [35]

Behind the disputed wording lay the legal question of what it actually was that constituted the commandment, blowing the *shofar* or hearing it. The matter is unclear from the pregeonic literature, and, in fact, the blessing itself is probably post-talmudic since the Talmud does not know of it. The only distinctively Rosh Hashanah blessings the Talmud recognizes are those within the *tefillah*. [36]

The impetus to define the commandment may have arisen from the fact that the Karaites denied the existence of any commandment at all connected with the *shofar*. [37] But beyond this possible factor, which may have provided a catalyst to geonic consideration, I see no particular polemic involved. With so late an innovation as this blessing, custom varied for some time, and geonic attention was drawn toward fixing its wording so as to reflect the correct conception of the commandment involved.

Sacrifice Verses in the Musaf Tefillah

This example of neutral responsa refers to the practice of citing biblical verses regarding sacrifices in the *musaf tefillah* of Sabbaths and holidays.[38] We have already seen that the daily *tefillot* were assumed to have been derived from the cultic cycle, and that the extra *tefillah*, or *musaf*, particularly, retained its theoretical connection with the Temple ritual. Thus, in our present rite, the middle blessing, or *kedushat hayom*, decries our inability to offer actual sacrifices any more, and then cites those biblical verses which specify the sacrifices that would be offered, were the Temple still standing.

Early authorities debated the wisdom of including biblical verses here. A talmudic statement (*R.H.* 35a) is used by Paltoi to prove that one need not say the verses in question: "Rav Chananel said in the name of Rav, As long as one says, 'It is written in Your Torah,' he need say nothing more." But, the gaon adds, "It is a *mitsvah* to mention them [the verses]."[39] According to his colleague Natronai, however, "In the academy we do not say the verses."[40] Sar Shalom concurs, since "They constitute a burden; we worry whether the worshipper's mind may be distracted,"[41] for he will not want to misquote the Bible and will be overly concerned about citing the verses accurately, to the detriment of the peace of mind necessary for true worship. But Saadiah, who includes the verses in his prayer book, felt that "it is nice to say in order all the verses relevant to each festival's sacrifice."[42] Amram has the verses too,[43] but considering Natronai's responsum and the unreliable nature of Amram's prayer text, the possibility exists that they are later accretions. The Palestinian rite has them regularly.[44]

The negative opinion by Sar Shalom and Natronai may be related to the development of the prayer book in their day. By Natronai's time some precentors had one, but certainly not the average worshipper; hence the burden which Sar Shalom and Natronai mentioned. Natronai's decision, to which Ginzberg refers,[45] in which a blind man is allowed to lead services but may not read from the Torah, is probably based, in part, on the assumption that such a precentor would have no Bible verses to say in the repetition of the *tefillah*, but could be allowed the luxury of a few mistakes in the prayer texts themselves.

But even Natronai and Sar Shalom do not forbid their inclusion in the *tefillah*. They seem to say only that their preference, given the prayer book situation as it is, is not to include the verses, especially since the Babylonian Talmud said there was no need to. Even Paltoi, who considered it a *mitsvah*, apparently avoided the practice. Saadiah, however, with his Palestinian background, was used to the recitation of the verses, and included them as a matter of course.

There is no polemic against anyone here, but simply a defense of the Babylonian tradition in the light of the situation that prevailed on account of the scarcity of prayer books; and a contrary opinion of Saadiah who had always recited the verses in Palestine, and continued to do so as a gaon.

Kiddusha' Rabbah

Our last example of a neutral responsum deals with the Saturday morning *kiddush*, known as *kiddusha' rabbah*.[46] Both *Sha'arei Teshuvah* and *Sefer Ha'ittim* carry nearly identical texts by an unknown gaon. The former reads:

> You asked about people who say in the morning "Who creates the fruit of the vine and sanctifies the Sabbath." [They follow] the path of error and ignorance [*ta'ut uborut*] and do not fulfill their obligation. Not only that, but they deserve corporal punishment [for disobeying] "You shall not take [the name of the Lord your God in vain]," since they say a blessing that is unnecessary, and also interrupt between the blessing [over wine] and drinking [the wine].[47]

However harsh this wording may be, that of the other version is even more severe. There, worshippers who use this formula are called "heretics," *chitsonim*.

It can readily be seen that the objection is to the eulogy, *borei' peri hagafen umekaddesh hashabbat*, "who creates the fruit of the vine and sanctifies the Sabbath." The latter clause, "and sanctifies the Sabbath," is considered superfluous; moreover, it comes between the blessing over wine and the drinking thereof.

It is impossible to be sure who advocated this formula. The later Karaite rite does not have it; nor does any Palestinian fragment to date. A Karaite kiddush formula does, however, connect the two phrases *borei' peri hagafen* and *mekaddesh 'et yom hashabbat*, possibly reflecting an earlier usage where they were said together.[48] Alternatively, since a double eulogy is called for, and dual forms characterized the Palestinian ritual, we may have here another example of Palestinian prayers. For that matter, the condemned phrase may once have been common to both Karaites and Rabbanites in Palestine. We can do no more than speculate, however.

Since neither the author nor the group he attacked is known, we can merely note the responsum and consider it "neutral."

In this chapter we have surveyed opinions regarding the disputed wording of a blessing in the *birkhot hashachar*; some variant *birkhot hatorah* which escaped geonic argument, but which were current in geonic times and indicate the breadth of Palestinian creativity; an attempt to define the commandment entailed in the *shofar* ritual by fixing the wording of its blessing; a debate over the wisdom of necessitating citation of biblical verses regarding sacrifices in the *musaf tefillah*; and an anonymous polemic against the custom of altering the morning *kiddush*. All of these may be classified as neutral issues in that whatever geonic discussion there was seems unrelated to the general perspective of each of the three periods so far discussed.

We have thus concluded the analysis of data regarding canonization attempts by the geonim. Nothing in this chapter indicates any necessity to alter our essential thesis of the canonization process. We are still left with three basic periods: the first, from Yehudai to Amram (and possibly a little beyond), in which strenuous attempts to fix the liturgy ran in direct opposition to Palestinian creativity; the second, actually Saadiah himself, for whom Palestinian and Babylonian sources were considered equally reliable, but whose antagonism to the Karaites and desire for grammatical and structural niceties provided criteria of liturgical propriety; and the third, beginning perhaps with Hai ben David, and stretching to Sherira and Hai bar Sherira, whose openness to alternatives was the general rule.

Every one of these periods corresponds to historical realities that permit us to deduce the causes for each gaon's general attitude. Our task now is twofold: to summarize the rulings we have seen so far, so as to provide a clear picture of each geonic period's hallmarks, and to discover the historical reasons which prompted the authorities in each period to make the decisions they did.

11: The Canonization Process

WE HAVE NOW ANALYZED THE PERTINENT GEONIC TEXTS, ONE BY ONE; IT remains only to consider them as a whole. To a great extent this has already been done in the foregoing chapters, but a full appreciation of the process of liturgical canonization awaits our drawing together this data and trying to explicate the pattern that emerges.

The process of fixing the liturgy in geonic times is easily divisible into three periods, each with its own tendencies, characteristic language, overall goals, and motivating features. While the second and the third stages are somewhat related, the first stands out as being unique.

Period 1 begins with Yehudai (757–761) and culminates with Sar Shalom, Paltoi, Natronai, and Amram (842–871). When it ends, one cannot say for sure, since the geonim from Amram to Saadiah are not sufficiently represented by our extant material to allow us to formulate their positions clearly. But by Saadiah (928–942) an entirely new approach is evident; it is as different from the period before it as *Siddur Saadiah* is different from *Seder Rav Amram*. Again, any hard-and-fast time limits on this period would be arbitrary and unwarranted, but by Sherira a third approach is evident, and by Hai it is fully discernible. Sherira and Hai (968–1038) represent the height of period 3, a time not entirely unlike that which preceded it, but unique enough in its own right to be considered separately.

To simplify discussion, the evidence has been summarized in tabular form in Appendix A. Because the choice of language is often crucial, exact quotations have been reproduced wherever possible. The left-hand column of the table lists all the liturgical variants condemned by the geonim, numbered in order, to facilitate reference to our discussion here. Beside each variant is another number in parentheses, representing the chapter from which the quotation is taken. Some are followed also by (P) or (K), indicating that the response in question has Palestinian or Karaite parallels. The other columns are divided into meaningful chronological units, whose significance will be manifested in the course of this discussion.

The table in Appendix A is complete except for three categories of geonic liturgical variants: (1) liturgical formulas for which no geonic opinion exists (e.g., some of the alternative *birkhot hatorah* discussed in chapter 10);

(2) formulas for which we have only anonymous geonic opinions (e.g., the *kiddush* response *borei' peri hagafen umekaddesh hashabbat* discussed in chapter 10); and (3) discussions of *piyyutim* and payyetanic inserts (such as those added for the High Holy Day period). Category 1 would have supplied no evidence whatever. Category 2 would have supplied evidence, but undatable, unattributable, and, therefore, unusable. Category 3 was deliberately omitted from this study for the reasons stated in chapter 4.

Clearly, the first two columns of the table comprise period 1. Yehudai and Amram, who form the outermost limits of the period, are remarkably alike. Nor do the geonim in the interim seem dissimilar in their approaches to the liturgy. All are marked by a distinctly anti-Palestinian bias. Yehudai discusses four responses (4, 15, 21, 46) in all, condemning three (4, 15, 21). Of these three, two (4, 21) are Palestinian. This is a very small sampling of evidence, of course, but the anti-Palestinian bias of Yehudai is independently established by Ben Baboi's famous letter to the Palestinians, where we saw him testify that Yehudai had urged Babylonian practice and the Babylonian Talmud on Palestine, only to have his protestations rebuffed.

Of the thirty-one potentially *polemical* remarks in column 2 of the table (i.e., those in which omission or inclusion of the response is accompanied by instructive discussion), nineteen are anti-Palestinian, almost two-thirds. With regard to no Palestinian custom do the geonim from Yehudai to Amram ever contradict one another. Moreover, only one distinctly Palestinian custom is advocated by them: Natronai allows *shirat hayam* (44), though he does not say it himself, because by his time it was already common to Babylonia as well as to Palestine. The only general exception to these observations is the *piyyut* with its various ramifications. Yehudai and Ben Baboi are unalterably opposed, and Amram hesitantly accepts them, but here we have a difference not in theory, but in practice. Yehudai failed to put an end to poetic innovation, and Natronai and Amram standardized their use as a necessary compromise with reality.

The responsa of this period are marked linguistically by the harshest of language. One becomes accustomed to finding all of these geonim calling their opponents fools, ignoramuses, and the like. The word *min*, "heretic," occurs twice (2 and 3); *ta'ut*, "error," is mentioned four times (4, 10, 39, 55); and other terms of disrespect (*chilluk lev*, "divisive-minded"; *kesilut*, "foolishness"; *hedyotut*, "simple-mindedness"; *borut*, "ignorance"; *shetut*, "nonsense"; *gena'i*, "unseemliness"; and *shevishta'*, "error") are the norm. Readers who ignore geonic requests are frequently subject to removal just as erring worshippers may find themselves silenced or asked to repeat their prayer properly. People are given a choice of procedure only in those instances where Babylonian practice itself varies. Local customs of other lands are uniformly treated as wrong. Respondents are routinely informed that they must, or must not, say or do things, and the general mode of classification is according to a presumed *halakhah* rather than a mere *minhag*. *Minhag* is cited only for variant practices which are usually deemed foolish, unseemly, and the like.

The Babylonian Talmud rules supreme in this period, though a subtle development from Yehudai to Amram is noticeable. We saw above that Ben Baboi quotes Yehudai as demanding two criteria for his decisions. They must be true to the *Babli* but must also have been handed down personally through the ages as the true tradition. Now in point of fact, Yehudai and Ben Baboi wish to treat both criteria as one. The point they want to make is that the *Babli* is equivalent to the true oral transmission. Unlike Amram, however, who could take this assumption for granted and quote the *Babli* without justification, Yehudai and Ben Baboi have to support their contention that the *Babli* represents the real guide for pious Jews.

Yehudai's dilemma was a result of the age in which he lived. The Babylonian Talmud was hardly a code yet. We have seen that many of its discussions do not end in any clear-cut decision; that those which do conclude with a statement of the *halakhah* are frequently treated even by later amoraim as something less than binding decisions, and that as a consequence, the geonim tended to codify the *Babli* as binding legal precedent. Yehudai, as the first powerful gaon and the heir to the *Babli* tradition, could quote his Talmud all he wanted to, but this could have no impact on people who accepted other sources of authority.

The Palestinians were such people. They followed practices rooted in their own tradition, going back to the *Yerushalmi* and often beyond, into tannaitic times. Their Passover *haggadahs*, for example, follow their own recension of the Mishnah, not the *Babli*'s, and their mourning customs probably date ultimately from the *Tosefta*. Moreover, one discovers from *Sefer Hama'asim* that a major source of Palestinian legal precedent in these early days was the *ma'aseh*, personal precedent. Both the *Babli* and the *Yerushalmi* use the *ma'aseh* as legal evidence, of course, and the Palestinian procedure was only an extension of that attitude. But the *ma'aseh* was clearly a bad precedent for Yehudai and the Babylonians. What good is a literary legal code if any prominent individual can claim his own source of personal authority? So Babylonian responsa cite only the individual practices of the amoraim (who are part of the literary code itself) and the customs of the great academies (who are presumed to base their practice on the code), but the authorities living in geonic times are mentioned so infrequently that unless they are geonim (or in a few cases, an *'av bet din* or prominent disciple), even their names are unknown to us. So the whole point of Yehudai and Ben Baboi's correspondence with the Palestinians is to prove that Yehudai's literary source, the *Babli*, is equivalent to his personal source, the transmission of the tradition through the generations.

The thrust of the Palestinian system was to decentralize authority and to allow for difference. *Minhag mevatel lehalakhah*, "custom nullifies law," as the Palestinians reminded Yehudai.[1] The Babylonian system, though, emphasizing one single literary precedent, and one institution, the gaonate, as the sole valid interpreter of that source, aimed at the very opposite goal: a centralized authoritative system which did away with local differences in custom.

All the geonim until Amram follow this approach to tradition. By Sar Shalom's time, no justification of the Babylonian Talmud is required, and they do away with Yehudai's attempts to claim an equivalent personal transmission of tradition. They quote the *Babli* and let it go at that. Those who differ are simply fools and ignoramuses. Their prayers are invalid, and their responsibility has not been discharged.

Now Yehudai and Ben Baboi wrote primarily to the Palestinians themselves. Their successors wrote to a variety of lands, Amram's prayer book having been sent as far away as Spain. Yehudai quite evidently failed to convince the Palestinians of their "errors," and these Palestinian practices found their way, along with Babylonian alternatives, to the other Jewish centers, whose leaders—often unaware of the origin of the options facing them—wrote to the geonim for guidance. The bulk of the responsa from Sar Shalom to Amram are in essence nothing more than an adjuration of these new communities to adopt Babylonian precedent rather than Palestinian.

This thesis depends on the assumption that Palestine was not moribund in the eighth and ninth centuries. Surely, there is sufficient evidence to support such a contention. Granted there are no Palestinian responsa from that period—or none that we know of—but this does not mean that native creativity had ceased. The liturgical fragments from the genizah are anything but a spiritual vacuum. The *piyyutim*, and the *midrash* on which they were often based, are certainly not signs of a cultural desert. If the development of authoritative legal pronouncements tantamount to the geonic legislation is lacking, it is because they were not desired in the first place. They were simply not part of the open-ended Palestinian system, which lacked institutional centralization, not to mention the necessary economic and executive means required to impose such a legal system, even if it had existed. Moreover, we do have such works as *Sefer Hama'asim* and *Massekhet Soferim* from this early period, and who knows what other writings might have reached us had the vicissitudes of history been as kind to Palestine as they were to Babylonia?

We can date the Palestinian cultural challenge to Babylonia as beginning about 800 with the first of the Ben Meir family succeeding Mar Zutra's dynasty as head of the academy.[2] In 835 Babylon was still dependent on Palestine for the fixing of the calendar.[3] In 868 the Tulunide revolt spurred on Palestinian independence, and the Fatimid revolution in 909 did likewise, as Ben Meir's assertion of Palestinian prerogative in 922 shows.

One further point should be made before turning to Saadiah and period 2. It is important to see how insignificant the Karaites were in these early years. Though Anan was a contemporary of Yehudai, it is by no means clear whether Anan himself achieved any but the most limited success. Nemoy points out that other than Anan we know of no conversion to Karaism from Rabbanism before the time of Saadiah.[4] Moreover, the Karaite sources up to that time are "permeated throughout by a spirit of profound pessimism," giving absolutely no hint of success.[5] Certainly no gaon even mentions them until Natronai, who heard of them only second-hand from a Spanish emigré who fell upon Anan's writings. Natronai even makes the grievous error of assuming that Karaites would read about Rabban Gamaliel in their *haggadah!* The only probable anti-Karaite stand taken in this period is the blessing over the candles (24), and even that is not absolutely certain. Even if the Karaites had been a force to contend with, very few of the liturgical formulas attacked could have been theirs, since by definition they limited their prayer texts to biblical passages, as is evident from the liturgy of Anan, Kirkisani, and even the bulk of today's Karaite rite, which—despite its many accretions from Rabbanite sources—is still basically a cumbersome collection of scriptural verses strung together in various ways.

Period 1 of the canonization process, then, is a reflection of the attempt by the geonim to impose their own Talmud and their own interpretation of that Talmud on Jewish communities everywhere. It brooks no compromise, claims the absolute authority of Babylonian precedent, admits the academies and their titular heads, the geonim, as the only post-talmudic guides, and argues almost exclusively against the one major alternative center of traditional authority, Palestine.

How different period 2, as represented by Saadiah, is. The very fact that a Palestinian could be elected gaon indicates a new trend. Saadiah, though born in Egypt, had lived extensively in Palestine and was well imbued with Palestinian lore. He had supported Babylonian claims of authority in the Ben Meir crisis though, and was therefore not automatically excluded from the gaonate. Still, the force of tradition was against him. As Ginzberg points out, the gaonate was almost exclusively hereditary, the prerogative of a small oligarchy of Babylon's first families.[6] Rivkin deals extensively with the sharp cleavage of tradition which Saadiah's appointment must have occasioned.[7]

One can hardly imagine such an honor being bestowed on a Palestinian in Yehudai's or Amram's time. Why it was necessary in this later period need not concern us here,[8] but one implication of the appointment is of the utmost significance: the Babylonian-Palestinian quarrel could not have been the central problem of the new age.

No wonder Saadiah has no qualms about including in his prayer book too many Palestinian responses to list. We have seen over and over again that Saadiah ruled with the *Yerushalmi* or with Palestinian precedent when no extenuating factors were in the way.

These extenuating factors have already been mentioned. Saadiah opposed deviations from the orderly structure of prayer, confusion of topics, and blessings without traditional talmudic support.

Now the last-mentioned consideration fits well with Saadiah's anti-Karaite bias, which marked his whole career. And the first two harmonize with the image of Saadiah the rationalist, the philosopher, the grammarian. These are the two keys to Saadiah.

Saadiah was raised in an age of reason, where orderliness and reasonableness were prime desiderata. In the Karaite world Kirkisani was attacking Daniel al Kumisi "as an example of an opponent to rationalism as applied to religion."[9] Kirkisani himself is concerned about the logical distinction between praise, petition, and thanksgiving, as his treatise on prayer shows.[10] Saadiah's approach to liturgy, then, is an expression of the *Zeitgeist*, wherein nothing irrational, unorderly, or out of place can be countenanced. To some extent this approach was necessary to combat Karaite criticism, but beyond this immediate necessity, Saadiah's approach was conditioned by the very intellectual world in which his mind developed, and Saadiah would have taken the same stand even if he had never heard of the Karaites. Though his battle with the Karaites was a major motivating factor—we have noted above his intense antipathy to *yein 'asis*, for example (1), even though other similar deviations meant nothing to him—a study of his prayer book indicates concern on a broader scale.

To begin with, the ordering of his *Siddur* is a defense of the rationality of the rabbinic rite. Unlike Amram's rather straightforward presentation of prayers in their natural liturgical order, Saadiah adopts an approach born of an a priori logical system superimposed on the prayer book. Yet this very systematic approach renders the book far less suitable for actual worship than Amram's *Seder*. The reading of the Torah, for example, falling in none of the logical categories set up by Saadiah, comes way at the end. Yom Kippur is set apart from Rosh Hashanah. Congregational prayer is rigidly separated from individual worship. As Elbogen perceives:

> Saadiah . . . presents a highly systematic elaboration of the different kinds of prayers. . . . The problem is how the unlearned man of whom he has so much to complain could find his way through this well-balanced system if he had not at his disposal an extended table of contents or a subject index like the present printed edition offers.[11]

So Saadiah was not writing for the average man, no matter what he may have contended to the contrary. He was writing for the intellectual, the philosopher, the logician, the man who wanted to know that his traditional worship fulfilled all the criteria demanded by an age of system and order. Karaites and other sectarians might mock the tradition for its anthropomorphism or its faulty understanding of the Bible—and these charges Saadiah answers elsewhere—but no reasonable person could look at Saadiah's *Siddur* and say the liturgy was irrational. Insertions on the subject of salvation are excised from the *yotser* and *birkat hashanim* (5 and 11); an irrelevant blessing by the priest at the *pidyon haben* ceremony is disallowed (50); superstitious waving of the *lulav* in all directions is condemned;[12] grammatical precision is adhered to scrupulously (13, 32, 41).

Saadiah's introduction tells us what to expect. He will not confuse the constituent liturgical elements of worship; he will restore the prayers to their original intentions, doing away with whatever may oppose them; he will trace the prayers to their biblical foundations.

Their biblical foundations, note! Though Amram cites the *Babli* almost exclusively, Saadiah rarely mentions rabbinic sources. Whenever possible, he finds scriptural warrant for his prayers. In his introduction, for example, he establishes the order of the blessings of the *tefillah*, "so as to reprove anyone who might possibly be presumptuous enough to alter their composition."[13] A ready reference for this purpose would have been *Megillah* 17b, where the order of the blessings is already established by the rabbis. But Saadiah virtually ignores this. He selects his own biblical quotations, and studiously avoids quoting any rabbinic maxims on the subject—such as Raba's justification for the seventh blessing, based on the *ge'ulah*'s expected arrival in the seventh messianic year (*Meg.* 17b). Surely Saadiah's attraction to the Bible and avoidance of ready-made rabbinic arguments are best explained by the other key to his thinking, his desire to answer the Karaites, for whom the citation of the Talmud would have been beside the point. If he was to champion the Rabbanite cause successfully, he had to meet his opponents on common ground, Scripture itself, and demonstrate the biblical basis for the rabbinic system.[14]

So he consciously chooses alternatives that are biblical in their basis. This is why he begins *'ahavah rabbah* with *'ahavat 'olam* (6); why he chooses *'or* not *ma'or* as the correct nominal form (13); and why he attacks the *mem* of *leshakhachem mitoratekha* (41). Since the Karaite liturgy differed so radically from the Rabbanite, not many Karaite responses were available options for attack. But what there was Saadiah singled out for comment. Since Karaites reserved priestly roles for priests alone, Saadiah was careful to side with Babylonian custom in having a nonpriestly reader recite the whole Priestly Benediction (14). Since Karaites treated Rosh Hashanah as just another *mo'ed*, he left out *mo'adim lesimchah* (27) and emphasized the rabbinic *yom hazikaron*. The blessing *yein 'asis* (1) and the *zimun* form *nevarekh menachem lev 'avelim* (55), both being similar to Karaite formulas, were similarly proscribed.

Saadiah, then, forms a new chapter in liturgical development. By his time geonic intolerance vis-à-vis the Palestinian tradition was an unaffordable luxury. Intellectual development had resulted in a new class of Jews who demanded "enlightened" justification of their ritual, as with every other aspect of their religion, according to the scientific and philosophic criteria of their time. The Karaites were tapping this intellectual discontent, presumably with some degree of success, and Saadiah answered the needs of this Jewish elite with his many writings. He provided them with a philosophical basis for faith, treatises on grammar and poetry, the intellectual arts of the day, and a defense of rabbinic worship. For the linguistic purist, he excises grammatical inconsistency. For the man of artistic temperament, he provides a generous supply of poetry. For the philosophically oriented, he includes original meditations—he calls them *bakashot*, "petitions"—on themes like the nature of God, the process of creation, divine retribution, redemption, and the like.[15] With calculated logic he edits the content and structure of every prayer, omitting the secondary, the irrelevant, the confusing. The practical is sacrificed to the intellectually acceptable, as the whole thing is packaged in a logical arrangement of radical conception, with an enticing prologue disclaiming any responsibility for illogical deviations which might accidently have crept into the "true" rabbinic service. Saadiah's *Siddur* was the best defense of his time against Karaite mockery, philosophical skepticism, and "scientific" logic.

After Saadiah our liturgical responsa again become all too few until Sherira. But Sherira and Hai are well represented, and form the last chapter of the canonization process. The overwhelming characteristic of their approach is their extraordinary acceptance of variation. Unlike Yehudai, Natronai, and Amram, they do not habitually condemn a practice out of hand. Their opponents are not called ignoramuses or fools, and contrary practices are generally judged to be bad customs at worst, not illicit deviations from *halakhah* which plunge their users into unfulfilled responsibility and sin. Hai is willing to quote the *Yerushalmi* with respect to the blessing *shelo' 'asani bor* (43). For *lishmor chukav* he says, "It is not our custom to say it, but if one wants to, he has the right to do it" (44). *Yein 'asis* is a "heretical custom," but nevertheless, "Since people like it . . . it is alright" (1). He dislikes *mishpetei tsidkekha*, but "if [a precentor] says it, we do not make him say the prayer over again" (28). The *'avodah* in *minchah* is misplaced but should not be changed since it is an old custom in some places (33). One may say the blessing for *milah* either before or after the operation (49). Sherira includes *'or chadash* in his prayers, but "someone who omits it loses nothing thereby" (5). The eulogy *mesameiach 'amo uvoneh yerushalayim* differs from the Babylonian one, but it is "a proper custom" (52). Both Sherira and Hai allow a confession in *selach lanu*, at *'erev Yom Kippur* since the people say "they need it" (30). And *kol nidre* becomes part of Hai's *Siddur* (29).

This openness to variety is not hard to explain. Rivkin has demonstrated the institutional crisis which faced the gaonate in its closing century.

At the end of the ninth century, three powerful, wealthy, and influential institutions flourished [Sura, Pumbedita, the exilarchate]. . . . Yet
in the space of fifty years in the tenth century an exilarch, Mar Ukbah,
was deposed and exiled; geonim and counter-geonim, exilarchs and
counter-exilarchs made their appearance; a world-renowned Academy
was closed; and the exilarchate dwindled into relative insignifi-
cance. . . . Though triumphant, Pumbedita was threatened with poverty and was compelled to beg piteously for alms and recognition from
Jewish communities that had once viewed her with veneration. [16]

That Sherira himself faced the crisis in all its severity is evident from the
following letter which he sent to Jews abroad.

Increased pressure has produced increasingly onerous pain for us and
we crouch under our burdens. There is no divine help and our own
strength flags. . . . Out of pressure and pain we write these words to you.
After long discussion and great frustration, we explain in full to you. If
the statutes of wisdom are denied, Torah will be abandoned. . . . For
from the time your ancestors turned a deaf ear, the academy began to
want, and now, behold, our poverty increases yearly. . . . If you really
should say to yourselves that you can remain detached with your own
devices, and that your academies will not fail while our [lit. the]
Academy goes down . . . how can the head fall leaving the body intact?
For after the head, the body goes.
    . . . So pursue your ancestral custom after the manner of your par-
ents; return things anew to the way they were. Inform us of your religious uncertainties so that you may behold responsa and flourish in
them, while, also, the heart of the Academy is strengthened. [17]

The gaonate under Sherira was under attack from all sides. Internecine
rivalry had ruined its reputation abroad. The Fatimid revolt had ripped away
half of the Jewish world, which was now subservient to powers in Egypt, not
Baghdad, and the Omayyad caliphate in Spain controlled the fortunes of the
most promising young Jewish center in Europe. Karaites flourished as never
before in Palestine. How Sherira rebuilt Pumbedita is chronicled by Lewin. [18]
His famous letter to Kairouan reestablished the traditional authority of geonic
tradition. Letters securing funds were dispatched all over. Scholarship was
intensified to regain the renown for which the gaonate had long been
acclaimed.

    But in the end, all was dependent on convincing foreign Jewry of its
responsibility to support Pumbedita economically and to accept its scholarly
opinions as decisive. Under such circumstances it hardly behooved Sherira
and Hai to downgrade foreign liturgical practices. So whenever possible they
did not do so. Regularly, they spoke highly of them.

    On some occasions, though, variants are attacked. Even if there were
no explanation for these instances, the above hypothesis would hold, since it

is enough to recognize the overwhelming preponderance of instances where variation is encouraged, especially when viewed in contrast to the severity of period 1. But as it happens, some of these exceptional outbursts of ire may be explicable. What follows, then, is a tentative attempt at such explanations, preceded by the caveat that they vary in their degree of certainty. Even if every one should prove to be incorrect, however, the novelty of Hai's permissiveness in so many cases remains firmly established.

Of the twenty-six quotations attributed to Hai or Sherira, twelve (1, 5, 21, 28, 30 [twice: by both Hai and Sherira], 38, 40, 44, 49, 50, and 52) are cases where Pumbeditan custom differed from that of the respondents, but the latter are permitted to maintain their practice, either by express geonic statement or by admission within the responsa that custom differs regarding the matter in question. Five more (22, 27, 29, 37, and 48) relate Hai's practice, without indicating whether the alternative was open to the questioner or not. One comment (43) is too short to know what Hai meant by it, except to note that he cited the *Yerushalmi*. And another (36) explains that a blessing is not talmudically based and thus unnecessary, though Hai says nothing about forbidding it. Another seven comments are left with some degree of polemic, actually dismissing the alternative or suggesting, in some other way, that Hai's practice is halakhically mandated and cannot be altered (6, 7, 15, 23, 24, 51 and 58). In one of these seven, however, the deprecatory phrase employed does not arbitrarily close off the alternative but merely shows strong disapproval: of *'ani 'adonai 'eloheikhem* (7), Hai says *'eino minhag yafeh*. We are left, then, with six responses which attract outright prohibition (6, 15, 23, 24, 51 and 58).

Many of Hai's denunciations may be tied to his fight against Karaism. His prohibition against reading the Torah at *musaf* (23) has already been discussed. In it he uses his most intense language; nowhere else does he appeal dramatically to the superior wisdom of earlier generations. Hai's antipathy for *veyitkales* (15) may be due to a desire to emphasize the rabbinic use of the word over the biblical, since the Karaites attacked rabbinic institutions by quoting biblical verses. With regard to Sherira's condemnation of *'ahavah rabbah* (6), it may be significant to note that Saadiah too avoided the phrase, preferring the biblically based *'ahavat 'olam*. For similar reasons Sherira, too, may have preferred to base the affirmation of God's love for the true Israel on a biblical foundation. Hai was led to specify the command to hear the *shofar* because the Karaites denied it; he chooses *lishmoa'* over *litkoa'* (58) because only the former is a practical possibility. He also opposes *mekaddesh yisra'el 'al yedei chuppah vekiddushin* (51) because of differences between Karaites and Rabbanites as to the binding nature of *kiddushin*.

The above explanations are not all offered as statements of fact. We can do no more than guess in some of the cases, though the *musaf* reading and the *kiddushin* formula (23, 51) seem relatively certain. Still one cannot but be impressed with the extent to which Hai and Sherira try to be lenient; they rarely use critically harsh language; most infrequently do they resort to words like *'asur*, "It is forbidden"; *chayyav*, "One must"; *halakhah*, "It is law"; and so on. Their overwhelming preference is *minhag*, "custom," and only when necessary do they absolutely condemn a *minhag*. Generally speaking, "customs" have their own inherent justification and command their own respect.

Our survey has shown that the geonim as a group are far from unanimous in their opinions. The harshest criticism came in the early years, when the gaonate was growing in strength and—like the Abbasid caliphate, which supported its existence—trying to bend the will of world Jewry to its own system of Jewish thought and practice. Yehudai's lack of success can best be estimated by the fact that Amram and the geonim surrounding his term of office felt constrained to repeat most of his admonitions or to compromise with reality. The Palestinian tradition did not disappear. Eventually it became part of Saadiah's prayer book, and it was in use in Hai's time. Saadiah may have accomplished his task of providing a *Siddur* for the enlightened, but its cumbersome organization was of no help in popularizing his opinions. Nor could its Arabic commentary compete with Amram's Rabbinic Aramaic in most of Western Europe, where the focus of Jewish life shifted by the end of the geonic age. Certainly, Hai and Sherira did not inherit a homogeneous ritual, common throughout Jewry, and they, as practical realists, virtually gave up the task of fixing the rite.

From the evidence in the geonic literature alone, it would seem that no great success was encountered by the geonim. It is fair to say, at least, that where success was attained, it was a result of the will of later communities themselves, not the authoritarian aspect of the gaonate. Whatever authority the geonim had for later generations, there is very little evidence, indeed, that the geonic will was venerated abroad during their own lifetimes. Later ages may have viewed the geonim as they themselves had viewed the amoraim, and only then were their mandates revived and respected, discussed ad infinitum, and acted upon one way or the other. But as for the geonic years themselves, the amount of variation faced by Yehudai seems in no way diminished by the time of Hai's death.

But the synagogue service was canonized, and in a sense by the geonim, particularly Amram, whose *Seder* became common currency in western Europe, citing, as it did, relevant *Babli* instructions for new communities hungry for roots in traditional sources. As Jews in Spain, Italy, Germany, and France accepted the Babylonian Talmud as their chief source of authority, and their primary legal text to study and act upon, so they were drawn to Amram's *Seder*. But the opinions of other geonim were considered too, as was Palestinian practice to the extent it was known.

It would, therefore, be truer to conclude that the geonim laid the groundwork for liturgical canonization, which then reached fruition in the several rites of the various Jewish communities that matured only after the geonic age had ceased. To a great extent ignored in their own time, the geonim were to achieve a posthumous victory, as their successors in Europe later decided to adopt their Talmud, to accept their authority, and to worship with their version of a canonized synagogue service.

Appendices

Appendices

A: Summary of Geonic Opinion

The following table summarizes the data in chapters 1–10, and is referred to in chapter 11. Whenever possible, exact quotations have been excerpted and reproduced.

Column 1 (on the left) cites the liturgical wording or custom at issue, the number of the chapter in which it is discussed, and, in some cases, the letter (P) or (K), indicating Palestinian or Karaite parallels.

Columns 2–5 cite geonic opinion. Where a column includes more than one gaon, the author's initial precedes his citation.

Of the two complete prayer books available to us—*Seder Rav Amram* and *Siddur Saadiah*—simple omission or inclusion of prayers is noted. Such a notation in column 3 refers to *Seder Rav Amram* unless otherwise indicated.

	Yehudai (Y) Ben Baboi (B)	Paltoi (P) Sar Shalom (S) Natronai (N) Amram (A)	Saadiah	Sherira (S) Hai (H)
1.	ז' עמים (I) (K)		אמור לפני	אמרן רבכנ (H) ... יבי ודיין ... יבי
2.	ואלהי, עת קוטש אמ	זו אריה (N)		
3.	ואלהי, (I) (P)	לב קוליהן אדי רבי בינן (N) ... מקצה כסכנך כברכי ליסבי יזה ... (A) quotes Natronai	omits	
4.	הניורדים מיים לברך על (I) (P)	על זה כמו זו (N) ... ברכי, מקשני אין (Y)		

גוי			
ואת ברזמ (H)			
ר׳א			
הטצמ ץראה (S)	omits		
	omits	omits	
	includes		
לא ויספמי	(3) הזד ןבו הבורמ	(3) הווארג הילבכמ	
יבר הצרמ יבר	(2) םט אלריב	ראד ,ילב	
אתמ, יומא...	אלונ יוברבל	(2) ינב ינב אתכלבמא,	
הפלש יתורבש (S)	(1) ירא ןביו דבור	ונ...	
המחנ הרבדמ		(A)(1) םאונ תאמוצ	
		םטמא	
		(A) ןיא הרונלצ	
		... הזמ אלש הזמ	

5.	אוה הרוד (2)
6.	רבד הוותא (2)
7.	הוותח האד םטמאירכ ,ה אלריא (2)
8.	םייח ינילב (2) (P)
9.	הזונב לבדא תובש (2) (P)
10.	רבדה הזד הבלה לבונ םיבש לאמטא (2) (P)

	Yehudai (Y) Ben Baboi (B)	Paltoi (P) Sar Shalom (S) Natronai (N) Amram (A)	Saadiah	Sherira (S) Hai (H)
11.	ונהגו לברך אלקה שבת (3) (P)	omits	זה מברך	וראוי ומצוה לברך (H)
12.	אחת (3)	מברך ובונה אלקינו (S)	אתה חונן לאדם דעת ...	
13.	מברכו ... (3)		ברכת שומע תפלה וכו' ואומר ואתה שומע תפלה כי אתה אלקינו וכו'	
14.	reader omits priestly blessing (3) (P)	disagrees, includes entire blessing	includes entire blessing	
15.	יאמר אבני גזר (3) (Y)	אך ברכת זה אך לא זה אלא זה (A)	includes	

				(H)
				אוהב ליה די מנוגו. חזי לקבל השני אסגולו אל (ב..בב..)
16.	אלאל אבי ינאל (5) (מ"ע)		איז מבגר (S) במקומות וכבבי לבני בסיביני (A) quotes Sar Shalom	omits
17.	(5) נאמר		same as above (16)	includes, adds ורבנן אמר יבין
18.	הוא הדם (5) (מ"ע)		(A) (S) omit (but others include)	omits
19.	מצרים ממס נמא שלום גדל לדי ליה בסא ממסם ינאל אלאי לבני נא... (5) (P) מצרים		אסור לחמם מן קם (N) (A) quotes Natronai	omits
20.	אאל כלה מעצמו (5) (P)		איז אמבר (N) (A) quotes Natronai	includes with יקאלוה עוד
21.	(5) (P) (ה"תנת) מהא בקמה וברובגא	אסור לחמם לבני (Y) נהגי, נמענו עובדא מהגא ובגדא ונהגי מהגא לחכמים	omits		

	Yehudai (Y) Ben Baboi (B)	Paltoi (P) Sar Shalom (S) Natronai (N) Amram (A)	Saadiah	Sherira (S) Hai (H)
22. שמע בקריאתה (כולם לה' בלבד) (5)				omits
23. קראת ההלל (במסכת) (5) (K)		includes	omits	
24. Blessing over Sabbath Candles (5) (K)		omits אין צריך להדליק (A/N)	אסור להדליקם על ידי נכרים כדי להדליקם מברכין עליה	ואין זה אלא שאומר לה ברוב המקומות ... הנוהגים לומר אותה אלא יש מקומות שאומרים אותה אנן דלא נהגינן כל מקומות לומר על המברכים ברכה ... אתה מקדש (H)
25. אין אנו יכולין להדליק (בליל) (ה"ט) (6)			אין לברך	

#		(Y) includes			
26.	והשיאנו (6) (ני, דב)	includes	includes	omits	
27.	באתונך לשמוח (6) (K) (ני, דב)		ארוך ליבך (P) includes	omits	אין (H) מברכתו להודות
28.	(6) ונבל בכנור		omits	omits ויי לא אבדי	ולא אחר מדברים (H) אין מברכין אותו אות
29.	(6) (P) יהיה כן וכו'		... היהיה אין (N) אלא יראו וכו (A) מברכין מברכין	includes	(H) includes
30.	(ממנהג) (6) (6) ה' זיע ליב דיר דבלה		includes	omits	(S) allows in את אתה ... כי את אומרים הם כל ... לך לו
31.	(6) המלך ונתון		includes at ne'ilah only	ואת מעשיו	אין (H) מברכין אותו
32.	... בתפילותיך (6) זאת אחת		omits	אסר ראו אבל לברך בתפילה לברך אלא	

	Yehudai (Y) Ben Baboi (B)	Paltoi (P) Sar Shalom (S) Natronai (N) Amram (A)	Saadiah	Sherira (S) Hai (H)
33. אברכה שהכל (6) בדברו		omits	אין מן המקרא	(H) allows אבינהו נאמר אל המקראות
34. במצבה הכל (6) (P) המצה לידי		omits		
35. לא יכבר כל (6) (P) המצא		(S) לא יעשו כן (A) omits	includes	יהודי ויהגה (H) יברכו אלוהיהו
36. (7) ואל הישיעני		omits	omits	
37. Blessing before hallel (7) (P)		(A and Tsemach ʾav bet din) אין לברך	omits	(H) quotes Amram and Tsemach ואין אלא אומר אמרו
38. (7) וברכם בהם ישמעי		(A) includes as optional	includes as optional	כל בשם (H) וברכם ובסום יי ואין לברך

#		includes / omits		
				נברשת חייב רבנן ל"י ... לברכה ולי, לא (H) לא חובה ני"ח אחם לפני מברכין (H) ...
39.	לתכבודנו (7)		דם ... מעלה (N) (A) quotes Natronai	
40.	הזכרת לפני מ"ר רב (7) (P)	includes	כל אחר ואמר (N) מקדם הזכרת הזכר (A) וכן אמר רב הזכרת צריכין לברך מעמד	
41.	למעמד מעלה (7)	אי לפניו מכ"ם	אי צריך לברך (A)	
42.	מעמד רבני הכוס (7) (P)	omits	אין לא צריך (A) אתכתבא	
43.	חובה (8) (P)	omits	לפני אך (P) מברכת לפני הברכה אין אך (P) (A) omits	
44.	למעמד וכו (8) (P)			

	Yehudai (Y) Ben Baboi (B)	Paltoi (P) Sar Shalom (S) Natronai (N) Amram (A)	Saadiah	Sherira (S) Hai (H)
45. שומ' רב הם (8) (P)		ובשבת "ש"וש' (N) ... גדיי לקרב יש אל (N) ואל ... אומר במצות עומדים מקום ברכה	... וננהג א' זאל על פי ואל אז' דו אל הג' נוהג בהללו בכלם	
46. ובכלם לקרב' ובשבת אחר ההללוי (8)	לא צריך (Y)	יש "ובא אומ' מכאן (N) (A) quotes Natronai	omits	
47. במצות ללולב מהמצוה (8) (P)		ונאמר נקט תהא ד"ית ... ובזה הקרן הח"ם (A)	omits	
48. צריך (9)		(S) said יהי המקרא לנהוג ? (A)	said יהי המקרא לנהוג	צריך (H)
49. להנהיג בכלל מקום המצוה אז אמרה (9)		אמרה (A)	אמרה	הנהיג המקרא אין אם (H) והנה ההיה מקום הנהגה יאמרה א אמרה

		omits	
(S) לבבה רבתא	כבד לבב		אל ביסטא.בי
לאחשורש	בד.ד ואין ... קבל		
כבס לחזור ואין	עול אמר ואין רמוה		
נלון? כבר ואשר			
אאנ פידא, ש.			
(H) יד.גיונא ד.אן		includes	
(H) נוניוני			
כבלכיני			

		omits
		(A) אל כבסי,
		לקבל קן ... קבלה
		(N) אין כבאד
		אורב לאל כבבל
		(A) quotes
		Natronai
		(P) פטפוה

50.	יהכל (פירוז נכ)	
	אם, ש. רמאי לכל	
	(9)	
51.	נשטא ונירורא.ן (6)	
	כנוס, ש. הל, ה.	
52.	ניהנה רמא נטבטש	
	(9) (P) הלאכ.ם	
	ייניא.ן	
53.	(9) (P) ניידראל?	
	להלריא	
54.	כ.הכהו ?אן	
	אנ כנול?	
	(9) (P)	
55.	כ ם.מם רמ.ל	
	הכל כנהה ריכ.ן	
	(K) (P)	

	Yehudai (Y) Ben Baboi (B)	Paltoi (P) Sar Shalom (S) Natronai (N) Amram (A)	Saadiah	Sherira (S) Hai (H)
56. מתם אלים ונהנה (9) (P) ירשיים'		(A) ?	includes optional	
57. הלילם (10)		הלילם לא יאבר (N)	omits	דליה הלכה (H) לזבוח אלא
58. להקרבן (10)		omits	omits	
59. בזבחים (10) מבטאך הלוים בגגות		מבטא הזבה לזלית (P) לא באבואב (N) אמרבן	נזבח בגבול בכל מקום זה' נמצא כל פסק'	
		(A) printed text has them		

B: Chronological List of Geonim Cited in This Study

	Pumbedita		*Sura*
		757–761	Yehudai
		765–775	Chaninai
		828–836	Moses
		838–848	Kohen Tsedak (bar Abomai)
842–857	Paltoi	848–853	Sar Shalom
		853–858	Natronai
860–869	Mattathias	858–871	Amram
		871–879	Nachshon
872–890	Tsemach bar Paltoi		
		879–885	Tsemach (bar Chayyim)
890–898	Hai (bar David)	885–896	Hai (bar Nachshon)
926–936	Kohen Tsedek (bar Joseph)	928–942	Saadiah
936–938	Tsemach (bar Kafnai)		
		944–988	(vacant)
968–998	Sherira	988–997	Tsemach (bar Isaac)
998–1038	Hai (bar Sherira)	997–1013	Samuel (bar Hofni)

Source: Based on chart given by Assaf in *Entsiklopidiah Ha'ivrit,* s.v. "Ga'on."

C: Glossary of Liturgical Rubrics and Related Terms

The following glossary contains only the rubrics and terms referred to in this work, and generally relates them only to the contexts here discussed. It gives (1) a translation of the term (in parentheses), (2) a general definition or explanation of the term, and (3) the number of the page (again in parentheses) where the prayer in question occurs in either the Birnbaum *Siddur* (S), the Birnbaum *Machzor* (M), or the Birnbaum *Haggadah* (H). In all cases references are to today's Ashkenazic rite, and the volumes cited are those used elsewhere in this book.

'*Aggadah.* A loose term, generally understood as implying rabbinic lore, as opposed to *halakhah*, rabbinic law.

'*Ahavah rabbah* (With great love . . .). One form of the *birkat hatorah* preceding the *shema*', now normative in the morning service of the Ashkenazic rite (S. 73–74).

'*Ahavat 'olam* (With everlasting love . . .). One form of the *birkat hatorah* preceding the *shema*', now normative in the evening service of the Ashkenazic rite (S. 123).

'*Al ha'arets* (For the land). The second blessing of the *birkat hamazon*; see *birkat hamazon* (S. 761–63).

'*Al hanissim* (For the miracles . . .). A prayer of thanksgiving for the miraculous salvation celebrated on Purim and Chanukah; inserted in the penultimate *tefillah* blessing (*hoda'ah*) and the second benediction of the *birkat hamazon* ('*al ha'arets*) (S. 91–93, 761–63).

'*Al yerushalayim* (For Jerusalem). The third blessing of the *birkat hamazon*; see *birkat hamazon* (S. 763–65).

'*Arami 'oved 'avi* (My father was a wandering Aramaean . . .). The midrashic embellishment of Deut. 26:5–8, recounting Israel's bondage and redemption from Egypt, and forming the central narrative portion of the Passover *haggadah* (H. 7?–84).

'*Arvit.* The evening service, known also as *ma'ariv*.

'*Avadim hayyinu* (We were slaves). The first of two introductions to the Passover *haggadah*'s central midrashic account of Israel's Egyptian bondage and deliverance, emphasizing physical servitude as the nadir of Israel's history (H. 64).

'*Avelut* (Mourning). Used here as a general category under which to subsume discussions of *birkat 'avelim* (blessing of mourners) and *tanchumei 'avelim* (comforting of mourners).

'*Avodah* (Worship). (1) The third-to-last blessing in the *tefillah*, requesting the rebuilding of the Temple and the reinstitution of the cultic worship practiced there (S. 89). (2) A liturgical rubric unique to Yom Kippur, wherein the cultic activity of the High Priest during Temple days is recalled (M. 811 ff.).

Barukh 'adonai le'olam (Blessed be the Lord forever). An extension to the *hashkivenu*, omitted on Sabbaths and holidays (S. 197); see also *yir'u 'eineinu*.

Barukh she'amar (Blessed be He who spoke). The introductory blessing to the *pesukei dezimrah* (S. 51).

Berakhah (Blessing). The unique literary prose genre of prayer favored by the rabbis in the tannaitic era, and thus attracting in time various rules regarding proper and improper *berakhah* structure.

Berakhah levatalah. (A blessing in vain). Any blessing which is unnecessary, superfluous, or unaccompanied by the act which it is intended to consecrate.

Berit Milah (Covenant of circumcision). The ritual marking the circumcision of every male child (S. 741–49).

Birkat 'avelim (Blessing for mourners). An ancient blessing, no longer extant.

Birkat ge'ulah. See *ge'ulah*.

Birkat hamazon. Grace after meals, composed essentially of four blessings: (1) *birkat hazan* (blessing [for God] who feeds [everyone]); referred to here as '*al hamazon* (blessing for food); (2) *birkat ha'arets* (blessing over the land), referred to here as '*al ha'arets* (for the land); (3) *birkat yerushalayim* (blessing for Jerusalem), referred to here as '*al yerushalayim*; and (4) *hatov vehametiv*, the blessing for "the One who is good, and does good." The introduction to the whole is (5) the invitation to join in the Grace, known as the *zimun* (S. 759–69).

Birkat hashir (Blessing of song). A blessing said upon the conclusion of a *hallel* (see *hallel*), celebrating God's praise and our duty to utter it. Our rite knows of several versions: (1) *yishtabach* (S. 69); (2) *nishmat* (S. 331–35); (3) *yehallelukha* (H. 120, S. 573).

Birkat hatorah (Torah blessing); pl. *birkhot hatorah*. A generic term for the benediction preceding the study of Torah. Used predominantly here for the blessing immediately preceding the *shema'* (S. 73–74, 191), but appearing also in other contexts (S. 13, 123).

Birkat hazan (Blessing [for God] who feeds [everyone]). The first blessing of the *birkat hamazon*, referred to, at times, as *ʿal hamazon* (for food); see *birkat hamazon* (S. 759).

Birkat kohanim (Priestly Benediction). The last blessing of the *tefillah*, recalling the trifold priestly benediction of Num. 6:24–26 (S. 94–95).

Birkat shalom (Blessing of peace). The last benediction of the *tefillah* (called also, and more accurately, *birkat kohanim*, or Priestly Benediction, after its first half); its theme is a petition for peace (S. 95). It appears alone, without the first part, in the evening *tefillah*, and (except for fast days) in the afternoon *tefillah* (S. 209, 173). The morning version (S. 95) is *sim shalom*, "Grant peace," and the evening-afternoon version (S. 209, 173) is *shalom rav*, "Great peace."

Birkat shanim (Blessing of years). The ninth benediction of the daily *tefillah*, requesting a bounteous harvest for the year (S. 87).

Birkhot hashachar (morning blessings). The first rubric of the morning service, originally intended for private home prayer but eventually included in the public liturgy. It is composed primarily of a series of blessings—hence the title—and passages, both scriptural and rabbinic, intended for study (S. 3–49).

Chatimah (seal). The conclusion, or seal, of a statutory benediction, translated throughout this book as "eulogy."

ʾEl melekh neʾeman (God, faithful King). Introduction to the *shemaʿ*, but said only by individuals in the absence of a quorum.

ʾEmet veyatsiv (True and enduring). The morning *geʾulah* (S. 77–81).

ʾErusin (Betrothal). The first part of the marriage ceremony, containing the formal act of *kiddushin* (S. 753); see *kiddushin*.

Geʾulah (Redemption). (1) The benediction immediately following the *shemaʿ*, emphasizing God's role as redeemer (S. 77–81, 195). (2) The seventh benediction of the *tefillah*, petitioning for redemption (S. 85). (3) The blessing for redemption said as part of the Passover *haggadah* liturgy, immediately after the recitation of the first section of the *hallel* (H. 100).

Haʿarev naʾ (Makes [the words of Your Torah] sweet). A form of the *birkat hatorah*, now said as part of the *birkhot hashachar* (S. 13).

Haggadah. The home liturgy for the Passover-eve *seder*.

Hakafot. The custom of circumambulating the synagogue or part thereof; discussed here with respect to carrying the *lulav* and *ʾetrog* around the room on Sukkot while chanting *hoshaʿnot*.

Halakhah. Translated here as "law."

Hallel (praise). A generic term for psalms of praise, there being three different such sets in the liturgy: (1) *hallel shebekhol yom* (daily *hallel*), today Pss. 145–50 (S. 57–65); (2) *hallel hamitsri* (Egyptian *Hallel*) Pss. 113–18 (S. 565–73, H. 97, 114–20); (3) *hallel hagadol* (Great *Hallel*), today Ps. 136 (H. 124, S. 313–15).

Hallel hagadol (The Great *Hallel*). See *hallel*.

Hallel hamitsri (The Egyptian *Hallel*). See *hallel*.

Hallel shebekhol yom (The daily *hallel*). See *hallel*.

Hashkivenu (Cause us to lie down). The fourth and last of the blessings accompanying the evening recitation of the *shema'* (S. 197).

Hatov vehametiv (He who is good and does good). The fourth blessing of the *birkat hamazon*; see *birkat hamazon* (S. 765).

Hoda'ah (Thanksgiving). The penultimate blessing in the *tefillah*, its theme being thanksgiving (S. 91–93).

Hosha'na' (Save!). See *hosha'not*.

Hosha'not. A specialized form of *piyyut* calling for salvation, and recited on Sukkot; frequently carrying the refrain *hosha'na'* or *hoshi'ah na'*, patterned after Ps. 118:25 (S. 679 ff.).

Hoshi'ah na' (Save!). See *hosha'not*.

Hasi'enu (Bestow upon us). See *vehasi'enu*.

Kaddish (Sanctification). A prayer praising God and looking forward to the coming of His kingdom, appearing in our rite in several contexts: *kaddish yatom* (Mourners' *kaddish*) (S. 215); *kaddish shalem*, i.e., "full" *kaddish*, also known as the reader's *kaddish*, marking the end of a major division in the service (S. 133–35); *chatsi kaddish*, i.e., "half" *kaddish*, an abbreviated form of the "full" *kaddish* used also to mark a division between two rubrics (S. 69); and *kaddish derabbanan*, the "rabbis'" *kaddish*, today being a form of the mourners' *kaddish* which includes an extra paragraph on behalf of students of Torah, and recited, therefore, after liturgical paragraphs intended primarily for study (S. 45–47). There is also a lesser-known version of the *kaddish* called *kaddish le'itchadata'* recited primarily at the graveside after burial; it is the only form containing an actual reference to resurrection of the dead (S. 737–79).

Kayem (Establish). A generic term used in this book to characterize many different but related liturgical formulas pleading for salvation, and inserted in the *ge'ulah* of the Palestinian rite.

Kedushah (Sanctification). A generic term for either *kedushat hayom*, celebration of the sanctity of Sabbaths and holidays (see *kedushat hayom*), or *kedushat hashem*, celebrating the sanctity of God (see *kedushat hashem*). It also occurs in this book as a geonic description of the state entered into by the bond of betrothal (see *kiddushin*).

Kedushah desidra'. A form of the *kedushah* petitioning redemption and marked by an Aramaic paraphrase of the key biblical citations which constitute the *kedushat hashem* (S. 131, 439). See *kedushat hashem*.

Kedushat hashem (Sanctification of the name [of God]). A stylized prayer occurring in several forms, praising God's sanctity; marked by the inclusion of Isaiah 6:3, "Holy, holy, holy...." It is found in the *yotser* (*kedushah deyotser*, S. 73); as the third benediction to every *tefillah* (S.

83), where, however, only the reader's repetition contains the full allusion to Isaiah's vision; and in a unique context requesting the messianic coming, known as *kedushah desidra*' (S. 131, 439).

Kedushat hayom (Sanctification of the day). Prayer proclaiming the sanctity of a Sabbath or holiday, occurring in several places and forms; but primarily as the fourth of the seven blessings which comprise the Sabbath or holiday *tefillah* (S. 353). See also *kiddush*.

Kiddush (Sanctification). Prayer declaring the sanctity of Sabbaths and holidays, *kiddush* standing for *kiddush hayom*, "sanctification of the day." When the word *kiddush* is used alone, it usually refers to *kiddush 'al hakos*, the *kiddush* that is said with wine. Customarily a home prayer inaugurating the evening of the day in question, it is also said in synagogue (S. 277–597).

Kiddusha' rabbah (Great *kiddush*). The morning recitation of a *kiddush 'al hakos* (with wine—see *kiddush*) on Sabbaths and holidays. *Rabbah*, "great," is actually a misnomer taken from the Talmud (*Pes.* 106a), in that the evening recitation is far better known and, liturgically, of more significance (S. 423).

Kiddushin (lit. sanctification). Act by which a man and a woman are legally sanctified to each other; thus, the first stage in marriage, translated loosely as "betrothal"; marked by the ceremony of *'erusin* (S. 753).

Kol nidre (All vows). Yom Kippur prayer requesting the divine annulment of certain vows (M. 489).

Korbanot (Sacrifices). Scriptural verses describing the sacrifices mandated for Sabbaths and holidays; though sacrifice itself ceased after the destruction of the Temple, the recollection thereof was maintained in the liturgy by relevant biblical instructions inserted, particularly, in the *musaf tefillah* (S. 395, 397).

Magen 'avot (Shield of the forefathers). A prayer following the Sabbath evening *tefillah* and comprising synopses of the themes of all of that *tefillah*'s blessings (S. 273–75).

Mayim 'acharonim (lit. last water). The practice of washing one's hands after eating.

Megillah (Scroll). Five books of the Bible are known as scrolls (*megillot*) and read on specified holidays. The only one discussed here is *megillat Esther*, the Book of Esther, read on Purim.

Minchah. The afternoon service, usually said late in the afternoon, immediately before evening, and thus along with the *'arvit* service.

Minhag. Custom

Minyan. Congregational quorum; the minimum presence necessary for certain prayers.

Mitechillah (At first [our ancestors were idolaters]). The second of two introductions to the Passover *haggadah*'s central midrashic account of Israel's Egyptian bondage and deliverance, identifying the primeval idolatry of the generations before Abraham as the nadir of Israel's history (H. 74).

Mitsvah. Commandment

Musaf. The additional service for Sabbaths and holidays, said immediately after the morning service (S. 391 ff.).

Ne'ilah. The concluding service, unique to Yom Kippur but originally customary for all fast days.

Nishmat kol chai (Every living soul [shall praise you]). A form of *birkat hashir.* See *birkat hashir.*

Nissu'in. The second part of the marriage ceremony (S. 753–55).

'Or chadash (May a new light [shine on Zion . . .]). An insertion near the end of the *yotser,* pleading for the light of Jerusalem rebuilt, in messianic days (S. 73).

'Over lifnei hatevah (Pass before the ark). A technical term used in ancient times to refer to the person who repeats the *tefillah;* see also *sheliach tsibbur.*

Payyetan (Poet). Liturgically, an author of certain poetry, *piyyutim,* inserted in the liturgy. See *piyyut.*

Pesukei dezimrah (Verses of song). An extended rubric composed of a lengthy series of loosely related prayers, their general theme being the praise of God. It precedes the official call to congregational prayer (S. 51–69).

Pidyon haben (Redemption of the [first-born] son). Ritual marking the redemption of first-born male children (S. 749–51).

Piyyut (Poem). Liturgical poetry, stylized according to various rules dependent on the time and place of the *piyyut's* origin and the liturgical function of the poem itself; not generally considered part of the statutory prayers demanded by tannaitic or amoraic legislation.

Pores 'al shema' (Lead the *shema'*). A technical term, dating from ancient times, referring to the person who leads the *shema'* and its benedictions.

Pores sukkat shalom 'alenu (. . . who spreads a tabernacle of peace over us). The altered conclusion of the eulogy for *hashkivenu* on Sabbaths and holidays (S. 263).

Seder (lit. order). (1) The ritual accompanied by the recitation of the Passover-eve home liturgy, the *haggadah.* (2) Any order of prayers, and hence a prayer book. Though the term *siddur* is generally preferred for this usage, the first prayer book known to us is *Seder Rav Amram,* the *seder,* or order of prayers, set down by Rav Amram Gaon (9th cent.).

Selach lanu (Pardon us). The opening words, and thus a geonic title, for the sixth benediction of the daily *tefillah;* known also as *selichah,* or "Pardon" (S. 85).

Selichot. Specialized *piyyutim* on the theme of pardon, intended particularly for Yom Kippur and the general period of time in which Rosh Hashanah and Yom Kippur fall, and for fast days generally.

Shacharit. The morning service.

Shalom rav (Great peace). The version of *birkat shalom* used in the evening and, if it is not a fast day, in the afternoon. See *birkat shalom.*

Sheliach tsibbur (Agent of the congregation). The prayer leader generally; more accurately, that individual who repeats the *tefillah* on behalf of those who cannot say it themselves. Thus, customarily, the *tefillah* is recited silently and then repeated aloud by the *sheliach tsibbur,* so that the unlettered may simply listen and say *'amen* to each benediction.

Shelosh regalim (Three pilgrimage festivals). Sukkot (Booths), Passover, Shavuʿot (Weeks).

Shemaʿ (Hear [O Israel]). Three biblical sections (Deut. 6:4–9, 11:13–21; Num. 15:37–41) said morning and evening (S. 75–77, 193–95), and accompanied by two introductory blessings and one concluding blessing (two in the evening). Parts of the *shemaʿ,* especially the first line itself, are now also found scattered throughout the prayer book in various contexts.

Shirat hayam (Song of the sea). Exodus 15:1–18, part of the *pesukei dezimrah* (S. 67–69).

Shofar. The ram's horn, blown primarily on Rosh Hashanah.

Shomer ʿamo yisraʾel laʿad (. . . who guards His people Israel forever). The daily eulogy to *hashkivenu,* altered on Sabbaths and holidays to read, *hapores sukkat shalom ʿalenu . . . ,* "who spreads a tabernacle of peace over us . . ." (S. 197).

Siddur (Order). An order of prayers, and thus a prayer book.

Sim shalom (Grant peace). The version of *birkat shalom* used in the morning and, if it is a fast day, in the afternoon. See *birkat shalom.*

Sukkah (Booth). The booth erected as a temporary dwelling during the festival of Sukkot.

Tanchumei ʾavelim (Comforting of mourners). An ancient practice associated with mourning, no longer extant.

Tefillah (Prayer). Though a generic term for prayer generally, the word is more accurately reserved for *hatefillah,* "The Prayer," a series of benedictions recited in each service. Our rite knows of nineteen on weekdays, of which the middle thirteen are removed on Sabbaths and holidays. In their place the *kedushat hayom* (see *kedushat hayom*) is said. Known also as *ʿamidah* ([the prayer said while] standing) and *shemoneh ʿesrei,* the eighteen benedictions, a mishnaic term referring to the standard Palestinian rite, wherein the *tefillah* has eighteen, not nineteen, benedictions (S. 81–95, 349–59).

Tekiyot. Specialized *piyyutim* which accompany the blowing of the *shofar* on Rosh Hashanah.

Vehasi'enu (Bestow upon us). The final section of the holiday *kedushat hayom* requesting the blessings of life, peace, and joy associated with holidays (S. 591–93).

Vehu' rachum (He is merciful). Biblical verse (Ps. 78:38) preceding the formal congregational call to prayer in the evening service (S. 191).

Veshameru ([The children of Israel] shall keep [the Sabbath]). Biblical recitation (Exod. 31:16–17) following the Sabbath eve *hashkivenu* (S. 263).

Vidui (Confession). Referring primarily to Yom Kippur liturgy. Today's liturgy contains both a long form (*vidui rabbah*, M. 551) and a short form (*vidui zuta'*, M. 547).

Ya'aleh veyavo' ([May the remembrance of us . . .] ascend and come). Part of the holiday *kedushat hayom* requesting God's remembrance of us and our merit, and consequently His granting deliverance to us (S. 591); found also inserted in the *birkat hamazon* (S. 765).

Yamim nora'im (Days of awe). Rosh Hashanah and Yom Kippur.

Yehallelukha ([All Your works] praise You). A form of the *birkat hashir*. See *birkat hashir*.

Yehei shemeih rabba' (May His great name be praised). The congregational response to the *kaddish* (S. 49).

Yir'u 'eineinu (May our eyes behold [the coming of the Kingdom]). An extension to the *hashkivenu*, following *barukh 'adonai le'olam*; omitted on Sabbaths and holidays (S. 199).

Yishtabach (May [Your name] be praised). A form of *birkat hashir*. See *birkat hashir*.

Yotser (Creator). The first of the benedictions accompanying the *shema'*, affirming divine creation (S. 71–73).

Zemirot (Songs). A general term for liturgical songs, but used here as a synonym for those songs which constitute the *pesukei dezimrah*. See *pesukei dezimrah*.

Zikhronot (Remembrance). The *kedushat hayom*, or fourth benediction, of the *musaf tefillah* for Rosh Hashanah is divided into three parallel parts, each devoted to a different theme. *Zikhronot*, or remembrance, is the second of the three (M. 385–89).

Zimun (Invitation). The invitation to join in the Grace after meals (S. 759).

Abbreviations

The following abbreviations for the names of journals are used in the Notes and in the Bibliography.

AAJR   *Proceedings of the American Academy for Jewish Research*
HTR   *Harvard Theological Review*
HUCA   *Hebrew Union College Annual*
JJS   *Journal of Jewish Studies*
JQR   *Jewish Quarterly Review*
MGWJ   *Monatsschrift für Geschichte und Wissenschaft des Judentums*
REJ   *Revue des Études Juives*

Notes

INTRODUCTION

1. On the *Wissenschaft* generally, see: Fritz Bamberger, "Zunz's Conception of History," *AAJR* 11 (1941): 1–25; Luitpold Wallach, "The Beginnings of the Science of Judaism in the Nineteenth Century," *Historica Judaica* 8, no. 1 (1946): 33–60; Michael A. Meyer, *The Origins of the Modern Jew* (Detroit, 1967), pp. 144–82; and idem, "Jewish Religious Reform and *Wissenschaft des Judentums*: The Positions of Zunz, Geiger and Frankel," *Leo Baeck Institute Yearbook* 16 (1971): 19–41.

2. Leopold Zunz, *Die Ritus des synagogalen Gottesdienstes* (Berlin, 1859).

3. At various points he mentions as factors: geographic isolation, cultural diffusion, the tendency to take the personal practices of revered rabbis as models, internal censorship by Jews in reaction to the non-Jewish community, scribal errors, and (after the sixteenth century) mistakes perpetuated on a large scale by ignorant printers.

4. The classic example is Zunz himself (*Haderashot Beyisra'el*, trans. Chanokh Albeck, p. 179), who unhesitatingly posits the original form of the benedictions accompanying the *shema'*.

5. Joseph Heinemann, *Hatefillah Bitekufat Hatannaim Veha'amoraim* (Jerusalem, 1966), p. 104, n. 12.

6. *Webster's Third New International Dictionary*, s.v. "canonization."

1: THE PASSOVER *HAGGADAH*

1. For Saadiah's life, see Henry Malter, *Saadiah Gaon* (1926; reprint ed., New York, 1969); and Ellis Rivkin, "The Saadiah–David ben Zakkai Controversy: A Structural Analysis," in *Studies and Essays in Honor of Abraham A. Neuman*, ed. Meir ben-Horin, Bernard D. Weinryb, and Solomon Zeitlin (Philadelphia, 1962), pp. 388–423.

2. See the introduction by Simchah Assaf in *Siddur Rav Saadiah Gaon*, ed. Simchah Assaf, Israel Davidson, and Issachar Joel, 2d ed. (Jerusalem, 1963), pp. 9–17 (hereafter cited as *SS*). For an English synopsis, see Ismar Elbogen, "Saadiah's Siddur," in *Saadiah Anniversary Volume of the American Academy for Jewish Research*, ed. B. Cohen (New York, 1943), pp. 247–63.

3. See, especially, Naphtali Wieder, "Fourteen New Genizah Fragments of Saadiah's Siddur Together With a Reproduction of a Missing Part," in *Saadya Studies*, ed. E. I. J. Rosenthal (Manchester, 1943).

4. *SS*, p. 11.

5. See Joseph Heinemann, "Yachaso Shel Rav Saadiah Gaon Leshinui Matbe'a Tefillah," *Bar Ilan Yearbook* 6 (1963): 220–33.

6. Ibid., p. 221.

7. Ibid.

8. Ibid., p. 222.

9. Petitions for the restoration of Zion in the *kedushat hayom* of the *musaf tefillah* were clearly beyond the original intent of the blessing, but they were too popular to be omitted. Similarly, Saadiah could not dispense with such well-established benedictions as *barukh she'amar* and *yishtabach* even though they may have been post-talmudic.

10. *SS*, p. 141. The structural distinction between long and short blessings is tannaitic. See M. *Ber.* 1:4.

11. The various translations are discussed in Naphtali Wieder, "Birkat Yein 'Asis," *Sinai* 20 (1947): 44–45. Cf. Heinemann, "Yachaso shel Saadiah," p. 221; Daniel Goldschmidt, *Haggadah Shel Pesach Vetoldeteha* (Jerusalem, 1960), p. 90.

12. For an analysis of the nature of Pumbedita and Sura in the Sassanian period, see David M. Goodblatt, *Rabbinic Instruction in Sasanian Babylonia* (Leiden, 1975).

13. Benjamin Manasseh Lewin, ed., *Otsar Hageonim* (Jerusalem, 1928–42), vol. 3, *Pes.* #278 (hereafter cited as OG).

14. Ibid., #279.

15. *Sefer Ha'ittim*, ed. Jacob Schor (Cracow, 1903), pp. 288–89.

16. Louis Ginzberg, ed., *Ginzei Schechter*, vol. 2 (1929; reprint ed., New York, 1969), p. 510; Lewin, OG, vol. 3, *Pes.*, p. 107, n. 8.

17. Ginzberg, *Ginzei Schechter*, vol. 2, p. 510.

18. Wieder, "Yein 'Asis," p. 46. See *Pes.* 106a for the incident of Rav Ashi; and Philip Birnbaum, ed., *Hasiddur Hashalem* (New York, 1949), p. 423, for the *kiddusha' rabbah* in today's ritual.

19. See discussion by Wieder, "Yein 'Asis," p. 46.

20. *Siddur Hatefillot Keminhag Hakara'im* (Eupatoria, 1836), p. 4b. The Karaite parallel cited by Wieder ("Yein 'Asis," p. 48) differs somewhat, but not significantly. A full text of the Rabbanite *yein 'asis* blessing is also given by him (p. 58) but is too long to reproduce here. It parallels the Karaite version in its general theme and some of its wording. It too draws on Ps. 104:15, and reads *umesameiach lev umatzhil panim*.

21. *Seder Rav Amram Gaon*, ed. Daniel Goldschmidt (Jerusalem, 1971), pp. 111–12 (hereafter cited as SRA). The liturgical rubrics referred to are: (1) the *kiddush* (see the *Birnbaum Haggadah*, ed. Philip Birnbaum [New York, 1967], pp. 54–57); (2) two interpretations of the concept of Israel's degradation, or *genut*, generally attributed to the third-century amoraim Rav and Samuel (*Birnbaum Haggadah*, pp. 64, 74), on which, see discussion and sources listed in Eugene Mihaly, "The Passover Haggadah as PaRaDiSe," *CCAR Journal* 13, no. 5 (April 1966): 3–27, and Menachem M. Kasher, *Haggadah Shelemah* (Jerusalem, 1960), pp. 21–30; (3) the paragraph introducing the *midrash* to Deut. 26:5 (*Birnbaum Haggadah*, p. 74); (4) the Deuteronomy passage itself and its midrashic embellishment (*Birnbaum Haggadah*, p. 76–84); (5) the interpretation of the Passover symbols attributed to Rabban Gamaliel (*Birnbaum Haggadah*, pp. 92–94); (6) the *birkat ge'ulah*, or Blessing of Redemption, from M. *Pes.* 10:6 (*Birnbaum Haggadah*, p. 100); (7) and the Egyptian *hallel*, Pss. 113–18 (*Birnbaum Haggadah*, pp. 96, 114–20).

22. On Elazar Alluf, see Arthur J. Zuckerman, *A Jewish Princedom in Feudal France: 768–900* (New York, 1972), p. 284.

23. See, for example, Israel Abrahams, "Some Egyptian Fragments of the Passover Haggadah," *JQR*, o.s. 10 (1898): 42; Goldschmidt, *Haggadah*, p. 74.

24. For a description of the find and its significance, see, particularly, S. D. Goitein, *A Mediterranean Society*, vol. 1 (Berkeley and Los Angeles, 1967), pp. 1–28.

25. See, for example, Louis Finkelstein, "The Development of the Amidah," in *Contributions to the Scientific Study of Jewish Liturgy*, ed. Jakob Petuchowski (New York, 1970), pp. 91–177.

26. Heinemann, *Hatefillah*, p. 82.

27. Abrahams, "Egyptian Fragments."

28. Ibid., p. 42.

29. See Joseph Heinemann, "One Benediction Comprising Seven," *REJ* 125 (1966): 110.

30. Abrahams, "Egyptian Fragments," p. 49; Goldschmidt, *Haggadah*, p. 78.

31. Abrahams, "Egyptian Fragments," p. 51.

32. For a discussion of the development of the Four Questions in Palestine and Babylonia, see Solomon Zeitlin, "The Liturgy of the First Night of Passover," *JQR*, n.s. 38 (1947–48): 437 ff. For citation of relevant sources, see Kasher, *Haggadah Shelemah*, pp. 112–17. For today's ritual, see *Birnbaum Haggadah*, p. 60.

33. Goldschmidt, *Haggadah*, p. 79.

34. Ibid., p. 75. It accompanies yet another elaboration of the *kiddush*, a section affirming, *ki vo ʿasah ʾadonai ʾeloheinu nissim*, "for the Lord our God wrought miracles for us on it [that day]." Typical of the Palestinian variety, this latter elaboration occurs in other fragments but without the *ʾasher kiddesh* addition, whereas the text known to Natronai contained the latter but not the former.

35. Ibid., p. 74.

36. *Tur, O.H.* #181; cf. citation from *Shibbolei Haleket* in Lewin, *OG*, vol. 1, *Ber.* #347; and Rabbenu Yonah to Alfasi, *Ber.* 44b, s.v. *uleʿinyan*.

37. *Sefer Halakhot Gedolot*, ed Azriel Hildesheimer (Jerusalem, 1972).

38. Louis Ginzberg, *Geonica*, vol. 1 (1909; reprint ed., New York, 1970), p. 104.

39. Simchah Assaf, *Tekufat Hageonim Vesifrutah* (Jerusalem, 1955), p. 169.

40. *Halakhot Gedolot*, Introduction, p. 21.

41. Ibid., p. 124.

42. *Shibbolei Haleket Hashalem*, ed. Solomon Buber (Jerusalem, 1962), p. 116.

43. Ginzberg, *Geonica*, vol. 2, p. 114.

44. *SRA*, p. 118.

45. Abrahams, "Egyptian Fragments," p. 47.

46. We have reserved some debates on the *haggadah*, too, for subsequent chapters, e.g., the question of saying a blessing over each and every cup of wine, the fifth cup, and the Great *Hallel*, or *hallel hagadol*.

2: DAILY LITURGY: THE *SHEMAʿ* AND ITS BLESSINGS

1. For today's rite, see Birnbaum, *Siddur*, pp. 71–81.

2. See the discussion by Elbogen, *Der jüdische Gottesdienst in seiner geschichtlichen Entwicklung* (Berlin, 1913), p. 25.

3. *Meg.* 17b.

4. See the summary statement by Heinemann, for example; *Hatefillah Beyisraʾel*, trans. Joseph Heinemann (Tel Aviv, 1972), p. 31.

5. For today's rite, see Birnbaum, *Siddur*, p. 73.

6. In fact, this extension of the *yotser* was only one of many. It had long been a favorite prayer for thematic elaboration, in part because of the motif of light contained

within it. Thus, the Merkavah mystics expanded it at length, taking light to refer to the created heavenly luminaries newly personified as angels, surrounding the heavenly throne and glorifying their creator. On light as a common religious symbol in the first century, see Irwin Goodenough, *By Light Light* (New Haven, 1935). On the Merkavah mystics, specifically, see discussion below, chap. 3.

7. *SRA*, p. 13.

8. Ibid. The same opinion is recorded of Saadiah in *Shibbolei Haleket*. See Lewin, *OG*, vol. 1, *Ber.* #65.

9. Lewin, *OG*, vol. 1, *Ber.* #65.

10. *Rokeach Hagadol* (Poland, 1806), *Hilkhot Berakhot*, end of #319.

11. Lewin, *OG*, vol. 1, *Ber.* #29.

12. Samuel Rosenblatt, ed., *Saadiah Gaon: "The Book of Beliefs and Opinions"* (New Haven, 1948), p. 310. It should be noted that Eleazer ben Nathan used the same biblical verse, but referred it to the light hidden away, the *'or ganuz*. He may simply have misunderstood Saadiah, but I think it likely that he deliberately changed the referrent to a light created in the past. According to Solomon ben Samson, an older contemporary of Eleazer's, and a leader in the same academy, "There are many people who do not want to say, 'May a new light shine upon Zion.' . . . They maintain that they should not say a blessing now over a light that will exist in Zion in the future." Against this view, Solomon argues that the distinction between past and future is irrelevant in blessings of deliverance. Perhaps his argument, which depended upon a creative interpretation of existing liturgical eulogies dealing with salvation, was not entirely successful, so Eleazer changed the reference to a different light completely. Though still eschatological, it was not the future light of God's presence, but the light stored away for the righteous, and in existence from the time of creation. See *Siddur of R. Solomon ben Samson of Garmaise*, ed. Moshe Hershler (Jerusalem, 1971), p. 98.

13. Ismar Elbogen, *Studien zur Geschichte des jüdischen Gottesdienstes* (Berlin, 1907), p. 23 ff.

14. "Elbogen's statement that Saadiah's attitude was in defense of the Palestinian rite should be modified, since our Palestinian texts show themselves different on this point" (Mann, "Genizah Fragments," p. 401).

15. Naphtali Wieder, "Fourteen New Genizah Fragments of Saadya's Siddur," in *Saadya Studies*, ed. E. I. J. Rosenthal (Manchester, 1943), p. 255.

16. Ibid., p. 260. The other controversies to which Wieder alludes are: (1) the inclusion of petitions for deliverance in *birkat shanim*, the ninth benediction of the *tefillah*; (2) a petition for future redemption in *'al hanissim*, this being a standard addition to the eighteenth benediction of the *tefillah*, intended for Purim and Chanukah, and meant to offer thanksgiving for the deliverance marked by these holidays; and (3) the fact that Saadiah, a native Palestinian, preferred the Babylonian eulogy, *ga'al yisra'el*, "who has saved Israel," rather than the parallel Palestinian one, *tsur yisra'el vego'ala*, "Rock of Israel and its savior," for the eulogy of the *ge'ulah* benediction. This implies that Saadiah knew the blessing to be about past redemption (Egypt), not future, and preferred a eulogy in the past tense. Yet the *kayem* formula is for the future and can be found in the same *ge'ulah* benediction. Thus Wieder has recourse to the technical distinction between the body of a blessing and its eulogy, or *chatimah*, arguing that only in the eulogy was Saadiah concerned about tense; otherwise he was content with making sure potential additions were on the same subject matter.

17. Joseph Heinemann, "Yachaso shel Saadiah," p. 221.

18. Cf. Mann, "Genizah Fragments," p. 433; Israel Levi, "Fragments de Rituels de Prières," *REJ* 54 (1907): 241; see also Mann, "Genizah Fragments," pp. 400–401,

where the dependence of *'or chadash* on Isaiah 40:1 is recognized; and Ginzberg, *Geonica*, vol. 1, pp. 127–28, where the same relationship is pointed out.

19. For discussions of the textual recension, see: Alexander Marx, "Untersuchungen zum Siddur des Gaon R. Amram," *Jahrbuch der Jüdisch-Literarischen Gesellschaft* 5 (1907): 341–66; Louis Ginzberg, *Geonica*, vol. 1, pp. 126–54; Daniel Goldschmidt, ed., *Seder Rav Amram Gaon*, pp. 11–22; and the summary, in English, of the manuscript research in David Hedegard, ed., *Seder R. Amram Gaon* (Lund, 1951), pp. xxi–xxiii.

20. See the discussion and sources listed by Goldschmidt, *SRA*, p. 13, note to line 19.

21. Cf. *Abudarham Hashalem*, ed. Solomon Wertheimer, p. 75; Baer, *Seder 'Avodat Yisra'el*, p. 79, s.v. *'or chadash*; and Daniel Goldschmidt, "Seder Hatefillah Shel Harambam 'al pi Ketav yad Oxford," p. 92; idem, "'Al Defus Kadum shel Machzor Sefardi," p. 712.

22. On the identification of this group as predominently Karaitic or, at least, proto-Karaitic, see Raphael Mahler, *Karaimer* (New York, 1947), and, more recently, Moshe Zucker, "Teguvot Litenu'at 'Avelei Tsiyon Hakara'im Besifrut Harabbanit," in *Sefer Hayovel Lerabbi Chanokh Albeck.* Cf. chap. 9, n. 47, below.

23. See chap. 10, pp. 152.

24. *Ber.* 11b.

25. *Teshuvot Hageonim*, ed. Jacob Musafiya (Lyck, 1864), #45.

26. Lewin, *OG*, vol. 1, *Ber.* #52.

27. Rashi's text read *lamdeni chukekha*. See discussion in chap. 10, pp. 153.

28. Cf. Lewin, *OG*, vol. 1, p. 28, n. 2; and idem, *Ginzei Kedem* 3 (1915): 44, n. 3.

29. The term is first cited in the Talmud itself (*Meg.* 29a, for example) and recurs frequently in geonic literature. Mann discusses the matter thoroughly in his *Texts and Studies*, vol. 1 (Cincinnati, 1931), p. 69, n. 16. It has been variously described as the synagogue of the exilarch, the academy of Nehardea, the ancient synagogue of Rav, the academy of Baghdad, and other institutions as well. See also David M. Goodblatt, *Rabbinic Instruction in Sasanian Babylonia* (Leiden, 1975), pp. 118–19.

30. Sherira's evidence in (E) would seem to disqualify both Tsemach bar Kafnai (936–938) and Tsemach bar Isaac (988–997) from consideration, since they lived close enough to Sherira (968–998) for him to have known about them, and whereas he does argue against Sar Shalom, he seems to be completely unaware of any adverse precedent set by Tsemach.

31. Cf. *Abudarham Hashalem*, ed. Solomon Wertheimer (Jerusalem, 1963), p. 75; *Shibbolei Haleket*, p. 13; Lewin, *OG*, vol. 1, *Ber.* #53.

32. As with the case of Tsemach, we would have to omit Kohen Tsedek bar Joseph (926–936) from consideration on the grounds that he lived too close in time to Sherira and was a Pumbeditan besides. See above, note 30, and below, responsum (E), where Sherira absolutely denies the practice for Pumbedita.

33. Lewin, *OG*, vol. 1, *Ber.* #54.

34. Adolph Büchler, "La Ketouba chez les Juifs du Nord de l'Afrique," *REJ* 50 (1905); 177–81.

35. *SS*, pp. 13–14.

36. See Birnbaum, *Siddur*, p. 75.

37. Elbogen, *Studien*, p. 27, n. 2. In fact, Elbogen does not stipulate precisely which form he considers Palestinian and which Babylonian. Both here and in his *Gottesdienst* (pp. 20–21), he says simply that there is a geographical difference. Presumably, since six of his eight manuscripts had *'ahavat 'olam*, he meant that to be the

Palestinian form. This is how Mann understood Elbogen's position (Mann, "Genizah Fragments," p. 401).·

38. *Ber.* 24b.

39. *Ber.* 64a; *M.K.* 25a; *'Iggeret Rav Sherira Gaon,* ed. Aaron Hyman (Jerusalem, 1967), pp. 70–71.

40. "Advanced rabbinic education in Babylonia was organized in disciple circles or apprentice groups rather than in (law) schools in the modern sense" (Goodblatt, *Rabbinic Instruction,* p. 280).

41. *SS,* pp. 13–14.

42. See, for example, Lewin, *OG,* vol. 13, *B.M.* pt. 2, #45.

43. *Abudarham,* p. 75.

44. For the present rite, see Birnbaum, *Siddur,* p. 77.

45. *Ber.* 14a–b.

46. Lewin, *OG,* vol. 1, pt. 2, *Ber.* #61.

47. The *shema'* as said in the Ashkenazic ritual is also outfitted with three preliminary words *'el melekh ne'eman* ("Lord, faithful King"). These words are to be said only by worshippers praying in solitude. Tradition ascribes the addition to numerology, the reasoning being that the *shema'* contains 245 words. In the congregational setting, the precentor repeats the last two words of the *shema'* plus the first word, "True," of the next blessing. He thus says 248 words in all, this sum being equal to the number of positive commandments in the Torah, and, incidentally, the number of bodily parts assumed to comprise a human being. Of course this is very late, post facto reasoning. As Elbogen points out, we have here an interesting development of folk ritual. Originally, every individual recited his *shema'* along with the next word, following Rabbi Judah's desire to emulate Jeremiah 10:10. It became customary for the reader to repeat three words, and these, together with the 245 of the *shema',* added up to 248. When the numerical significance of this became known to certain unspecified "mystics," they fell on the fact that without the reader's repetition the words recited would number but 245; so they conceived of the strategy of adding three words more for the individual. These were placed at the beginning of the *shema',* so that the individual praying alone would himself now recite the requisite total of words (Elbogen, *Gottesdienst,* pp. 21–22). We might surmise that the "mystics" who worried most about the practice were the *chassidei ashkenaz* and their precursors in Italy, since the custom is only true for Ashkenazic lands, and we know that the early Jewish communities in the Rhineland fostered an intense interest in numerology. See Israel Ta-Shema, "'El Melekh Ne'eman; Gilgulo Shel Minhag," *Tarbits* 39 (1969/70): 185–94. Yet Hai was aware of the numerological concern, at least insofar as repeating the last words was concerned. That such motivation had nothing to do with the original practice of joining the first word of the *ge'ulah* to the individual recitation of the *shema'* can be proved from the fact that even the Palestinians did it, and they did not include the last paragraph of the *shema'* at all in the evening. Yet even then, according to the same *Babli* source, they were careful to add the word, though, of course, without the last paragraph being recited, the total number was nowhere near 248. As for the choice of the three introductory words, *'el melekh ne'eman,* Elbogen surmises they are dictated by the *Babli*'s decision that *'amen* stands for those three words, each letter of *'amen* being the first letter of one of the three words in question. It would seem, then, that after the *Babli*'s identification of *'amen* as *'el melekh ne'eman,* the "mystics," in search of three appropriate words, chose these three. Their choice was hastened by the fact, says Elbogen, that some ancient rituals had the word *'amen* itself immediately before the *shema'.* As we shall see (chap. 10), the practice of concluding a blessing with *'amen* is an ancient Palestinian custom, and a blessing before the *shema'* (*birkat hatorah*) other

than the ones we have looked at so far did indeed conclude this way. To the extent that German congregations had before them these early Palestinian alternative *birkhot hatorah*, including the one with *'amen* at the end, they might indeed have drawn on the *Babli* identification of *'amen* with *'el melekh ne'eman*, and transmuted the simple *'amen* into three different words, which together with the 245 of the *shema'* made up the required 248. In passing, it might be noted that a number count of the words in the *shema'* arrives at 245 only without the word "True" from the next blessing. Thus the mystics must have lived at a time when the original purpose of the whole custom was forgotten and the custom itself was not followed. Had the individual worshipper actually read the *shema'* plus the extra word plus *'el melekh ne'eman*, he would have said 249 words, not 248. The number of synonyms, incidently, for "True" in the opening lines of the *ge'ulah* is fifteen, equal to the number of words in the original proof-text of Jeremiah 10:10. So although the original practice of including the first one in the individual recitation of the *shema'* must have vanished, the biblical basis for it did not. It survived in another form. See *Siddur* of Rabbi Solomon ben Samson, pp. 95–96.

48. See for example, *Siddur Rashi*, ed. Solomon Buber (1911; reprint ed. Jerusalem, 1963), p. 16; and *Abudarham*, p. 87.

49. *Sefer Ha'eshkol*, ed. B. H. Auerbach, *Hilkhot Tefillah Ukeriyat Shema'*, p. 9.

50. Ginzberg, *Geonica*, vol. 2, p. 91. Cf. Ginzberg, *Ginzei Schechter*, vol. 2, p. 515, where he identifies this gaon as a Suran on the grounds that the responsum contains a reference to *bet rabbenu*, an institution which Ginzberg thinks is mentioned only by Surans. On the other hand, as we have already noted, *bet rabbenu* will not be used here as the basis for determining a given responsum's provenance since its identification is by no means a matter of scholarly consensus. See above, n. 29.

We have yet to examine the role of the *piyyutim*, liturgical poetical expansions dating at least as far back as the fifth century, and owing their provenance, to a large extent, to similar activity in the Byzantine world. The latest general scholarly survey of the *piyyut* in all its historical development is Ezra Fleischer, *Shirat Hakodesh Ha'ivrit bimei Habenayim* (Jerusalem, 1975). See also Joseph Heinemann with Jakob J. Petuchowski, *Literature of the Synagogue* (New York, 1975), especially, for our context, sec. 3 by Petuchowski, "The Poetry of the Synagogue." pp. 203–83. It was customary to insert poetical embellishments in blessings, ending these additions just before the final lines of the blessing in question. Thus our geonic author cites the latter section of the *ge'ulah*, "May the Lord reign forever and ever," as the only part that he says, meaning that he does not insert poetical expansions before it.

51. See above, p. 27–28, and n. 17.

52. See Mann, "Genizah Fragments," pp. 413, 431. Text 7, for example, reads, "May the Lord our God establish His glory and His might and His greatness, and His holiness, and the holiness of His great name, and may He bring us complete redemption after which there is no enslavement." And text 11 reads, "May the Lord establish for us His might and His greatness and His glory and His holiness and the holiness of His great name. He is the Lord our God. May He act graciously, compassionately, and mercifully towards us, relieving us from our troubles, and may He bring complete redemption, and may He rule over us quickly, forever. Blessed art Thou, O Lord, who redeemed Israel. Amen." The latter text ends with the typically Babylonian eulogy *ga'al yisra'el*, "who redeemed Israel," rather than the Palestinian equivalent, *tsur yisra'el vego'alo*, "Rock of Israel and its Redeemer." On the other hand, the inclusion of *'amen* after it indicates Palestinian influence (see *Babli, Ber.* 45b, and Mann, "Genizah Fragments," p. 372). This, then, is from a mixed rite influenced by both major centers. Cf. Israel Levi, "Fragments de Rituels de Prières," *REJ* 53 (1907):

236–67, for other variations. Levi's fragment also displays the Babylonian *ga'al yis-ra'el*, and a Babylonian form of the *tefillah* on the verso. It probably originated in a Babylonian-oriented congregation in Palestine whose members constituted recent immigrants there. According to one witness, Ben Baboi, such immigrants maintained their own congregations and adhered scrupulously to the customs of their homeland (see Ginzberg, *Ginzei Schechter*, vol. 2, p. 556). But in the course of time they would naturally have been influenced by their environment to accept certain local forms. Hence the incorporation of a Palestinian *kayem* formula here.

53. Cf. Levi, "Fragments de Rituels," p. 236; Ginzberg, *Ginzei Schechter*, vol. 2, pp. 515–16.

54. *SRA*, p. 20.

55. On the basis of the formulae known to us, compared with other similar strings of like adjectives or nouns, it seems to me that we are dealing here with a literary genre in which the specific content of each individual word had lost any particular semantic meaning. They all become synonymous expressions for the experience of redemption, symbolized by the establishment of the Kingdom, God's power, glory, might, etc. They are Palestinian, possibly ancient, allied with tannaitic prayers which formed paradigms for later forms of the *kedushah*. The *kedushah*, too, is a complex of ideas like kingship, glory, might, etc., as can be seen most clearly in the *kedushah* that has been inserted into the *yotser* (see Birnbaum, *Siddur*, pp. 71–73). There is some connection here with the activity of the *merkavah*, or throne, mystics, about whom we shall speak later.

56. *SS*, pp. 13–14.

57. See the discussion by Wieder, above, p. 28.

58. *SS*, p. 110.

59. Ginzberg (*Ginzei Schechter*, vol. 2, p. 515) holds that the verb read originally in the perfect, and that it was this verbal form that Amram knew. Amram's objection, therefore, could have had nothing to do with the notion of inserting petitions for the future in a blessing intended for the past. Rather, says Ginzberg, Amram was opposed to a change in the text of the blessing itself (*nusach haberakhah 'atsmah*). For a refutation of this position and references to manuscripts of Saadiah's *Siddur*, see Wieder, "Fourteen Saadya Manuscripts," pp. 250–51, especially p. 251, n. 2. Ginzberg also maintained that Saadiah was opposed to *biglal 'avot*, but, of course, he was unaware of Wieder's later discovery of manuscripts indicating that in benedictions about deliverance, Saadiah had no objections to insertions on the same theme. Ginzberg relied on a discussion in the thirteenth-century European compendium *Orchot Chayim*, section *Keriyat Sefer Torah*, end of subsection 58, where we are, in fact, told that Saadiah opposed *biglal 'avot*. The issue there, however, is not the same at all. There the discussion has absolutely nothing to do with a *ge'ulah* insertion, but a benediction of thanks to be said after the conclusion of the reading of the prophetic section, or *Haftarah*, on Sabbath morning. Saadiah is said to have opposed an insertion which was not talmudically warranted, and Amram is said to have included it. *SRA* as we have it, however, displays the blessing in only one manuscript, so it is hard, if not impossible, to know what exactly Amram thought of the blessing. As for Saadiah, even if he did oppose it, this says nothing about his opinion of the entirely different matter of *biglal 'avot* in the *ge'ulah*. As it happens, however, Saadiah did not oppose the *Haftarah* blessing anyway. This blessing was originally just a poetic expansion of the Torah blessing, only later becoming associated with the *Haftarah*, having been relegated to a position nearer the end of the service on account of its being an optional poem (*piyyut*) and far from obligatory (see Heinemann, "Yachaso Shel Saadiah," p. 222, n. 6).

60. Ginzberg, *Ginzei Schechter*, vol. 2, p. 516.

61. Cf. Ismar Elbogen, "Studies in the Jewish Liturgy," *JQR*, o.s. 18 (1906), reprinted in Petuchowski, *Contributions*, pp. 1–34; Ezra Fleischer, "Towards a Clarification of the Expression *Poreis 'Al Shema'*" (Hebrew), *Tarbits* 41 (1972): 145–50.

62. *SRA*, pp. 16–17.

63. Ibid., p. 17.

64. Ibid., p. 15.

65. Ibid.

3: DAILY LITURGY: THE *TEFILLAH* AND THE *KADDISH*

1. For discussion see Heinemann, *Hatefillah Bitekufat Hatannaim Veha-'amoraim*, chap. 2; idem, notes to *Hatefillah Beyisra'el* by Elbogen, pp. 31–32; and prior studies cited in Heinemann's discussions.

2. See M. *Tamid* 5:1, 7:2. On the significance of the Temple cult as precedent for this, as well as the two blessings before it, see particularly, M. Liber, "Structure and History of the Tefilah," *JQR*, n.s. 40 (1950): 331–57.

3. For today's rite, see Birnbaum, *Siddur*, p. 87 (*birkat shanim*), p. 95 (*birkat kohanim*), p. 95 (*sim shalom*), and p. 209 (*shalom rav*). The Priestly Benediction is said in another extended form on holidays. For a synopsis of the regulations regarding this form as they pertain to different rites, see Idelsohn, *Jewish Liturgy*, pp. 192–94.

4. Heinemann, "Yachaso shel Saadiah," p. 222.

5. A. Marmorstein, "A Misunderstood Question in the Yerushalmi," *JQR*, n.s. 20 (1929–30): 319. Text 4 is not cited, since it is the same as part of text 5 but lacks the crucial last half.

6. *SS*, p. 19, and note to 1. 9 there.

7. *SS*, p. 19.

8. *Shibbolei Haleket*, p. 22. Cf. citation, in part, by Assaf, *SS*, p. 19, n. 9; and Lewin, "Review of Mann's *Genizah Fragments*," *Hatsofeh Lechokhmat Yisra'el* 11 (1807–8), pt. B, pp. 187–88.

9. *SS*, p. 19. Although Saadiah says that the use of *'or* is prevalent throughout Babylonia, it does not follow that in Palestine the alternative nominal form was utilized. The genizah manuscripts reviewed by Lewin vary, and so, for that matter, do those of *Seder Rav Amram*. Nor should *'echad*—as opposed to *'achat*—be seen as a Babylonian rather than a Palestinian reading. *'Echad* is common to all genizah fragments to date, and appears in all but one manuscript of *Seder Rav Amram*, the exception having neither *'echad* nor *'achat*. And, with one exception, all manuscripts of *Siddur Saadiah* read *'echad*.

10. For today's rite, see Birnbaum, *Siddur*, p. 95.

11. See Joel Müller, *Chilluf Minhagim Ben Bavel Ve'eretz Yisra'el* (1878; reprint ed., Jerusalem, 1970), #29.

12. *SRA*, pp. 36–37; *SS*, p. 42. See also *SS*, p. 42, note to 1. 14. Our manuscript of *SS* is confirmed by Abudarham.

13. Leon Nemoy, "The Liturgy of al-Qirqisani," in *Studies in Bibliography, History, and Literature in Honor of I. Edward Kiev*, ed. Charles Berlin (New York, 1971).

14. See also various related excerpts from other Karaites, translated into English by Leon Nemoy in *Karaite Anthology* (New Haven and London, 1952), pp. 271–320.

15. Jacob Mann, "Anan's Liturgy and His Half-Yearly Cycle of the Reading of the Law," *Journal of Jewish Lore and Philosophy* 1 (1919): 320–53; reprinted in *Karaite*

Studies, ed. Philip Birnbaum (New York, 1971), pp. 283–309, and in *The Collected Articles of Jacob Mann,* vol. 3 (Israel, 1971), pp. 1–26.

16. Ibid., p. 344, n. 26.

17. Ibid., p. 333.

18. The classical study is David de Sola Pool, *The Old Jewish Aramaic Prayer: The Kaddish* (Leipzig, 1909). Cf. Elbogen, *Gottesdienst,* pp. 92–98, and Heinemann with Petuchowski, *Literature of the Synagogue,* pp. 81–84.

19. Our present form of the *kaddish* lacks the word. See Birnbaum. *Siddur,* p. 135.

20. *Shibbolei Haleket,* p. 8. For the negative intent inherent in biblical usage, see Brown, Driver, and Briggs, *Hebrew and English Lexicon of the Old Testament,* p. 887. For the rabbinic idiom, see Eliezer ben Yehudah, *Milon Halashon Ha'ivrit,* vol. 12, p. 5961, n. 1. The change in meaning resulted from the contact of the Semitic word with Greek.

21. *SRA,* p. 12.

22. See Pool, *The Kaddish,* Appendix D. Cf. Jakob J. Petuchowski and Michael Brocke, eds., *The Lord's Prayer and Jewish Liturgy* (New York, 1978).

23. For discussion of these "mystics," or *yordei merkavah,* cf. Philipp Bloch, "Die Yordei Merkavah, die Mystiker der Gaonenzeit und ihr Einfluss auf die Liturgie," *MGWJ* 37 (1893): 18–25, 69–74, 257–66, 305–11; Gershom Scholem, *Jewish Gnosticism, Merkabah Mysticism and Talmudic Tradition* (New York, 1960); Alexander Altmann, "Shirei Kedushah Besifrut Hahekhalot Hakadumah," *Melilah* 8 (1951): 1–25; Morton Smith, "Observations on *Hekhalot Rabbati,*" in *Biblical and Other Studies,* ed. Alexander Altmann (Cambridge, 1963), pp. 142–61. For their relevance to the study of *piyyutim,* see Chayyim Schirmann, "Yannai Hapayyetan Shirato Vehashkafat 'Olamo," *Keshet* 6 (1964): 45–66; and Ithamar Gruenwald, "Piyyutei Yannai Vesifrut Yordei Merkavah," *Tarbits* 36 (1966–67): 257–78.

24. We customarily say *yitbarakh veyishtabach veyitpa'ar veyitromam veyitnase' veyithadar veyit'aleh veyithallal,* eight words in all. Amram says that he includes *yitbarakh* in his count plus six other words, but which six does he mean? Saadiah (*SS,* p. 35) has: *yitbarakh yishtabach yitpa'ar yitromam yit'aleh veyitnase' veyitkales,* seven terms in all, including *veyitkales.* But a variant manuscript of Saadiah has *yitbarakh veyishtabach veyitpa'ar veyitromam veyitnase' veyithadar veyit'aleh veyitkales.* Here we find eight terms, seven if *yitbarakh* is not counted, a formula differing from our own only in the exchange of *yitkales* for *yithallal.* Schechter ("Nusecha' Bekaddish," in *Gedenkbuch zur Erinnerung an David Kaufmann,* ed. M. Brann and F. Rosenthal [Breslau, 1900]. pp. 52 ff.) published a genizah fragment ending with *yit'aleh veyitkales.* It is probable, then, that Amram read the response as we do, but without *veyithallal,* thus with seven terms in all. The "others" of whom he speaks added *veyitkales* but did not count *yitbarakh* and, therefore, considered their version also to have the required seven terms. It is possible, on the other hand, that Amram had no particular wording in mind, since in his day the number of words may have been more important than the actual choice of what those words were to be. Thus any one synagogue might have been the locus of various wording in the *kaddish.* We do find variations in the genizah fragments. An eleventh-century Palestinian *kaddish*—it can be dated because of the mention of Abiathar Hakohen, *rosh yeshivah,* and Solomon Hakohen, his *'av*—reads *yitbarakh veyishtabach yitpa'ar yitromam yitnase' yit'aleh veyithadar,* the same seven words that we use, but with the last two interchanged. It too, however, lacks *yithallal.* There seems to be no way of determining any exact group who used *veyitkales.* Amram could not have had Pumbedita in mind because we know from a Pumbeditan *machzor* extract dating from the gaonate of Tsemach bar Paltoi (872–890) that *veyitkales* was not said in Pumbedita, at least not according to

this manuscript. It also lacks *yithallal* but has *yitkadash* instead. See Benjamin Manasseh Lewin, *Ginzei Kedem* 3 (1925): 53.

25. Lewin, *Ginzei Kedem* 3 (1925): 53.

26. *Shibbolei Haleket*, p. 8. Our editions of *Targum Onkelos* read *vekulas denech-ash*. Hai's point is the common root *kls* in *yitkales* and *kulsa'*.

27. Ginzberg, *Ginzei Schechter*, vol. 2, p. 163.

28. Adolph Büchler, "Le Mot Veyitkales dans le Kaddish," *REJ* 54 (1909): 194–204.

29. *Massekhet Soferim* does use the term and derivatives of the same root frequently; 19:7 for example. But *mekallesin* here is equivalent to saying a *kedushah*, in this case the *kedushat hayom* of the holiday involved. Cf. the comments by Elbogen in Ismar Elbogen, "Die Tefilla für die Festtage," *MGWJ* 55 (1911): 42.

30. See above, n. 17.

31. Mann, "Genizah Fragments," p. 383, for example, does not have *yitkales*.

32. Ginzberg, *Ginzei Schechter*, vol. 2, p. 161.

33. See above, n. 23.

34. See Scholem, *Jewish Gnosticism*, p. 66.

35. See the responsum by Hai in *Teshuvot Hageonim*, ed. Musafiya, #99.

36. Cf. Bloch, "Yordei Merkavah"; Gershom Scholem, *Major Trends in Jewish Mysticism* (1941; Schocken ed., New York, 1946), pp. 57–58.

37. Joseph Caro, his best example perhaps, wrote a logical, rational, intelligible code of law, but also composed *Magid Mesharim*, a book purporting to be the mystical secrets vouchsafed to him by an angel while he slept.

38. See, for example, E. E. Urbach, "The Traditions About Merkabah Mysticism in the Tannaitic Period" (Hebrew) in *Studies in Mysticism and Religion Presented to Gershom G. Scholem*, ed. R. J. Zwi Werblowsky and Ch. Wirszubski (Jerusalem, 1967); and Jacob Neusner, "The Development of the Merkavah Tradition," *Journal for the Study of Judaism in the Persian, Hellenistic and Roman Periods* 2 (1971): 149–62.

39. Excellent examples are: the acrostic *'el barukh* in the daily *yotser*, an alphabetic acrostic with both rhythm and rhyme (*a a b b c c b*); or the *kedushah* which follows it, especially the introductory lines which feature several synonymous verbs of which *shem ha'el* is the object. Taken together all the synonyms produce an effect on the worshipper. Individually each has cognitive meaning, but that meaning is lost during the moment of worship.

40. See, for example, Scholem, *Merkabah Mysticism*, p. 115, #31; p. 116, #32.

41. That the amoraim saw the intimate relationship between the two prayers in question can be gleaned from Rava's famous statement that in a deteriorating world the only hope is the *yehei shemeih rabbah de'aggadeta'* and the *kedushah desidra'* (*Sotah* 49a). The former is the congregational response to the *kaddish*, and the latter is a form of the *kedushah* still associated, at least in name, and probably also in practice in the academy, with study. It is clearly messianic, beginning as it does with "A redeemer shall come to Zion" (see Birnbaum, *Siddur*, pp. 131–33).

42. See discussion by Heinemann, *Hatefillah*, p. 163.

43. See discussion by Elbogen, *Gottesdienst*, p. 79.

44. See Ben Zion Wacholder, Prolegomenon to *The Bible as Read and Preached in the Old Synagogue*, by Jacob Mann (New York, 1971), p. xxvi.

45. See above, n. 41.

46. See discussion below, chap. 10.

47. A paradigm for such antiphonal recitation of a doxology is given in *Sifre* to Deut., #306.

48. See above, n. 24.

49. See references above to research by Schirmann and Gruenwald, n. 23.

50. Ginzberg, *Ginzei Schechter*, vol. 2, p. 546.

51. Assaf holds that "Sura was attracted to mysticism more than Pumbedita" (Simchah Assaf, *Tekufat Hageonim Vesifrutah*, pp. 261 ff.). He bases his case on Hai's opposition to the legend of Natronai's *kefitsat haderekh* and to the custom of *tokeia‘ lashed*. But Hai's debunking of popular superstition is no index for any opposition to mystical cosmology or theophany. Moreover, his remarks regarding the customs and beliefs of the masses are equally well explained by the late period in which he lived, so that there is no valid reason to invent a Pumbeditan tradition for him to have followed. Saadiah, a Suran, was no less antagonistic to popular superstition, as his opposition to the waving of the *lulav* in all four directions indicates (see *SS*, p. 237, note to l. 17). Similarly, Saadiah tried to limit the influence of crude anthropomorphic beliefs, such as those contained in *Shi‘ur Komah* (see his responsum in Lewin, vol. 1, *Ber.* #29). But neither gaon was necessarily opposed to all forms of mysticism as such. Their only reservation about the mystical tradition was the possibility of its degeneration into popular magic and superstition. Both geonim lived at a time when Karaites and others mocked any sign of superstition in the Rabbanite tradition. Thus Hai's opposition to the items cited by Assaf should be seen as his defense of the rationality of the tradition, a rationality not necessarily incongruous with mystical speculation.

52. See above, n. 51.

53. *SS*, pp. 35–36.

54. See, for example, Lewin, *OG*, vol. 6, *Suk.* #194.

55. Gerson D. Cohen, ed., *Sefer Ha-Qabbalah: The Book of Tradition by Abraham ibn Daud* (Philadelphia: 1967), pp. 59–60.

56. Cf. B. M. Lewin, "Rav Sherira," in B. M. Lewin, *Mechkarim Mitekufat Hageonim* (reprint ed., Tel Aviv, 1971), pp. 27–31; and Gerson D. Cohen, *Sefer Ha-Qabbalah*, p. 132, notes to ll. 196 and 199.

4: THE *PIYYUT*

1. For general discussion, see Heinemann and Petuchowski, *Literature of the Synagogue*, pp. 203–13, and the bibliography referred to in the notes, pp. 279–80. The flavor of the *piyyutim* can be grasped by Petuchowski's translation and notes, pp. 215–77. A theological treatment of some medieval *piyyutim* is given in Petuchowski's *Theology and Poetry* (London, 1978). See also, Ezra Fleischer, *Shirat Hakodesh Ha‘ivrit Bimei Habenayim* (Jerusalem, 1975), and the comprehensive bibliography contained therein.

2. Fleischer, *Shirat Hakodesh*, p. 11.

3. See above, pp. 63.

4. Ginzberg, *Ginzei Schechter*, vol. 2, p. 544.

5. The passage is from *Kid.* 49a and concerns someone who translates incorrectly. See Ginzberg, *Ginzei Schechter*, vol. 2, p. 545, n. 8, where Ginzberg points out that Ben Baboi's use of the citation is typical of him; that is, he utilizes *Babli* material in a loose, homiletical way.

6. For identification of *vayavo’ ‘amalek*, see Ginzberg, *Ginzei Schechter*, vol. 2, p. 547, n. 8. Ginzberg is unable to identify *’eikhah ’evkeh*.

7. Ibid., p. 550.

8. Ibid., pp. 556–57.

9. Ibid., pp. 559–60.

10. Ibid., p. 553.

11. Lewin, *OG*, vol. 1, *Ber.* #178.

12. Alternatively, the first one mentioned, *bekibbuts geluyot*, should be translated "in the blessing known as *kibbuts geluyot*," i.e., the tenth benediction of the *tefillah*, and he would be warning against only one *piyyut* known as *behikabets betulot*. We would then assume it was said in the tenth benediction because of the commonality suggested by its opening words, but was judged on the whole to be irrelevant to the subject matter of the blessing itself. My translation follows the suggestion by Lewin, who holds the first term to be a *piyyut* in its own right, by Kalir. Ginzberg doubts the identification, since our version of the Kalirian parallel fits Natronai's criteria, and should have been allowed by him. Cf. Lewin, *OG*, vol. 1, *Ber.*, p. 70, n. 4; Ginzberg, *Ginzei Schechter*, vol. 2, p. 515.

13. *SRA*, p. 32.

14. *SRA*, pp. 167–68. The recitation of *piyyutim* "is neither fixed nor obligatory, but depends on the extent to which the congregation wishes to say them."

15. M. *Ber.* 4:3.

16. Ginzberg, *Ginzei Schechter*, vol. 2, p. 553.

17. Ginzberg (ibid., p. 559) treats the term as if it were used the same way by all geonim, as if Amram's and Natronai's positive use of the concept were present already in Ben Baboi's thinking. The fact is, though, that Ben Baboi uses the argument of *me'en berakhah* only as an additional proof against the validity of *zokhrenu*. There is no reason to believe that he made the conceptual jump from allowing personal petitions in the middle benedictions, for which there is some talmudic warrant, to permitting publicly recited additions throughout the prayers generally, a practice for which no such warrant can be found.

18. *Sefer Chemdah Genuzah*, ed. Zeev Wolfenssohn, #145, attributes a similar decision to the Rif, but Ginzberg (*Ginzei Schechter*, vol. 2, p. 509) thinks it is geonic, and attributes it to Sar Shalom, Natronai's predecessor. If Ginzberg is correct, the compromise was even earlier than Natronai.

19. Lewin, *OG*, vol. 1, *Ber.* #179.

20. The problem arises from the fact that the author cites the responsum from *Sefer Ha'ittim*, but our version of this work does not have it. See Y. N. Epstein, "Sur les chapitres de Ben Baboi," *REJ* 75 (1922): 184. Epstein thinks that Nachshon did write the responsum but guesses that the author who carried the report, R. Yochanan of Ochrida (Bulgaria), found it in some Spanish sources other than *Sefer Ha'ittim* but equally as reliable. Mistakenly, he said it was from *Sefer Ha'ittim*.

21. Ginzberg, *Ginzei Schechter*, vol. 2, p. 510.

22. Ibid., pp. 510–11. Ginzberg admits that no Pumbeditan says explicitly that he opposes *piyyutim*, but he holds that they accepted them grudgingly, unlike the Surans, who had been under Palestinian influence ever since the days of Rav, and therefore took to them willingly. This whole idea of Rav's everlasting influence in Sura seems to me unfounded. Amram and Natronai—as should be evident by now, and will be made manifest in our concluding chapter—are staunchly opposed to Palestinian customs; and they are Surans. Then, too, Ben Baboi represents Yehudai's opinion as anything but accepting of Palestinian practices, most particularly *piyyutim*. Ginzberg rests his case on what he takes to be Sherira's opposition to Saadiah's acceptance of *piyyutim*. Since Saadiah rejected *'or chadash*, he should have rejected *piyyutim* as well, or so Ginzberg understands Sherira's argument. Certainly he is right to think these words are directed against Saadiah, but the force of the argument is not that Saadiah should have prohibited *piyyutim*. On the contrary! Sherira's point is the very reverse. Since Saadiah did not ban *piyyutim*, he should have permitted *'or chadash*

too. This understanding of Sherira's responsum harmonizes with his and Saadiah's stand on *'or chadash,* as we have seen. Ginzberg also maintains that only Sura said *zohkrenu* (Remember us for life . . .)" and the other High Holiday insertions in the *tefillah,* which we mentioned earlier with respect to Yehudai and Ben Baboi. This contention is debatable, but even if correct, it would say nothing about Pumbedita's attitude toward *piyyutim* per se.

23. *SS,* pp. 225, 264, for example.
24. See, for example, *SS,* p. 289. "Were this *piyyut* not so beautifully composed, I should not have included it."
25. Ibid., pp. 291 ff.
26. Ibid., p. 225.
27. Ibid., p. 156.

5: SABBATH LITURGY

1. For today's rite, see Birnbaum, *Siddur,* p. 290.
2. For today's rites, see Birnbaum, *Siddur,* p. 191; and (for the Sefardi parallel) see Moses Gaster, ed., *The Book of Prayer and Order of Service According to the Custom of the Spanish and Portuguese Jews,* vol. 1 (London, 1901), pp. 67, 83. Gaster's ritual has dispensed with it for Sabbath eve (p. 83). But see Baer, *Siddur 'Avodat Yisra'el* (1868; reprint ed., New York, 1937), p. 183, note to *barekhu.*
3. Cf. Birnbaum, *Siddur,* pp. 197, 263.
4. Ibid., pp. 197–98.
5. Ibid., p. 199.
6. Ibid., p. 263.
7. Ibid., p. 267.
8. Ibid., pp. 273–75; cf. the discussion by Joseph Heinemann, "One Benediction Comprising Seven," *REJ* 125 (1966): 101–11.
9. Liebreich dismisses this sort of reasoning since it is "unscientific" (Leon J. Liebreich "The Liturgical Use of Psalm 73:38," pp. 367–68). But such "unscientific" notions were accepted as reality in amoraic and geonic times and may well have prompted the adoption of liturgical customs.
10. Baer, *Seder 'Avodat Yisra'el,* pp. 163, 183. For other opinions cited here, see *Sefer 'Or Zarua',* Zhitomir ed., pt. 2, p. 47; and *Shibbolei Haleket,* ed. Buber, p. 41.
11. *SRA,* p. 61.
12. *Abudarham,* p. 137.
13. Cited in Lewin, *OG,* vol. 1, *Ber.* #14.
14. *SRA,* p. 63.
15. *Machzor Vitry,* ed. Simon Horowitz, p. 81.
16. See Natronai's remarks, for example, *SRA,* p. 62.
17. *Tanchuma,* ed. Buber, *Ha'azinu* (beginning), and for discussion of *kaddish,* see *midrash* on Rabbi Akiba, *Machzor Vitry,* pp. 112–13; earlier sources of the same tale, some of geonic vintage, are cited in the notes.
18. Mann, "Genizah Fragments," pp. 421 ff.
19. Ibid., p. 430. The *Yerushalmi* version of the eulogy reads *pores sukat shalom 'alenu ve'al 'amo yisra'el ve'al yerushalayim.* The same *'aggadah,* however, which yields this version of the eulogy is cited in variant texts of both the *Yerushalmi* and *Shir Hashirim Rabbah* with *boneh yerushalayim.* See Levi, "Fragments," p. 232. The *Yerushalmi* reference is *Ber.* 4:5 (8c); cf. Baer Ratner *'Ahavat Tsion Virushalayim,* 1:113. It is important to realize that Palestinian eulogies with *boneh* as the verb and

yerushalayim as the object frequently interchange this verb for various prepositions—in this case, the preposition *'al*. Other examples, to be discussed later, include *birkat chatanim* and *birkat 'avelim* which at times conclude *mesameiah (menachem) 'amo birushalayim* (or *be'iro*); and at times *mesameiach (menachem) 'amo uvoneh yerushalayim*. Wieder holds, moreover, that even the *boneh* form is attested to as being in the *Yerushalmi* in the time of Isaiah di Trani (see Wieder, "Fourteen Saadya Fragments," pp. 270–71).

20. For a discussion of the extent to which such dual eulogies are favored by the Palestinian tradition, see Ginzberg, *Ginzei Schechter*, vol. 2, p. 519, and the discussion below, chap. 9. For a discussion on ending one's blessing with *'amen*, see Mann, "Genizah Fragments," p. 399.

21. *SRA*, p. 130. Natronai and Sar Shalom are on record in sources other than *SRA* as being opposed to this dual eulogy (see the sources cited by Wieder, "Fourteen Saadya Fragments," p. 271).

22. Assaf has published an excerpt from a Babylonian *siddur*, probably from a Babylonian congregation housed in Palestine or Egypt. He points out that many of the remarks follow Amram; others come from *Halakhot Gedolot*. Now this excerpt has *vehu' rachum* and *veshameru* but not *shomer 'amo yisra'el*. For proof that the latter is not to be said, the author cites Sar Shalom, but whereas Amram quoted Sar Shalom as being opposed to *veshameru*, this author thinks Sar Shalom held the very reverse opinion. Moreover, he makes the mistake of calling Sar Shalom *rosh yeshivah ge'on yisra'el*. Even if *ge'on yisra'el* is a scribal error for *ge'on ya'akov*—as it probably is, since both *yisra'el* and *ya'akov* begin with a *yod*, and the *roshei tevot, gimel yod*, could easily be confused—the author would still be in error, since *ge'on ya'akov* always means Pumbedita, and Sar Shalom was a prominent Suran. At times, too, this *siddur* bears a resemblance to Saadiah, having, for example, *'asher kilah ma'asav*, and is probably under the influence of its Egyptian or Palestinian environment. I tend, therefore, to date it very late, post-Saadiah anyway, and due to its confusion of Babylonian precedent and its combination of Babylonian and Palestinian practices, I leave it out of the discussion here. See Simchah Assaf, *Misifrut Hageonim*, pp. 71 ff.

23. *SS*, pp. 110–11.

24. Rosenblatt, *Beliefs and Opinions*, pp. 157 ff.

25. Ibid., p. 158. The other quotation there is an addition by Ibn Tibbon. See p. 158, n. 2.

26. Ibid., p. 171.

27. Ibid., p. 158.

28. *SS*, p. 110.

29. Assaf, *Misifrut Hageonim*, p. 75. See above, n. 22.

30. *SRA*, p. 61.

31. See the parallels listed by Assaf in *Misifrut Hageonim*, p. 75, n. 4, and his identification of the phrase as Palestinian; cf. Elbogen, *Gottesdienst*, p. 109, and Mann, "Genizah Fragments," p. 422. Elbogen concurs with Assaf. Mann is a bit more cautious, suggesting that it may be either Palestinian or Egyptian. It is not Babylonian in any case.

32. *SS*, p. 110.

33. According to Saadiah's interpretation, God too calls it *'oneg*. *Machzor Roma* carries the phrase, *'asher kilah ma'asav* and follows Saadiah's precedent of including *veyikra'ehu 'oneg*.

34. For a discussion of these legal considerations and their relation to the concept of *'oneg shabbat*, see Bernard Revel, *Inquiry into the Sources of Karaite Halakah*, pp. 48–49.

35. *Sefer 'Eshkol Hakofer* (Eupatoria, 1836), p. 56d.

36. *SS*, p. 117.

37. For today's rite, see Birnbaum, *Siddur*, p. 393.

38. Ben Baboi notes that during the period of persecution, the Palestinians had been allowed to pray at certain times, and among the places where they inserted the *shema'* was the *musaf* (*tefillah?*). Yet he also says that they did not say the *kedushah* during *musaf*. Ginzberg's original attempt to solve the contradiction posited a novel use of the word *musaf*. Ben Baboi meant not the *musaf* service but simply additional prayers. Mann accepted this hypothesis. Later Ginzberg changed his mind, since it seemed implausible that Ben Baboi would use a technically precise term such as *musaf* in any but its usual sense. So Ginzberg now held that the authorities watching over the service depended on Jewish converts to Christianity, who left the service before *musaf* since they knew there was no *shema'* there anyway. Palestinian Jews, therefore, improvised a *kedushah* containing the *shema'* in *musaf*. After the persecutions ceased, they reverted to their regular custom of saying the *kedushah*—with the *shema'* now—in *schacharit* alone (see Ginzberg, *Ginzei Schechter*, vol. 2, p. 524).

39. Ginzberg, *Ginzei Schechter*, vol. 2, pp. 551–52, 554–56, 559–60.

40. *SRA*, p. 30; see also p. 171, where Amram vouches for the fact that he himself still says the *shema'* in the Yom Kippur *ne'ilah* service as well.

41. *Teshuvot Geonim Mizrach Uma'arav*, ed. Joel Müller (1888; reprint ed., New York, 1959), #122; and notes there. English words in italics represent Müller's emendation.

42. *Sha'arei Simchah*, ed. Isaac Bamberger, vol. 2 (Fürth, 1861), p. 20.

43. Jacob Mann, "Changes in the Divine Service Because of Religious Persecution," *HUCA* 4 (1927): 251–59.

44. Ibid., p. 255, n. 26.

45. Ginzberg, *Ginzei Schechter*, vol. 2, pp. 525–26.

46. *SS*, p. 121.

47. See above, chap. 4, n. 22.

48. *O.H.* 127. He calls the expanded *kedushah*, *kedushah rabbah*.

49. *SRA*, p. 30.

50. Lewin, *OG*, vol. 5, *Meg*. #250.

51. See Anan's *Sefer Hamitsvot* in Harkavy, *Studien und Mittheilungen*, vol. 8 (St. Petersburg, 1903), p. 38; and Leon Nemoy, "Studies in the History of the early Karaite Liturgy," p. 320. Kirkisani followed Anan here.

52. *Ber*. 12a; P. T. *Ber*. 1:5 (3c).

53. Harkavy, *Studien*, vol. 8, p. 142.

54. Mann, "Genizah Fragments," p. 392.

55. *Siddurei Hatefillot Lekhol Hashanah Khefi Minhag Hakara'im* (Kale, 1804–6), pp. 9b–10b.

56. Harkavy, *Studien*, vol. 8, p. 38; Mann, "Anan's Liturgy," p. 330.

57. Harkavy, *Studien*, vol. 8, p. 38.

58. M. *Eduyot* 1:5.

59. Jacob Z. Lauterbach, "The Sabbath in Jewish Ritual and Folklore," in Jacob Z. Lauterbach, *Rabbinic Essays*, pp. 454 ff.

60. Since Lauterbach's essay, we have uncovered more evidence for the importance of the custom in Rabbanite-Karaite relations. When mixed marriages took place between the two groups, the *ketubot* reflected concern over lighting candles for the Sabbath. One *ketubah* in our possession stipulates that the Karaite husband will allow his Rabbanite wife to light candles (see Simchah Assaf, "Letoledoth Hakara'im Be'artsot Hamizrach," reprinted in Assaf's collection of essays, *Be'oholei Ya'akov* [Jerusalem, 1943], p. 183). Another gives a Karaite wife the right to remain away from

her Rabbanite husband whose room is aglow with Sabbath lights (see Jacob Mann, *Texts and Studies*, vol. 2 [Philadelphia, 1935], p. 159).

61. Lauterbach, "The Sabbath," p. 430.

62. Two texts are from *Halakhot Gedolot* and *Chemdah Genuzah*. They parallel each other, but the latter adds the name of Natronai and Paltoi. Both are cited by Lewin, *OG*, vol. 2, *Shab.* #83. A third text is from *SRA*, p. 61, and is repeated almost verbatim in Assaf, *Misifrut Hageonim*, p. 74. Cf. n. 22, above.

63. My own leaning is toward Amram, for the reason given above. Paltoi should be discounted since—as the first Pumbeditan gaon to write responsa—he seems to have been less innovative than either of his Suran contemporaries. He may, however, have repeated the words of Amram or Natronai and hence have been included in the *Chemdah Genuzah*'s list of authors.

64. The object of the verb *lehadlik* varied in any case, however. *SS* manuscripts display *ner shel shabbat*, *ner hashabbat*, and *ner shabbat*. Saadiah, moreover, indicates that he knows versions differ (*SS*, p. 109).

65. Our text of the Talmud, however, reads "Rav," not "Samuel." See *Machzor Vitry*, p. 80, n. 2, which explores the opinion of some medieval authorities to the effect that such a blessing was found in the *Yerushalmi*. Cf. Lauterbach, "The Sabbath," p. 459, n. 98, which discusses the same putative sources.

66. *Shab.* 23b.

67. Lewin, *OG*, vol. 2, *Shab.* #85. Cf. *Teshuvot Hageonim*, ed. Jacob Musafiya, #82, where the same responsum is cited in the name of both Hai and Sherira.

68. *Sha'arei Teshuvah*, ed. Leiter, #92.

69. *SS*, p. 109. The text reads *mevarekhin 'alav lehadlik*. Whether we translate using the definite article "the" or the indefinite "a" makes considerable difference. The former implies, "Most people say blessing X but others say blessing Y. Everyone says a blessing, however." The latter could mean, "Most people say a blessing, X being what it is, but some do not say a blessing at all." I prefer the former since Saadiah would not have admitted so casually that some people did not keep the commandment.

70. Solomon Schechter, "Notes on the Hebrew Manuscript in the University of Cambridge," *JQR*, o.s. 4 (1892): 253.

71. Tos. to *Shab.* 25b, s.v. *chovah*.

72. *SS*, p. 109.

73. See n. 60, above. *Ketubot* had to take the right to light candles into consideration. See also the discussion of *'oneg Shabbat*, above, pp. 80. Sabbath light symbolized *'oneg*.

6: FESTIVAL AND HOLIDAY LITURGY: ROSH HASHANAH, YOM KIPPUR, AND FAST DAYS

1. See *Machzor Hashalem Lerosh Hashanah Veyom Kippur*, ed. Philip Birnbaum (New York, 1951), pp. 201–2, 217–18.

2. *SS*, pp. 219–20. For today's rite, see Birnbaum, *Siddur*, pp. 659–61. The relevant phrase is wanting both here and in Gaster's Sefardic ritual. See *The Order of Service for the New Year*, ed. Moses Gaster (London, 1903), p. 89.

3. *SS*, p. 220, n. 10, where Assaf cites Hai's words from *Sefer Hapardes*.

4. Quoted by Goldschmidt, *SRA*, p. 136, n. 33.

5. *Massekhet Soferim*, chap. 19, is inconclusive but does not mention any distinctive Rosh Hashanah wording, and probably would have if such had existed, since it

does stipulate unique words for Yom Kippur, saying it may not be called a *mo'ed* or a *yom tov*, but a *tsom* ("fast"). Similarly, neither Mann ("Genizah Fragments") nor Elbogen ("Die Tefilla für die Festtage") notes distinctive Rosh Hashanah wording along the lines of what Saadiah and Amram refer to.

6. *SS*, p. 151.

7. Ibid., p. 221. For today's rite, see Birnbaum, *Siddur*, pp. 613–15, and idem, *Machzor*, p. 331.

8. *Abudarham*, p. 264.

9. *SRA*, pp. 140, 166.

10. See Elbogen, *Gottesdienst*, p. 146, for a discussion of this theoretical consideration.

11. M. *R.H.* 4:1, *'Eruv.* 3:9.

12. Cf. *SRA*, p. 136; *SS*, pp. 219, 150.

13. *Abudarham*, p. 264.

14. Ibid.

15. The responsum, however, is addressed not to Meshullam but to "Moses the son of Meshullam." If this is not a scribal error, and if, as seems probable, Abudarham was referring to this responsum, then the actual correspondence would have been with Moses ben Meshullam ben Kalonymus, who functioned at Mayence during the eleventh century, the same time that Elijah and Abiathar were active in Jerusalem. Moses' father died in 985, so his son could well have written to Elijah and Abiathar early in their careers. Alternatively, Abudarham may be correct, and the German correspondent would then be not Moses' father, who died too soon, but the later Meshullam ben Moses (1010–1080).

16. Lewin, *OG*, vol. 1, *Ber.*, p. 125. Nerhardea probably refers to Pumbedita, as we shall see.

17. *SRA*, p. 137.

18. Elbogen states, "From Soferim on, all authorities agree that it [*vehasi'enu*] is said, and all rites except the German rite have it" (*Gottesdienst*, p. 146). Idelsohn, however, knew of the recitation of *vehasi'enu* on Rosh Hashanah only in the Italian rite (Idelsoh, *Jewish Liturgy*, p. 208). Abudarham (p. 265) follows Amram in saying it, but this is not necessarily true of all later Sefardi rites. See, for example, the *Machzor* published in Livorno according to the rite of Constantinople (1887), where it is lacking.

19. Lewin, *OG*, vol. 1, *Ber.*, p. 125.

20. According to Sherira, the amora Samuel established Nehardea while Rav built Sura. Pumbedita was established after Nehardea was sacked by Odenathus (263). In the geonic age, the Nehardea-Pumbedita line of descent was maintained by referring to Pumbedita from time to time as Nehardea. But Sura had its own history and would not generally be so referred to.

21. See Elbogen's text in Elbogen, "Die Tefilla für die Festtage." Text 2 for Rosh Hashanah (p. 434) lacks *vehasi'enu*. His Yom Kippur text for *musaf* (p. 442) has it, but the parallel Rosh Hashanah *musaf* text (p. 441) lacks it. Mann's fragment 14 ("Genizah Fragments," p. 439) is for Rosh Hashanan *musaf* and lacks it. It is also missing in text 17 (p. 441). Fragments 15 and 16 (pp. 440–41) have it in *ma'ariv* of Yom Kippur.

22. *Massekhet Soferim*, ed. Higger, 19:5. We have already seen the term *kilus* to refer to *kedushah*-like praise. See the discussion of the *kaddish*, above, pp. 56–64.

23. *Sefer Ma'aseh Hageonim*, ed. Abraham Epstein (Berlin, 1909), p. 37.

24. Baer Ratner, *Sefer 'Ahavat Tsiyon Virushalayim*, vol. 1 (Vilna, 1901), pp. 203–4.

25. *SRA*, p. 137. We have already remarked that one cannot assume every passage in *Halakhot Gedolot* to be by Yehudai. But in this case, *Halakhot Gedolot* tallies with what Amram says of Yehudai. Amram's precise wording is not the same as that given by Elijah in the name of *Halakhot Gedolot*, however, so we are probably dealing with two variant recensions of the original Yehudai source.

26. Jacob Mann, *The Jews in Egypt and Palestine under the Fatimids*, vol. 1, p. 178.

27. Ibid., p. 42.

28. Ibid., pp. 181–83. *Megillat Evyatar* portrays Daniel as being hated by the Palestinians, but Mann demonstrates the tendentious nature of this account. The only hostility directed against Daniel was the result of the political battle between him and the others who aspired to the Palestinian gaonate. Elijah himself was opposed to Daniel for that reason, but ultimately he accepted the compromise of becoming his *'av*. There was no nascent Palestinian nationalistic fervor at work, and no hostility toward Daniel's Babylonian ancestry or his probable penchant for Babylonian customs.

29. Ibid., vol. 2, p. 224.

30. *Sefer Pardes Hagadol*, ed. Michael Levi Frumkin (Jerusalem, 1964), p. 34b; cf. the similar opinion attributed to Paltoi in *SRA*, p. 136; and in *Chemdah Genuzah* (Jerusalem, 1963), #99.

31. *SS*, p. 219; *SRA*, p. 137. Samuel bar Hofni, Hai's father-in-law and gaon of the newly opened Sura, also supported Hai. See the Rosh to *R.H.* 4:13.

32. M. *R.H.* 4:5, *Ta'an.* 3:3.

33. *R.H.* 4:1 (59b).

34. See Leon J. Liebreich, "Aspects of the New Year Liturgy," *HUCA* 34 (1963): 136–39. Liebreich notes that the concept applied equally to all holidays in biblical times, but does not consider the role of the geonim in emphasizing the remembrance aspect of Rosh Hashanah. Cf. Joseph Heinemann, "Birkat 'Boneh Yerushalayim' Begilguleha," in *Sefer Chaim Schirmann*, ed. Shraga Abramson and Aaron Mirsky, p. 101, n 31. Heinemann seems to consider the equation of Rosh Hashanah with *yom hazikaron* as an early rabbinic concept, on the grounds that no other holiday has a celebration of *zikhronot* within the *'amidah*. The issue is one of emphasis. Certainly Heinemann is right with regard to the *'amidah*, but it does not follow that the concept of *zikhronot* was specific to Rosh Hashanah alone in the early period.

35. Saadiah omits *mo'adim lesimchah* naturally. Amram includes the clause, thus indicating that despite Rosh Hashanah's unique characteristics, it is still just another *mo'ed*. Both geonim, though, conclude with the eulogy: *barukh . . . mekadesh yisra'el veyom hazikaron.*

36. *Massekhet Soferim* 19:5; Elbogen, "Die Tefilla für die Festtage," p. 434.

37. Harkavy, *Studien*, vol .8, pp. 69 ff; *'Eshkol Hakofer*, p. 136a. For a discussion of Hadassi's contention, see Bernard Revel, "Karaite Halakah," reprinted in Birnbaum, *Karaite Studies*, pp. 78–79, and references there. A later Karaite authority, Aaron ben Elijah (d. 1369), indicates quite clearly that for Karaites, in the Byzantine period of their glory, Rosh Hashanah was not a day of judgment at all, but a day of rejoicing like every other holiday. He says it is not a festival, but he means the Hebrew *chag*, not *mo'ed*. See Aaron ben Elijah's discourse for Rosh Hashanah in Nemoy, *Karaite Anthology*, pp. 172–74.

38. For the present rite, see Birnbaum, *Machzor*, p. 489.

39. The origin of *kol nidre* has been discussed elsewhere and need not be reiterated in detail here. Joseph Bloch (*Kol Nidre und seine Entstehungsgeschichte*) argued for its origin in the West Gothic kingdom in the reigns of Scintilla and Recceswinth. Poz-

nanski (*Eine neue Hypothese über die Entstehung des Kol Nidre*) countered Bloch's argument and dated it in post-talmudic Palestine. Elbogen (*Gottesdienst*, p. 54) agreed with Poznanski, as did Mann (*Texts and Studies*, vol. 2, pp. 51–35), who added that it came into being before the eighth century.

40. Ginzberg, *Ginzei Schechter*, vol. 2, p. 120. See also Lewin, *OG*, vol. 11, *Ned.* #56, for a manuscript paralleling Ginzberg's text. The latter is also carried in *Sefer Hapardes.*

41. Poznanski, *Kol Nidre*, p. 4.

42. He says *la' garsinan nedarim.* Yehudai's precise words are *la mefarshin massekhta' dinedarim.*

43. Lewin, *OG*, vol. 11, *Ned.* #63 and 64.

44. *SRA*, pp. 162–63.

45. *Sha'arei Teshuvah*, ed. Wolf Leiter (1802; reprint ed., Pittsburgh, 1946), #143.

46. Lewin, *OG*, vol. 11, *Ned.* #64.

47. Ginzberg, *Ginzei Schechter*, vol. 2, p. 120. Ginzberg would seem to be confirming Aptowitzer's view that "the geonim of Pumbedita were lenient with respect to the annulment of vows but the geonim of Sura were stringent." Avigdor Aptowitzer, "Teshuvot Meyuchasot Lerav Hai Ve'einan Lo," *Tarbits* 1 no. 4 (1929/30): 63–105.

48. See Ginzberg, *Geonica*, vol. 1, p. 41; and above, chap. 2, n. 29.

49. Mann, *Texts and Studies*, vol. 2, p. 52, n. 99.

50. Lewin, *OG*, vol. 11, *Ned.*, #68. The report then cites the version of the prayer that refers to the past, *miyom tsom kippurim she'avar 'ad yom tsom kippurim hazeh.*

51. *Sha'arei Teshuvah*, ed. Leiter, #38.

52. Lewin, *OG*, vol. 11, *Ned.*, #62.

53. See n. 39 above. The genizah as reported by Mann ("Genizah Fragments," p. 437) does not have *kol nidre*, but this may be due to the unrepresentative nature of our fragments. Alternatively, *kol nidre* may have been excluded because, like Saadiah, the Palestinians accepted it only as an adjunct to the actual service, for unusual circumstances.

54. "Hai seems to have yielded to popular pressure" (Jacob Mann, *Texts and Studies*, vol. 2, p. 52, n. 99).

55. It occurs in two major forms in today's ritual, both of which are repeated several times during Yom Kippur day. See Birnbaum, *Machzor*, pp. 475–81. The second paragraph, beginning with *'ashamnu*, is an alphabetic acrostic known as the *vidui zuta'*, "the small confession." The lengthy litany which begins with *'al chet'* is called the *vidui rabbah*, "the large confessional." Our responsa are concerned with the *vidui rabbah.*

56. M. *M.S.* 5:10–13.

57. See, for example, *Yoma* 87a.

58. Indeed Amram recommends the practice daily after the *tefillah*, not just on Yom Kippur. *SRA*, p. 28.

59. Lewin, *OG*, vol. 6, *Yoma*, #100.

60. Ibid., p. 37, n. 5.

61. Birnbaum, *Machzor*, p. 469.

62. Lewin, *OG*, vol. 6, *Yoma*, #99.

63. *SRA*, p. 162.

64. Ibid., p. 162.

65. See Elbogen's pioneer studies, "Pores 'al Shema'" and "'Over Lifnei Hatevah," reprinted in Petuchowski, *Contributions*, pp. 2–51.

66. Birnbaum, *Machzor*, p. 469.

67. *Teshuyot Hage'onim Mitokh Hagenizah,* ed. Assaf, p. 86. Assaf suggests that the placement of this *vidui* was one of the differences between the two academies. I doubt that there is enough evidence to go that far.

68. T. *Yoma* 4 (5): 14. For a discussion of the passage, see Saul Lieberman, *Tosefta Kifshutah,* vol. 4 (New York, 1962), p. 830, and, more recently, Zevi Groner, "Haberakhah 'al Havidui Vegilguleha," *Bar Ilan Yearbook* 13 (1976): 158–68.

69. This variation is evident even in later sources. Rashi to *Yoma* 87b interprets the *Tosefta* passage as referring only to *ne'ilah.* Thus, the English rite included the eulogy only at *ne'ilah.* See J. Kaufman, "The Prayer Book According to the Ritual of England Before 1290," *JQR,* o.s. 4 (1892); reprinted in Petuchowski, *Contributions,* pp. 459–502. The *Rokeach* [Poland, 1806,] p. 346), however, adds it at every *vidui.* See also Groner, "Haberakhah 'al Havidui," for an extensive survey.

70. *SS,* p. 260.

71. Heinemann, "Yachaso Shel Rav Saadiah," pp. 228 ff.

72. Later authorities confused Saadiah and Amram. Zerachiah Halevi thought it was Saadiah who favored the eulogy while both the Rosh and Jacob ben Asher quote Saadiah's deprecatory statement but attribute it to Amram. See Lewin, *OG,* vol. 6, *Yoma* #101/2; *SRA,* p. 170, n. 2.

73. *SS,* p. 261; *Abudarham,* p. 285. See also the texts reproduced in Naphtali Wieder, "Lecheker Minhag Bavel Hakadmon," *Tarbits* 37 (1967–68): 243.

74. "If one act was done out of order, it was as if it were not done at all" (M. *Yoma* 5:7). For the role of the Confession in the day's proceedings, see M. *Yoma* 3:8, 6:2.

75. Ecclesiasticus 50:1–10; translation taken from Ellis Rivkin, *The Shaping of Jewish History* (New York, 1971), pp. 45–46.

76. M. *Yoma* 3:4, 7; 7:4.

77. M. *Yoma* 6:1–6.

78. M. *Yoma* 5:4–6.

79. M. *Yoma* 5:1.

80. For today's rite, see Birnbaum, *Machzor,* pp. 811 ff., but especially p. 815. For a discussion of its development, see Daniel Goldschmidt, *Machzor Layamim Hanora'im,* vol. 2 (Jerusalem, 1970), Introduction, pp. 18–25.

81. Cf. Lewin, *OG,* vol. 6, *Yoma',* #119/20, and *SS,* p. 263.

82. *SS,* p. 76. *'Ein min ha'ikar.*

83. Lewin, *OG,* vol. 6, *Yoma',* #122.

84. Lewin, *OG,* vol. 6, *Yoma',* #121. Hai is also involved in a dispute over the wording of the *'avodah.* I have relegated the matter to a footnote because I do not think his interest was in a liturgical practice of the day, but rather in establishing the correct text of what the High Priest said during Temple times. His statement is: *'ana' hashem velo 'ana' bashem* (see Lewin, *OG,* vol. 6, *Yoma* #39). The wording was problematic since both the Mishnah and the *Tosefta* vary with respect to the prefix. See *Tosefta Kifshutah,* 4:753 ff. Hai's point seems to be that the High Priest used the ineffable name itself, a name which he says is still known in the academies of his own time, but, of course, not used any more. The Bach, *O.H.* #621, is probably correct in saying that since the name was not used any more anyway, the whole matter was purely academic. The only liturgical consequence would have been that Hai's preference would have been *hashem* rather than *bashem* in the *'avodah.* It is hard to say what geonic custom was, since this part of the prayer book was usually copied by a scribe who stopped after the first few words, saying, "etc." Amram, assuming that everyone knows the Mishnah, gives us no wording at all. Our text of Saadiah reads *bashem,* but this may be corrupt, since the *Tur, O.H.* #621, records him as favoring *hashem* throughout the *'avodah.*

Hai's father, Sherira, is involved in a similar problem, stemming also from the

Tosefta, Yoma 2:1. The *Babli, Yoma* 36b, tries to determine what the High Priest said, whether *ʿaviti fashaʿti vechataʿti* or *chataʿti vaʿaviti ufashaʿti*. The former is Meir's opinion, and the latter is that of the sages. Sherira rules against the individual, Meir, in favor of the majority, advising people that if they pray in the order recommended by Meir, they are wrong. Here, of course, liturgical custom was at issue, but again I believe the main consideration to have been the historical one, determining what the High Priest said, and setting the precedent of depending on the Talmud, with its rules of individual versus majority, and the like, to decide issues. The Talmud and the rabbinic tradition were under attack by the Karaites, and the veracity of the historical information contained in those sources had to be defended at all costs. This was the motivation behind *ʾIggeret Sherira Gaon* as well as such similar works as Ibn Daud's *Sefer Hakabbalah*. For Sherira's responsum, see Lewin, *OG*, vol. 6, *Yoma* #43. For a discussion of the Karaite attack on rabbinic historical traditions, see Gerson D. Cohen, *Sefer Ha-qabbalah: Ibn Daud, "The Book of Tradition,"* Introduction p. liii. Lewin (*OG*, vol. 6, *Yoma* #41) quotes the Spanish version of *Halakhot Gedolot* as recording Saadiah in favor of Meir's interpretation, but this is most unlikely, considering the motivations discussed here, and, in fact, his *Siddur*, p. 261, does follow the majority.

85. On the sorry state of the gaonate and its internecine quarreling, see: *ʾIggeret Sherira Gaon*, pt. 3, chap. 8; and *Ibn Daud*, ed. Gerson Cohen, p. 58. For discussion see Ellis Rivkin, "The Saadiah-David ben Zakkai Controversy: A Structural Analysis," in *Studies and Essays in Honor of Abraham A. Neuman*, ed. Meir ben-Horin, Bernard D. Weinryb and Solomon Zeitlin (Philadelphia, 1962), pp. 388–423; and below, in this book, chap. 10. For Sherira's restorative influence, see Lewin, "Rav Sherira," in *Mitekufat Hageʾonim*, sec. 3.

86. For its use in the Yom Kippur rite, see Birnbaum, *Machzor*, p. 869. For a summary of its development, see Idelsohn, *Jewish Liturgy*, pp. 192 ff.

87. M. *Taʿan.*, chap. 4.

88. *Taʿan.* 26b.

89. Lewin, *OG*, vol. 5, *Taʿan.* #73.

90. *SRA*, p. 97.

91. *Geʾonei Mizrach Umaʿarav*, #46.

92. Ibid., #48.

93. Lewin, *OG*, vol. 5, *Taʿan.* #80, and n. 11, there.

94. Müller, *Chilluf Minhagim*, p. 21.

95. *O.H.* 580:2.

96. *SRA*, p. 95.

97. Mann, "Genizah Fragments," pp. 405–6.

98. *SS*, p. 317.

7:   FESTIVAL AND HOLIDAY LITURGY:
PILGRIMAGE FESTIVALS, CHANUKAH, AND PURIM

1. Cf. *SRA*, p. 177; *SS*, p. 237.

2. *SS*, p. 238.

3. See *Manhig, Hilkhot ʾEtrog*, #42. For the early origin of the liturgical and paradigmatic use of Ps. 118, see Jakob J. Petuchowski, "*Hoshiʿah Naʾ* in Psalm CXVIII:25—A Prayer for Rain," *Vetus Testamentum* 5 (1955): 265–71; and for an early dating of the *hoshaʿnot* generally, see Heinemann, *Hatefillah*, chap. 6.

4. *Manhig* (Jerusalem, 1950), *Hilkhot 'etrog* #43. Though there is a paucity of polemical responsa, considerable data regarding various customs are at hand. For the geonic ritual generally, see *SRA*, p. 176, and *Sha'arei Simchah*, 1:114 ff. An interesting comment by Saadiah is carried in *SS*, p. 237, n. 17. He objects to interpreting the talmudic maxim, *molikh umevi' lemi she'arba' ruchot shelo* (*Suk.* 37b) in such a way as to imply waving in all four directions. One who does so is a *chitsoni*, a "heretic." One should wave it in two directions only, upward and to the east. Another question of interest is the saying of *hosha'not* on the Sabbath. Hai rules against the existing custom of saying *hosha'not* then, since children might infer that carrying the *lulav* to the synagogue on the Sabbath was also permitted. See Lewin, *OG*, vol. 6, *Sukkot* #154, and *Toratan shel Rishonim*, ed. Horowitz, vol. 2, p. 42. For a thorough discussion of the development of the institution of *hakafot*, see Ginzberg, *Ginzei Schechter*, 2:252ff.

5. *Meg.* 21b.

6. It is part of the standard Ashkenazi rite too. See Birnbaum, *Siddur*, p. 727. Amram's inclusion of this blessing in his *Seder* shows how much he relied on the *Babli* as his prototype, since elsewhere he is opposed to dual eulogies. The contradiction between this blessing and the *Babli*'s generally negative opinion of dual eulogies did not elude the geonim. Moses Gaon felt constrained to explain why it was that both parts were necessary. The first refers to God's act of vengeance against Israel's enemies, and the second denotes His act of saving us. Both acts are part of the deliverance process, so both are mentioned in the eulogy. See Lewin, *OG*, vol. 5, *Meg.* #113.

7. *Sha'arei Simchah*, ed. Bamberger, vol. 2, pp. 114–15.

8. M. *Pes.* 5:7.

9. M. *Pes.* 10:6.

10. For a thorough discussion, see *Entsiklopidiah Talmudit*, s.v. *hallel*. See, especially, vol. 9, p. 421, n. 450 and 454, where contradictory texts are compared. See also Menachem Kasher, *Haggadah Shelemah*, pp. 135–39, especially p. 135, n. 1; and Lewin, *OG*, vol. 3, *Pes.*, pp. 124–25 and notes there.

11. *Sha'arei Teshuvah*, ed. Leiter, #102. The identity of this Tsemach is problematic. Some parallel versions call him Tsemach bar Solomon, the *'av bet din* or *dayyana' debava'* of Amram's Sura. Others call him Tsemach Gaon. *SRA* carries the same citation in Amram's name (p. 122) without even mentioning Tsemach. It may be that the responsum originated in the *Seder*, which is prefaced with greetings from both Amram and Tsemach, his *'av* (p. 1). Later authorities quoted the *Seder* in the name of both men. Later still, this Tsemach was incorrectly assumed to be the gaon of the same name. See Lewin, *OG*, vol. 3, *Pes.*, p. 124, and notes there.

12. Ibid., #102.

13. The Palestinian practice goes back to the *baraita'* quoted in the *Soferim* passage. It gives the time for which the *hallel* is appropriate. This *baraita'* appears first in *Tosefta Sukkah* 3:2, where *'erev pesach* is included in the list of appropriate occasions. The same reading is carried in the *Yerushalmi*, *Sukkah* 4:5. The *Babli*, though, both in *Ta'anit* 28b and *'Arkhin* 10a, omits the mention of *'erev pesach*. Early medieval authorities who argue with the geonim and advocate a blessing before the *hallel* at the *seder* all quote the *Yerushalmi* version of the *baraita'*. See Lieberman, *Tosefta Kifshutah*, vol. 4, p. 872, for discussion.

14. *Pes.* 118a.

15. It was Rashi's interpretation of the Talmud which made this *hallel* obligatory for Ashkenazic Jewry. Jacob ben Asher provided the same service for the Sefardim. See Goldschmidt, *Haggadah*, p. 66.

16. *SRA*, p. 148.

17. *SS*, p. 148.

18. Lewin, *OG*, vol. 3, *Pes.* #251 and 353.

19. *Sha'arei Simchah*, vol. 2, pp. 100–101; *Tur, O.H.* #481. The end of a responsum by Sherira (Lewin, *OG*, vol. 3, #354) seems to indicate that Sherira sided with the majority of his geonic predecessors and permitted the fifth cup as a licit alternative for those who desired it. He could not, therefore, have opposed the custom. But the last sentence of the responsum which provides this indication is really not by Sherira at all, but a quotation from Sar Shalom. See Lewin's note #7, p. 127.

20. *Pes.* 118a. For the Blessing of Song in the present rite, see Birnbaum, *Haggadah*, pp. 120, 126.

21. Büchler explains Hai's distaste for the fifth cup by his being a Pumbeditan. "One notes immediately that all the geonim cited who assume the fifth cup to be permissible are without exception from Sura, that is: Moses, Kohen Tsedek, Sar Shalom, Amram and Saadiah. On the other hand, Hai standing alone against all [the others] adopts another attitude and declares that with them—Pumbedita—that usage is not practiced" (Büchler, "La Ketouba chez les Juifs du Nord de l'Afrique," *REJ* 50 [1905]: 162). Hai and Pumbedita, he thinks had our emended text, while Sura possessed R. Tarfon's original words.

But Hai never says that the fifth cup is nontalmudic, and he surely would have, had he believed that to be the case. So if this is a difference between the two academies, another basis must exist for it. It is, however, dangerous to argue for a difference between Sura and Pumbedita when we have only Hai's testimony for Pumbedita. Imagine the errors that would accrue if we were to attribute every statement by Saadiah to a tradition of Sura! One gaon is never evidence enough for a school tradition.

22. *Sha'arei Teshuvah*, #102.

23. *Sha'arei Simchah*, vol. 2, p. 100.

24. *Sefer Ha'eshkol*, ed. Albeck, vol. 2, p. 92.

25. *SRA*, p. 111. The introduction to the *hallel* to which he refers can be found in Birnbaum, *Haggadah*, p. 96.

26. See Goldschmidt, *Haggadah*, p. 6, where this identification is made.

27. Ibid., p. 75; cf. p. 6, n. 12, where two other manuscripts are cited. In passing, it might be noted that a similar *'al hanissim* formula occurs elsewhere in our fragments and ends with *barukh . . . zokher haberit*; see, for example, Israel Abrahams, "Some Egyptian Fragments of the Passover Haggada," *JQR*, o.s. 10 (1898): 48. Heinemann (*Hatefillah*, p. 101) calls this a long form of the normal blessing over *matsah* and *maror*. It follows *hamotsi'* in the Abrahams fragment and precedes it in the Goldschmidt text. Amram's opposition, though, was expressly directed against the *she'asah nissim* of the *kiddush*. The similar phrase in the expanded blessing for *matsah*, in fact, is lacking in some forms of the expansion—Abrahams's fragment 5, for example. As it happens, the blessing over *matsah* was not set until very late and, therefore, provides an excellent illustration of the thesis that exact wording fluctuated long after the tannaitic period and often the amoraic as well. Thus *zokher haberit*, normally for Rosh Hashanah (see Birnbaum, *Machzor*, p. 389), was also available to be used here. Both holidays, it may be recalled, competed for the distinction of remembrance. Even after the form of the blessing over *matsah* crystallized into our short formula—Babylonia may never have used the long one—practice varied between *'al 'akhilat matsah* and *le'ekhol matsah*. The latter, though not used today, is found in *Ma'aseh Hage'onim*, ed. Epstein, p. 18, and even *SRA*, p. 112. Also, Ibn Giyyat cites its use by Amram and Moses (see *Sha'arei Simchah*, vol. 2, p. 103). Apparently, the two forms were used interchangeably for some time. *Pardes*, ed. Frumkin, p. 176, urges *le'ekhol* and calls the *'al* form *ta'ut*. For *maror*, though, Pardes uses the *'al*

form and devotes a long explanation to the theoretical differences between the formulas (see *Pardes* 17b, 27b, 28b).

28. *SS*, p. 142.

29. *Sha'arei Simchah*, vol. 2, p. 99.

30. Ginzberg, *Geonica*, vol. 2, p. 185, and discussion, p. 178.

31. Goldschmidt, *Haggadah*, p. 83; cf. MS references, p. 6, n. 13.

32. These events—Egyptian slavery, exodus, and entry into the promised land—represent the sacred history, as recorded in Deut. 26:5–9, a passage singled out in Temple times as a yearly affirmation of faith to be recited by pilgrims bringing their first fruits to the Temple (M. *Bik.* 3:6). It also became the essence of the folk history related at the *seder* (M. *Pes.* 10:4), outfitted eventually with a midrashic exposition. Even by itself, however, it telescoped Israel's history into significant epochs, moving with divine purpose; as the Mishnah describes it (M. *Pes.* 10:4), *matchil bigenut umesayem beshevach*, "beginning with degradation and concluding with glory."

33. *SRA*, p. 124.

34. For today's rite, see Birnbaum, *Siddur*, pp. 91–94.

35. *Shab.* 21b.

36. *Massekhet Soferim* 34:6.

37. *Abudarham*, p. 201.

38. *Toratan shel Rishonim*, ed. Horowitz, vol. 1, p. 18. On the identification of *Halakhot Ketsuvot* and *Sefer Hama'asim*, see Y. N. Epstein, "Ma'asim Livnei 'Erets Yisra'el," *Tarbits* 1, no. 4 (1929–30): 34. The earliest reference to *Sefer Hama'asim*, as far as we know, is by Hai. But the book was subsequently lost, and was recovered, in part, only in recent times. See Benjamin Manasseh Lewin, "Ma'asim Livnei 'Erets Yisra'el," *Tarbits* 1, no. 1 (1929/30); Epstein, "Ma'asim"; and Jacob Mann, "Sefer Hama'asim Livnei 'Erets Yisra'el," *Tarbits* 1, no. 3 (1929–30). Both Epstein (p. 33) and Mann (pp. 1–2) date the work at the end of the Byzantine period, and most scholars agree. See, for example, Simchah Assaf, *Tekufat Hage'onim*, p. 177. Ginzberg goes further and postulates two versions, an original Palestinian one and a later Babylonian adaptation of that original, in which Babylonian customs were integrated into the original Palestinian text (see his *Perushim*, 1:88). In any event, the responsa published by Horowitz under the title *Halakhot Ketsuvot* are not by Yehudai and not Babylonian at all, but Palestinian.

39. *Abudarham*, p. 201.

8: PRELIMINARY MORNING SERVICE

1. For today's rite, see Birnbaum, *Siddur*, pp. 51–69.

2. The introductory blessing, *barukh she'amar*, is in Birnbaum, *Siddur*, p. 51; the *birkat hashir* is on p. 69. The title of the former is somewhat of a misnomer. Though today's prayer does indeed begin with these words, it originally contained only the last half of the present text.

3. See Heinemann, *Hatefillah*, p. 100, n. 2.

4. *Shab.* 118b.

5. Elbogen, *Gottesdienst*, p. 82; for these psalms in today's rite, see Birnbaum, *Siddur*, pp. 57–65.

6. *Massekhet Soferim* 18:1.

7. Alfasi to *Shab.* 118b.

8. See *Siddur Rashi*, ed. Solomon Buber (Berlin, 1911), p. 6.

9. Rashi to *Shab.* 118b, s.v. *pesukei dezimrah.*

10. Mann, "Genizah Fragments," p. 386.

11. *SRA*, p. 9; *SS*, p. 43.

12. For today's rite, see Birnbaum, *Siddur*, pp. 3–50.

13. For a thorough discussion, see Solomon Freehof, "The Structure of the Birchos Hashachar," *HUCA* 23 (1950–51), pt. 2, pp. 359–64. But note Heinemann's critical note, Heinemann, *Hatefillah*, p. 111.

14. Most of the blessings are from the *Babli, Ber.* 60a. The blessing under discussion, however, is from *Men.* 43b = P.T. *Ber.* 9:2 (13b).

15. T. *Ber.* 6:18.

16. *Men.* 43b–44a.

17. On the origin of the rejection, see Louis Ginzberg, *Perushim Vechidushim Birushalmi*, vol. 3 (New York, 1941), p. 229. Ginzberg argues that originally the word *bor* read *behemah*, "cow." Though the strong reaction against *behemah—kulei ha'i namei*, "Must you go so far?"—led to the later substitution of the word *bor*, the *Babli* maintained an alternative solution, the reading of *'eved* = "servant." The Palestinian rite still shows signs of the original word.

18. *SRA*, p. 5.

19. *Sha'arei Teshuvah*, #327.

20. Ginzberg, *Perushim*, vol. 1, pp. 99–100, 102; idem, *Geonica*, vol. 1, p. 146.

21. See above, chap. 6, p. 94, and n. 16.

22. Lewin, *OG*, vol. 1. *Ber.* #283.

23. Ibid., #284.

24. *Ber.* 2:3 (4c).

25. Lewin, *OG*, vol. 1, *Ber.* #198. For today's rite, see Birnbaum, *Siddur*, p. 67.

26. *SS*, p. 34.

27. Lewin, *OG*, vol. 1, *Ber.* #197.

28. *Mishneh Torah, Hilkhot Tefillah* 7:13. Some people read *shirat hayam*; others read *ha'azinu* (Deut., chap. 32); still others recited both.

29. See Harkavy, *Studien*, vol. 8, p. 20, n. 1; Mann "Anan's Liturgy," p. 333.

30. *SRA*, p. 60. cf. *Likkutei Hapardes* (Amsterdam, 1715), 8b, where the same responsum is found, but simply in the name of Moses Gaon.

31. *Teshuvot Hage'onim*, ed. Musafiya, #45.

32. Birnbaum, *Siddur*, p. 13. For other Torah Blessings, see discussion below, chap. 9.

33. Cf. Elbogen, *Gottesdienst*, p. 83; Mann, "Genizah Fragments," p. 386.

34. *Teshuvot Hage'onim*, ed. Musafiya notes to #45, p. 13. The reference in *'Or Zarua'* is to *Hilkhot Keriyat Shema'*, #22.

35. *Tosafot* to *Ber.* 11b, s.v. *shekhevar niftar.*

36. For the reference to the *vatikin*, see *Ber.* 9b, 26a; the *ge'ulah* referred to is the blessing immediately succeeding the *shema'*, and immediately before the *tefillah* in the morning service. See Birnbaum, *Siddur*, pp. 77 (bottom)–81.

37. *SRA*, p. 11.

38. The Palestinian response to Yehudai, in Louis Ginzberg, *Ginzei Schechter*, vol. 2, pp. 559–60.

39. *Massekhet Soferim* 14:15.

40. See Heinemann, *Hatefillah*, pp. 103 ff., where the lack of order in these blessings is discussed.

41. *SRA*, p. 8. For today's rite, see Birnbaum, *Siddur*, p. 69.

42. Birnbaum, *Siddur*, p. 51.

43. *Ta'an.* 6b.

44. Simchah Assaf, "Misefer Hatefillah Mei'erets Yisra'el," *Sefer Dinabourg*, p. 122; Mann, "Genizah Fragments," p. 389.

45. Birnbaum, *Siddur*, p. 69.

9: LIFE–CYCLE AND GRACE AFTER MEALS

1. For a general survey of blessings that were canonized, see Ze'ev Yabetz, *Sefer Mekor Haberakhot* (1910; reprint ed., Jerusalem, 1976). For a fine collection of source citations on blessings generally, and the life-cycle and Grace after meals rubrics specifically, see Issachar Jacobson, *Netiv Binah*, vol. 3 (Tel Aviv, 1973).

2. See Heinemann, *Hatefillah*, pp. 73–77, for a discussion of early sources and secondary literature.

3. For a straightforward traditionalist account of the four blessings, see Eliezer Levi, *Yesodot Hatefillah* (Tel Aviv, 1963), pp. 293–99, and idem, *Torat Hatefillah* (Tel Aviv, 1967), pp. 223–28. For scholarly bibliography, see relevant entries in Heinemann, *Hatefillah*, pp. 196–97.

4. See sources in Lewin, *OG*, vol. 8, *Ket.*, pp. 14–15.

5. For today's rite, see Birnbaum, *Siddur*, pp. 741 ff.

6. T. *Ber.* 6: 12–13.

7. *Shab.* 137b.

8. SRA, p. 179.

9. SS, p. 98.

10. Lewin, *OG*, vol. 2, *Shab.* #409.

11. See Baer, *Seder ʿAvodat Yisra'el*, p. 583. Baer prefers the imperative. Cf. Shakh to *Y.D.* 265:5: "It seems to me it is a petitionary prayer for the future."

12. Lewin, *OG*, vol. 2, *Shab.* #408.

13. Ibid., #412.

14. Ibid., #378. The question put to him was, Which patriarch does *yedid* refer to? He argues that *yedid* is Jacob rather than Abraham or Isaac. Hai contradicts the *Babli* in this identification. *Men.* 53a–b gives several interpretations of *yedid*, including Abraham, but not Jacob. For later discussions see *Tosafot* to *Men.* 53b and *Shab.* 137b.

15. The time element was tied to Samuel's saying, in *Pes.* 7b and elsewhere, that we always bless ʿ*over laʿasiyatan*, "before the act." The Palestinian Talmud *Ber.* 9:3 (14a), quotes the same phrase in the name of Yochanan while Samuel is cited as recommending *beshaʿat ʿasiyatan*, "at the time of the act." Whatever Samuel's actual statement was, and whatever he may have meant by it, Babylonian tradition assumed him to have posited the general rule of saying the blessing prior to the act of performing the commandment. The Ashkenazic practice with regard to *milah* originally followed Amram, Saadiah, and Sar Shalom, but Rabbenu Tam reverted to what he considered the proper custom of saying it before the operation (*Tosafot* to *Shab.* 137b). When the geonic concern for saying the blessing after the operation came about is a puzzle, since neither the *Babli* nor the *Yerushalmi* makes *milah* an exception to the general rule formulated by Samuel. In fact the Talmud's own objection (*Pes.* 7b), ʾ*i hachi ʾafilu shechitah umilah nami*, presumes *milah* to be included in the rule.

16. For today's rite, see Birnbaum, *Siddur*, pp. 749 ff.

17. See Jacobson, *Netiv Binah*, vol. 3, p. 155, for full biblical citations.

18. For citation of rabbinic discussion, see Levi, *Yesodot Hatefillah*, p. 285; Jacobson, *Netiv Binah*, vol. 3, p. 156.

19. *SS*, p. 100. Cf. discussion by Israel Ta-Shema, "Nispach" in Mordecai Margoliot, *Hilkhot 'Erets Yisrae'el min Hagenizah* (Jerusalem, 1973), pp. 32–38.

20. *Sha'arei Teshuvah*, ed. Leiter, #47.

21. See, however, chap. 5, n. 1 above. Heinemann identifies the objection as having its basis in the fact that the blessing is not talmudic.

22. For today's rite, see Birnbaum, *Siddur*, pp. 753–55.

23. *Ket.* 7b.

24. *SRA*, p. 181.

25. *SS*, p. 97.

26. Lewin, *OG*, vol. 8, *Ket.* #70 and 71. Cf. Ginzberg, *Ginzei Schechter*, vol. 2, p. 510, where Ginzberg recognizes that Hai had no objections to liturgical additions per se, but was uniquely disturbed by this one.

27. See Rabbenu Nissim to Alfasi, *Ket.* 7b, s.v. *ve'asar*, and Meiri, ad loc.

28. If so, the problem may have arisen because the eulogy was originally no eulogy at all, but an alternative blessing in itself. By talmudic times it had coalesced with another form of the blessing and—since it was the shorter one—became the eulogy for the alternative. Those who received the new form later discovered that the "eulogy" did not fit very well, and added a repetition of the phrase found in the body of the blessing, in order to make it fit better.

29. *SRA*, p. 181; *Abudarham*, p. 359.

30. *Simchah Assaf*, "Chalifat She'elot Uteshuvot ben Sefarad Uven Tsorfat Ve'ashkenaz," *Tarbits* 8 (1936/37): 167.

31. Ginzberg, *Ginzei Schechter*, vol. 2, p. 510.

32. Hai, of course, did not actually have the word *nesu'ot* in his Talmud and did not use it for his blessing (see Lewin, *OG*, *Ket.* #70). But the sentence in which it occurred says God "allowed us" to have intercourse with (*hanesu'ot*) those who have passed through *chuppah* and *kiddushin*. So even without the technical noun *hanesu'ot*—in fact, particularly without it—the sense of the blessing at that point demanded the complete qualifying phrase, lest people think intercourse was rabbinically acceptable after only *kiddushin*. Though, technically speaking, intercourse with one's betrothed was not "illegal," the rabbis had frowned on it from tannaitic times onward.

33. See Bernard Revel, "The Karaite Halakah," in *Karaite Studies*, ed. Philip Birnbaum (New York, 1971), p. 71, n. 102, for citations from these authorities.

34. See Mann, *Texts and Studies*, vol. 2, pp. 156–66.

35. *Ket.* 8a.

36. *SRA*, p. 181.

37. *SS*, p. 108.

38. Lewin, *OG*, vol. 8, *Ket.* #87.

39. See Lieberman, *Tosefta Kifshutah*, vol. 1, p. 250, for discussion.

40. See above, chap. 5, nn. 19 and 20.

41. For today's rite, see Birnbaum, *Siddur*, p. 759.

42. Ibid.

43. Ibid., pp. 761–63.

44. Ibid., pp. 763–65.

45. Ibid., p. 765.

46. M. *Ber.* 7:3. Yose and Akiba debate what is to be the *halakhah*. The *Babli* (*Ber.* 50a) cites Raba as declaring Akiba to be correct, but apparently there was still no unanimity on the subject. R. Hama still followed Yose, as that was the exilarch's practice; and other localities, such as Be Gobar and Nehar Bel, are mentioned, each with its own tradition. See also P.T. *Ber.* 7:3 (11c) for a similar variety of opinion.

47. Alfasi's Mishnah text read with the *Yerushalmi*, as did some texts of the Tosafot. Thus, the Tosafot felt compelled to point out that the proper reading was without the *lamed*. As evidence, the Tosafot cite Amram. See Tosafot to *Ber*. 49b beginning with the words *nevarekh 'eloheinu*. Their comment is: *nevarekh 'eloheinu garsinan vela' garsinan nevarekh le'loheinu belamed*.

48. *SRA*, p. 45.

49. *SS*, p. 105.

50. *SRA*, p. 46.

51. *SS*, p. 102.

52. *Toratan shel Rishonim*, vol. 1, p. 34.

53. See above, chap. 7, n. 38.

54. Mann, "Genizah Fragments," pp. 445–48. See also his discussion, p. 443, n. 129.

55. Louis Finkelstein, "Birkat Hamazon," p. 253.

56. P.T. *Pes*. 8:8 (36b).

57. *Ket*. 8b.

58. Lieberman, *Tosefta Kifshutah*, vol. 1, p. 50.

59. T. *Ber*. 3:24.

60. Lieberman, *Tosefta Kifshutah*, vol. 1, p. 50. It should be noted that it was characteristic of the Palestinians to add the words *'al hamazon* to the *zimun*, and that this addition distinguished the Palestinian form of the *zimun* from the Babylonian version. See Müller, *Chilluf Minhagim #24*.

61. Cf. *Toratan Shel Rishonim*, vol. 1, p. 34; and *'Eshkol Hakofer* 14b. Hadassi's formula reads *barukh menachem lev ha'agumim veha'avelim*. It was originally part of the general Palestinian milieu from which the earlier Karaites drew. Hadassi himself refers to the Karaites as *ba'alei mikra' 'avelei tsiyon* (p. 13a). Some scholars—see for example Moshe Zucker, "Teguvot Litenu'at 'Avelei Tsiyon Hakara'im Besifrut Harabbanit," in *Sefer Hayovel Lerabbi Chanokh Albeck*—have therefore identified all *'avelei tsiyon* as Karaites. I should think it more likely that there were many groups in Palestine who yearned for the restoration of the Temple, and practiced a strict regimen of fasting and the like. The Karaites found their way of life congenial and became one of many such groups. Thus, to the extent permitted by the self-imposed limits of the Karaite liturgy, rabbinic idiom carried over to Karaite texts and from there became part of the standard Karaite rite in Byzantium.

62. See, above, p. 211, n. 19.

63. Lieberman speculates, though, that when the blessing was said independently—i.e., separate from the *birkat hamazon*—on the first two days of mourning, there may have been the following eulogy: *Barukh . . . gomel sechar tov legomelei chasadim*.

64. *Massekhet Soferim* 19:9.

65. Ginzberg, *Geonica*, vol. 2, p. 37, and notes on p. 24.

66. *Teshuvot Ge'onim Kadmonim*, ed. David Cassel (1848; reprint ed., New York, 1959), p. 7b. The blessing is not given in its entirely, but its identifiable characteristics are cited: "In our place, when we return from the graveside with a mourner, we say a blessing over a cup [of wine]: Blessed art Thou, Lord, King, [and] merciful judge ['adonai, melekh, dayyan harachamin]." This blessing is quoted by Lewin in its entirety (*OG*, vol. 8, *Ket*. #106) from *Midrash Sekhel Tov*: "On the way back from the cemetery, upon entering the mourner's house, we mix him a cup of wine and say a blessing over the cup of consolation, that is, the *birkat rechovah*, thusly: 'Blessed . . . merciful judge, judge of faithfulness, who had judged us according to His truthful judgment. . . . Blessed art Thou Lord, who comfort the heart of mourners.'"

Though the Cassel version is cited anonymously, it also appears in Ibn Giyyat's *Sha'arei Simchah*, vol. 2, p. 65a, where it is attributed to Natronai.

67. Lewin, *OG*, vol. 8, *Ket.* #110.

68. Ibid., vol. 1, *Ber.* #404.

69. The former is the traditional *zimun* when there is no quorum present. With a quorum, however, the latter form, i.e., the one containing God's name, is customary. Note that Natronai omits the preposition *lamed* typical of Palestinian practice, and condemned, as we saw, by Amram, though not, of course, by Saadiah.

70. Lewin, *OG*, vol. 8, *Ket.* #108.

71. *SS*, p. 104, n. 15; and p. 105.

72. *SRA*, p. 187.

73. See above, chap. 5, n. 21.

10: MISCELLANEOUS DEBATES AND LITURGICAL ALTERNATIVES

1. For today's rite, see Birnbaum, *Siddur*, p. 14.

2. Ginzberg, *Geonica*, vol. 2, p. 114; *Tur, O.H.* 6:1.

3. *SRA*, p. 2.

4. *SS*, p. 88.

5. *O.H.* 6:1.

6. Mann, *Texts and Studies*, vol. 2, p. 310.

7. *Abudarham*, p. 37.

8. Baer, *Seder 'Avodat Yisra'el*, p. 36.

9. P.T. *Ber.* 9:4 (14b); cf. Baer Ratner, *'Ahavat Tsiyon Virushalayim*, vol. 1, p. 213.

10. For today's rite, see Birnbaum, *Siddur*, p. 13.

11. For today's rite, see Birnbaum, *Siddur*, p. 369.

12. Rashi to *Ber.* 11b, s.v. *barukh 'atah 'adonai hamelamed*; cf. Tosafot and *Mordecai*, ad loc., and *'Or Zaru'a, keriyat shema'*, sec. 24.

13. See *Dikdukei Soferim* to *Ber.* 11b, and the discussion by Heinemann, *Hatefillah*, p. 105, n. 14.

14. Scholem, *Jewish Gnosticism*, p. 13, n. 8.

15. *'Eshkol Hakofer*, pp. 11a and 17b, for example.

16. See discussion by Ginzberg, *Perushim*, vol. 1, pp. 200 ff.

17. Cf. Mann, "Genizah Fragments," p. 396; Assaf, "Miseder Hatefillah," p. 128; Solomon Schechter, "Genizah Specimens," *JQR*, o.s. 10 (1898): 54; Mann ("Genizah Fragments," p. 366) doubts that the Schechter specimen is really Palestinian in its entirety, but the benediction is admittedly so.

18. The bedtime *shema'* in today's rite can be found in Birnbaum, *Siddur*, p. 779.

19. Ginzberg, *Geonica*, vol. 1, pp. 136–38.

20. For the location of *'el melekh ne'eman* in today's rite, see Birnbaum, *Siddur*, p. 75.

21. Abraham I. Schechter, *Studies in Jewish Liturgy*, p. 109.

22. Mann, "Genizah Fragments," p. 397.

23. Jonathan Rosenbaum, "A Reconstruction and Analysis of the Palestinian Rite for the Sabbath Evening, Morning and Additional Services" (M.H.L. thesis, Hebrew Union College, 1972), p. 21.

24. See, for example, Lewin, *OG*, vol. 1, #19, and n. 4 there.

25. See discussion by Zuckerman, *A Jewish Princedom*, p. 322, and n. 14 there.
26. See above, Introduction, n. 5.
27. Rosh to *Ber.* 11b.
28. Assaf, "Misefer Hatefillah," p. 123.
29. Mann, "Genizah Fragments," p. 405.
30. Lewin, *Ginzei Kedem* 3 (1925): 44.
31. For today's rite, see Birnbaum, *Machzor*, p. 317.
32. Cf. *Sha'arei Teshuvah*, ed. Leiter, #79; and Ginzberg, *Ginzei Schechter*, vol. 2, p. 84, for examples.
33. *Machzor Vitry*, p. 385, n. 5; Rosh to *R.H.* 4:13.
34. *SRA*, p. 139, and references in n. 2.
35. Lewin *OG*, vol. 5, *R.H.* #111.
36. See *Hama'or* to *Rosh Hashanah*, chap. 4. Zerachyah Halevi argues that the blessing is post-talmudic, and Nahmanides, in *Milchemet 'Adonai*, disagrees.
37. See discussion in Selvin Goldberg, *Karaite Liturgy and Its Relation to Synagogue Worship* (Manchester, 1957), pp. 115 ff.
38. See Birnbaum, *Siddur*, p. 395, for example.
39. Lewin, *OG*, vol. 5, *R.H.* #136.
40. Ginzberg, *Geonica*, vol. 2, p. 119.
41. *Sha'arei Simchah*, vol. 2, p. 26b.
42. Ibid.
43. *SRA*, pp. 78, 89.
44. Elbogen, "Die Tefilla." His texts include them consistently.
45. Ginzberg, *Geonica*, vol. 1, pp. 119 ff.
46. For today's rite, see Birnbaum, *Siddur*, p. 423.
47. *Sha'arei Teshuvah*, ed. Leiter, #115; cf. Lewin, *OG*, vol. 3, *Pes.* #276.
48. *Siddur Hatefillot Keminhag Hakara'im* (Eupatoria, 1836), p. 46.

11: THE CANONIZATION PROCESS

1. See also evidence from *Sefer Hama'asim*. Zvi Meir Rabinowitz, "*Sepher Ha-Ma'asim Livnei Erez Yisra'el*—New Fragments," *Tarbits* 41 (1972): 279; and Mordecai Margoliot, *Hilkhot 'Erets Yisra'el min Hagenizah* (Jerusalem, 1973).
2. Mann, *The Jews in Egypt and Palestine*, vol. 1, p. 58.
3. Ibid., pp. 52–54.
4. Leon Nemoy, "Early Karaism (The Need for a New Approach)," *JQR*, n.s. 40 (1949–50): 312.
5. Ibid., p. 311.
6. Ginzberg, *Geonica*, vol. 1, pp. 9–10.
7. Rivkin, "The Saadiah–David ben Zakkai Controversy," p. 393.
8. Rivkin deals extensively with the problem. Ibid., pp. 393 ff.
9. W. Bacher, "Qirqisani the Karaite and His Work on Jewish Sects," in Birnbaum, *Karaite Studies*, p. 267.
10. Leon Nemoy, "The Liturgy of al Qirqisani," in *Studies in Bibliography, History and Literature for I. Edward Kiev*, ed. Charles Berlin pp. 314 ff.
11. Ismar Elbogen, "Saadia's Siddur," in *Saadia Anniversary Volume of the American Academy of Jewish Research*, pp. 252–53.
12. SS, p. 237, n. 17. See above, chap. 7, n. 4.
13. SS, Introduction, pp. 6–7.
14. The significance of Saadiah's dependence on the Bible throughout his writings

has been noted by Malter (Henry Malter, *Saadia Gaon: His Life and Works*, p. 148, n. 324).

15. Here, too, he was careful to include anti-Karaite messages. The first *bakashah*, for example, includes a statement of faith in the divine origin of "Scripture and Mishnah, the written [Torah] and its [oral] exposition" (*SS*, p. 57).

16. Rivkin, "The Saadiah–David ben Zakkai Controversy," pp. 402, 423.

17. Ibid., p. 423. The citation is from Solomon Schechter, *Saadyana*, pp. 118–21.

18. Lewin, "Rav Sherira Gaon," pp. 4 ff.

Bibliography

Abrahams, Israel. "Some Egyptian Fragments of the Passover Haggada." *JQR*, o.s. 10 (1898): 41–51.

Abudarham Hashalem. Edited by Solomon Wertheimer. Jerusalem: Usha Press, 1963.

Ankori, Zvi. *Karaites in Byzantium*. New York: Columbia University Press, 1959.

Aptowitzer, Avigdor. "Teshuvot Meyuchasot Lerarv Hai Ve'einan Shelo." *Tarbits* 1 (1929/30).

Assaf, Simchah. *Be'oholei Ya'akov*. Jerusalem: Mosad Harav Kook, 1943.

————. "Chalifat She'elot Uteshuvot bein Sefarad Uvein Tsorfat Ve'ashkenaz." *Tarbits* 8 (1936/37): 162–70.

————. "Misefer Hatefillah Mei'erets Yisra'el." In *Sefer Dinabourg*, edited by Isaac Baer. Jerusalem: Kiryat Sefer, 1949.

————. *Tekufat Hage'onim Vesifrutah*. Jerusalem: Mosad Harav Kook, 1955.

Bacher, Wilhelm. "Qirqisani the Karaite and His Work on Jewish Sects." In *Karaite Studies*, edited by Philip Birnbaum. New York: Hermon Press, 1971.

Baer, [Seligman]. *Seder 'Avodat Yisra'el*. 1868. Reprint. New York: Schocken, 1937.

Bamberger, Fritz. "Zunz's Conception of History." *AAJR* 11 (1941): 1–25.

Birnbaum, Philip, ed. *Hasiddur Hashalem*. New York: Hebrew Publishing Co., 1949.

————. *Karaite Studies*. New York: Hermon Press, 1971.

————. *Machzor Hashalem Lerosh Hashanah Veyom Kippur*. New York: Hebrew Publishing Co., 1951.

————. *The Birnbaum Haggadah*. 2d ed. New York: Hebrew Publishing Co., 1976.

Bloch, Joseph. *Kol Nidre und seine Entstehungsgeschichte*. Vienna, 1917.

Bloch, Philipp. "Die Yordei Merkavah, die Mystiker der Gaonenzeit und ihr Einfluss auf die Liturgie." *MGWJ* 37 (1893).

Brocke, Michael, and Petuchowski, Jakob J. *The Lord's Prayer and Jewish Liturgy.* New York: Seabury Press, 1978.

Büchler, Adolf. "La Kedouscha de Yozer chez les Geonim." *REJ* 53 (1907): 220–30.

———. "La Ketouba chez les Juifs du Nord de L'Afrique." *REJ* 50 (1905): 145–81.

———. "Le Mot Veyitkales dans le Kaddisch." *REJ* 54 (1907): 194–204.

Butin, Romain. "Some Leaves of an Egyptian Jewish Ritual." *JQR*, n.s. 9 (1918–19): 259–303.

Chemdah Genuzah. Edited by Shneer Shneerssohn and Zeev Wolfenssohn. 1863. Reprint. Jerusalem, 1967.

Cohen, Gerson D. *Sefer Ha-qabbalah: "The Book of Tradition" by Abraham Ibn Daud.* Philadelphia: Jewish Publication Society, 1967.

Davidson, Israel. *'Otsar Hashirah Vehapiyyut.* 4 vols. 1929. Reprint. New York: Ktav, 1970.

———. "Seder Hibbur Berakot." *JQR*, n.s. 21 (1930–31): 241–79.

Elbogen, Ismar. *Der jüdische Gottesdienst in seiner geschichtlichen Entwicklung.* 1913. Reprint. Hildesheim: Georg Olms, 1962.

———. "Saadiah's Siddur." In *Saadia Anniversary Volume of the American Academy for Jewish Research*, edited by B. Cohen, pp. 247–63. New York, 1943.

———. *Studien zur Geschichte des jüdischen Gottesdienstes.* Berlin, 1907.

———. "Die Tefillah für die Festtage." *MGWJ* 55 (1911): 586–99.

Epstein, Y. N. "Maʿasim Livnei 'Erets Yisra'el." *Tarbits* 1, no. 2 (1929/30).

———. "Sur les Chapitres de Ben Baboi." *REJ* 75 (1922).

Finkelstein, Louis. "The Birkat Hamazon." *JQR*, n.s. 19 (1928–29): 211–62.

———. "The Development of the Amidah." In *Contributions to the Scientific Study of Jewish Liturgy*, edited by Jakob Petuchowski, pp. 91–177. New York: Ktav, 1970.

———. "Pre-Maccabean Documents in the Passover Haggadah." *HTR* 35 (1942): 291–332.

Fleischer, Ezra. *Shirat Hakodesh Haʿivrit Bimei Habenayim.* Jerusalem: Keter Publishing House, 1975.

———. "Towards a Clarification of the Expression *Poreis 'Al Shema'*" (Hebrew). *Tarbits* 41 (1972): 145–50.

Freehof, Solomon. "The Structure of the Birchos Hashachar." *HUCA*, pt. 2, 23 (1950–51): 339–55.

Galis, Jacob. *Minhagei 'Erets Yisra'el.* Jerusalem: Mosad Harav Kook, 1968.

Ginzberg, Louis. *Geonica.* 2 vols. 1909. Reprint. New York: Hermon Press, 1968.

————. *Ginzei Schechter*, vol. 2. 1929. Reprint. New York: Hermon Press, 1969.

————. *Perushim Vechidushim Birushalmi*. 3 vols. New York: Jewish Theological Seminary, 1941.

Ginzei Kedem. 6 vols. Edited by Benjamin Manasseh Lewin. Palestine, 1922–44.

Goitein, S. D. *A Mediterranean Society*. 2 vols. Berkeley and Los Angeles: University of California Press, 1967–71.

Goldberg, P. J. *Karaite Liturgy*. Manchester: Manchester University Press, 1957.

Goldschmidt, Daniel. *Haggadah Shel Pesach Vetoldoteha*. Jerusalem: Bialik, 1960.

————. *Machzor Layamim Hanora'im*. 2 vols. Jerusalem: Mosad Bialik, 1970.

————. "Seder Hatefillah Shel Harambam ʿal pi Ketav Yad Oxford." *Yediot Hamakhon Lecheker Hashirah Haʿivrit* 7 (1958).

Goodblatt, David. *Rabbinic Instruction in Sasanian Babylonia*. Leiden: E. J. Brill, 1975.

Goodenough, Irwin. *By Light Light*. New Haven: Yale University Press, 1935.

Greenwald, Ithamar. "Piyyutei Yannai Vesifrut Yordei Merkavah." *Tarbits* 36 (1966/67): 257–78.

Groner, Zevi. "Haberakhah ʿal Havidui Vegilguleha." *Bar Ilan Yearbook* 13 (1976): 158–68.

Harkavy, A. *Studien und Mittheilungen*. Vol. 4. Berlin, 1887. Vol. 8. St. Petersburg, 1903.

Heinemann, Joseph. "Birkat Boneh Yerushalayim Begilguleha." In *Sefer Chaim Schirmann*, edited by Shraga Abramson and Aaron Mirsky, pp. 93–101. Jerusalem: Schocken, 1970.

————. *Hatefillah Bitekufat Hatannaim Veha'amoraim*. Jerusalem: Magnes Press, 1966.

————. "Ketaʿim Misiddur Rav Saadiah." *Tarbits* 34 (1964/65): 363–65.

————. "One Benediction Comprising Seven." *REJ* 125 (1966): 101–11.

————. "Yachaso shel Rav Saadiah Gaon Leshinui Matbeiʿa Tefillah." *Bar Ilan Yearbook* 6 (1963): 220–33.

————. trans. *Hatefillah Beyisra'el*. Tel Aviv: Dvir, 1972.

————, and Petuchowski, Jakob J. *Literature of the Synagogue*. New York: Behrman House, 1975.

Hershler, Moshe, ed. *Siddur of Rabbi Solomon B. Samson of Garmaise*. Jerusalem, 1971.

Idelsohn, Abraham Z. *Jewish Liturgy and Its Development*. 1932. Reprint. New York: Schocken, 1967.

'*Iggeret Rav Sherira Gaon*. Edited by Aaron Hyman. Jerusalem, 1967.

'*Iggeret Rav Sherira Gaon*. Edited by Benjamin Manasseh Lewin. Haifa, 1921.

Jacobson, Issachar. *Netiv Binah*. 3 vols. Tel Aviv: Sinai Publishing Co., 1968–73.

Kasher, Menachem M. *Haggadah Shelemah*. Jerusalem, 1967.

Kaufman, J. "The Prayer Book According to the Ritual of England Before 1290." *JQR*, o.s. 4 (1892).

————. "The Ritual of the Seder and the Aggadah of the English Jews Before the Expulsion." *JQR*, o.s. 4 (1892).

Lauterbach, Jacob Z. *Rabbinic Essays*. Cincinnati: Hebrew Union College Press, 1951.

Levi, Eliezer. *Torat Hatefillah*. Tel Aviv: Abraham Zioni Publishing House, 1967.

————. *Yesodot Hatefillah*. Tel Aviv: Abraham Zioni Publishing House, 1963.

Levi, Israel. "Fragments de Rituels de Prières." *REJ* 53 (1907): 231–43.

Lewin, Benjamin Manasseh. "Maʿasim Livnei ʾErets Yisraʾel." *Tarbits* 1, no. 1 (1929–30): 79–101.

————. "Mitekufat Hageʾonim: Rav Sherira Gaon." 1917. Reprinted in *Mitekufat Hageʾonim*. Tel Aviv: Zion, 1971.

————. Review of "Genizah Fragments," by Jacob Mann. *Hatsofeh Lechokhmat Yisraʾel*, pt. B, 11 (1927/1928).

Liber, M. "Structure and History of the Tefilah." *JQR*, n.s. 40 (1950): 331–57.

Lieberman, Saul. *Tosefta Kifshutah*. Vols. 1, 3–6. New York: Jewish Theological Seminary, 1955–67.

————. "Shuv Lesefer Hamaʿasim." *Tarbits* 42 (1972/73): 90–96.

Liebreich, Leon J. "Aspects of the New Year Liturgy." *HUCA* 34 (1963): 125–76.

————. "Insertions in the Third Benediction of the Holy Day ʿAmidoth." *HUCA* 35 (1964): 79–101.

————. "The Liturgical Use of Psalm 78:38." In *Studies and Essays in Honor of Abraham A. Neuman*, edited by Bernard D. Weinryb, and Solomon Zeitlin, pp. 365–74. Leiden: E. J. Brill, 1962.

Machzor Vitry. Edited by Simon Halevi Hurwitz. Nuremberg: Mekitsei Nirdamim, 1923.

Mahler, Raphael. *Karaier*. New York: Eliahu Schulman, 1947.

Malter, Henry. *Saadia Gaon*. 1962. Reprint. New York: Hermon Press, 1969.

Mann, Jacob. "Anan's Liturgy." *Journal of Jewish Lore and Philosophy* 1 (1919): 329–53.

———. "A Polemical Work Against Karaites and Other Sectaries." *JQR*, n.s. 12 (1921–22): 123–50.

———. "Changes in the Divine Service of the Synagogue Due to Religious Persecutions." *HUCA* 4 (1927): 241–311.

———. "Genizah Fragments of the Palestinian Order of Service." 1925. Reprinted in *Contributions to the Scientific Study of Jewish Liturgy*, edited by Jakob Petuchowski. New York: Ktav, 1970.

———. "Les Chapitres de Ben Baboi et les Relations de R. Jehoudai Gaon avec la Palestine." *REJ* 70 (1920): 113–48.

———. "Misrat Rosh Hagolah Bevavel." In *Sefer Zikaron Lichvod Shemuel Avraham Poznanski*, pp. 18–32. Warsaw, 1927.

———. "Responsa of the Babylonian Geonim as a Source of Jewish History." *JQR* n.s. 7 (1916–17): 457–90; n.s. 8 (1917–18): 339–66; n.s. 9 (1918–19): 139–79; n.s. 10 (1919–20): 121–51, 309–65; n.s. 11 (1920–21): 433–71.

———. "*Saadiah Gaon, His Life and Works* by Dr. H. Malter—A Review." *REJ* 73 (1921): 105–12.

———. "Sefer Hama'asim livnei 'Erets Yisra'el." *Tarbits* 1, no. 3 (1929/30): 1–14.

———. *The Jews in Egypt and in Palestine Under the Fatimid Caliphs.* 2 vols. 1920–22. Reprint. New York: Ktav, 1970.

———. *Texts and Studies in Jewish History and Literature.* 2 vols. Cincinnati: Hebrew Union College, 1931; Philadelphia: Jewish Publication Society, 1935.

Margoliot, Mordecai. *Hilkhot 'Erets Yisra'el min Hagenizah.* Jerusalem: Mosad Rav Kook, 1973.

Marmorstein, Arthur. "A Misunderstood Question in the Yerushalmi." *JQR*, n.s. 20 (1929–30): 313–20.

———. "Inyanim Shonim Lecheker Tekufat Hage'onim." *Tarbits* 1, no. 5 (1929/30).

Marx, Alexander. "Untersuchungen zum Siddur des Gaon R. Amram." *Jahrbuch der Jüdisch-Literarischen Gesselschaft* 5 (1907).

Massekhet Soferim. Edited by Michael Higger. 1937. Reprint. New York: Makor Press, 1970.

Meyer, Michael A. "Jewish Religious Reform and Wissenschaft des Judentums: The Positions of Zunz, Geiger, and Frankel." *Leo Baeck Institute Yearbook* 16 (1971): 19–41.

_____. *The Origins of the Modern Jew.* Detroit: Wayne State University Press, 1967.

Mihaly, Eugene. "The Passover Haggadah as PaRaDiSe." *CCAR Journal* 13, no. 5 (April 1960): 3–27.

Mirsky, Aaron. "Mekorah shel Tefillat Yotser." In *Sefer Hayovel Lerabbi Chanokh Albeck*, pp. 324–31. Jerusalem: Mosad Harav Kook, 1963.

Misifrut Hageonim. Edited by Simchah Assaf. Jerusalem: Darom Press, 1933.

Müller, Joel. *Chilluf Minhagim bein Bavel Ve'erets Yisra'el.* 1878. Reprint. Jerusalem: Mekor, 1970.

_____. *Mafteiach Liteshuvot Hage'onim.* Berlin, 1891.

Munk, Leo. "Die Pessach-Hagada der Bne Israel." In *Festschrift für David Hoffman*, vol. 2, pp. 257–66. Berlin, 1914.

Nemoy, Leon. "Early Karaism (The Need for a New Approach)." *JQR*, n.s. 40 (1950): 307–15.

_____. *Karaite Anthology.* New Haven: Yale University Press, 1952.

_____. "The Liturgy of al-Qirqisani." In *Studies in Bibliography, History and Literature in Honor of I. Edward Kiev*, edited by Charles Berlin. New York: Ktav, 1971.

Neusner, Jacob. "The Development of the Merkavah Tradition." *Journal for the Study of Judaism in the Persian, Hellenistic and Roman Periods* 2 (1971): 149–62.

'*Or Zarua'.* Edited by Akiba Lehrn. Zhitomir, 1862.

'*Otsar Hage'onim.* vols. 1–3, 5–6, 8, 11. Edited by Benjamin Manasseh Lewin. Palestine, 1928–42.

Petuchowski, Jakob J. *Contributions to the Scientific Study of Jewish Liturgy.* New York: Ktav, 1970.

_____. "'Hoshi'ah Na' in Psalm CXVIII: 25—A Prayer for Rain." *Vetus Testamentum* 5, no. 3 (July 1955): 265–71.

_____. *Theology and Poetry.* London: Routledge and Kegan Paul, 1978.

_____, and Brocke, Michael. *The Lord's Prayer and Jewish Liturgy.* New York: Seabury Press, 1978.

_____, and Heinemann, Joseph. *Literature of the Synagogue.* New York: Behrman House, 1975.

Pool, David de Sola. *The Old Jewish Aramaic Prayer: The Kaddish.* Leipzig, 1909.

Poznanski, Samuel. *Eine Neue Hypothese über die Entstehung des Kol Nidre.* Vienna, 1918.

_____. *Karaite Literary Opponents of Saadiah Gaon.* London: Luzac and Co., 1908.

_____. *Schechter's Saadyana.* Frankfurt a.M.: J. Kaufmann, 1904.

Rabinowitz, Zvi Meir. "*Sepher Ha-Ma'asim Livnei 'Erets Yisra'el*—New Fragments." *Tarbits* 41 (1972): 275–305.

Ratner, Baer. *Sefer 'Ahavat Tsiyon Virushalayim*. Vol. 1. Vilna, 1901.

Revel, Bernard. *The Karaite Halakah and Its Relation to Sadducean, Samaritan, and Philonian Halakah*. Philadelphia: Dropsie College, 1913.

Rivkin, Ellis. "The Saadiah–David ben Zakkai Controversy: A Structural Analysis." In *Studies and Essays in Honor of Abraham A. Neuman*, edited by Meir ben-Horin, Bernard D. Weinryb, and Solomon Zeitlin, pp. 388–423. Philadelphia: Dropsie College, 1962.

―――. *The Shaping of Jewish History*. New York: Charles Scribner's Sons, 1971.

Rosenbaum, Jonathan. "A Reconstruction and Analysis of the Palestinian Rite for the Sabbath Evening, Morning, and Additional Services." M.H.L. dissertation, Hebrew Union College, 1972.

Rosenblatt, Samuel, trans. *Saadia Gaon: "The Book of Beliefs and Opinions."* New Haven: Yale University Press, 1948.

Rosenthal, E. I. J., ed. *Saadya Studies*. Manchester: Manchester University Press, 1943.

Schechter, Abraham I. *Studies in Jewish Liturgy*. Philadelphia: Dropsie College, 1930.

Schechter, Solomon. "Genizah Specimens." *JQR*, o.s. 10 (1898): 654–59.

―――. "Nusecha' Bekaddish." In *Gedenkbuch zur Erinnerung an David Kaufmann*, edited by M. Brann and F. Rosenthal. Breslau, 1900.

―――. "Notes on Hebrew Manuscripts in the University Library at Cambridge." *JQR*, o.s. 4 (1892): 90–101, 245–55.

―――, ed. *Saadyana*. Cambridge: Deighteon and Bell, 1903.

Scheiber, Alexander. "Elements fabuleux dans l'Eshkol Hakofer de Juda Hadassi." *REJ* 53 (1943).

―――. "Siddur Rabbani hamuva' 'al yedei Kirkisani." In *Ignace Goldziher Memorial Volume*, edited by Samuel Loewinger and Joseph Somogyi, vol. 1, pp. 27–41. Budapest, 1948.

Schirmann, Chayyim. "Yannai Hapayyetan Shirato Vehashkafat 'Olamo." *Keshet* 6 (1964): 45–66.

Scholem, Gershom. *Jewish Gnosticism, Merkabah Mysticism and Talmudic Tradition*. New York: Jewish Theological Seminary, 1960.

―――. *Major Trends in Jewish Mysticism*. New York: Schocken, 1946.

Seder Rav Amram Gaon. Edited by Daniel Goldschmidt. Jerusalem: Mosad Harav Kook, 1971.

Sefer 'Eshkol Hakofer. Gozlov, 1836.

Sefer Ha'eshkol. Edited by Benjamim Zevi Auerbach. Halberstadt, 1867.

Sefer Ha'Ittim. Edited by Jacob Schorr. Cracow, 1913.

Sefer Halakhot Gedolot. Edited by Azriel Hildesheimer. Jerusalem: Mekitsei Nirdamim, 1972.

Sefer Hamanhig. Edited by Isaac Goldman. Jerusalem: Lewin-Epstein Brothers, 1951.

Sefer Harokeach Hagadol. Edited by Barukh Shimon Schneerson. Jerusalem, 1967.

Sefer Ma'aseh Hage'onim. Edited by Abraham Epstein and Jacob Freiman. Berlin, 1909.

Sefer Pardes Hagadol. Edited by Michael Levi Frumkin. Jerusalem, 1964.

Sefer Sha'arei Simchah. Edited by Isaac Dov Halevi Bamberger. Fürth, 1861.

Sha'arei Teshuvah. Edited by Wolf Leiter. Pittsburgh, 1946.

Sha'arei Tsedek. 1792. Reprint. Jerusalem, 1966.

She'elot Uteshuvot Hage'onim. Edited by Mordecai Elijah Rabinowitz. 1884. Reprint. Jerusalem, 1966.

Shibbolei Haleket Hashalem. Edited by Solomon Buber. 1886. Reprint. Jerusalem: Alef Publishing Co., 1962.

Siddur Rashi. Edited by Solomon Buber. 1911. Reprint. Jerusalem: Kiryah Ne'emanah, 1963.

Siddur Rav Saadiah Gaon. Edited by Simchah Assaf, Israel Davidson, and Issachar Joel. 2d ed. Jerusalem: Mekitsei Nirdamim, 1963.

Smith, Morton. "Observations on *Hekhalot Rabbati.*" In *Biblical and Other Studies,* edited by Alexander Altmann, pp. 142–61. Cambridge, 1963.

Ta-Shema, Israel. "'El Melekh Ne'eman Gilgulo Shel Minhag." *Tarbits* 39 (1969/70): 185–94.

————. "Nispach." In Mordecai Margoliot, *Hilkhot 'Erets Yisra'el min Hagenizah,* pp. 32–38. Jerusalem: Mosad Rav Kook, 1973.

Tchernowitz, Chaim. *Toldot Haposkim.* Vol. 1. New York: Va'ad Hayovel, 1946.

Teshuvot Ge'onei Mizrach Uma'arav. Edited by Joel Müller. 1888. Reprint. New York: Menorah Press, 1959.

Teshuvot Ge'onim Kadmonim. Edited by David Cassel. 1848. Reprint. New York: Menorah Press, 1959.

Teshuvot Hage'onim. Edited by Simchah Assaf. 1942. Reprint. Jerusalem: Makor Press, 1971.

Teshuvot Hage'onim. Edited by Nachman Coronel. 1871. Reprint. Jerusalem, 1967.

Teshuvot Hage'onim. Edited by Arthur Marmorstein. 1928. Reprint. Jerusalem, 1968.

Teshuvot Hage'onim [Lyck]. Edited by Jacob Musafiya. 1864. Reprint. Jerusalem, 1967.

Teshuvot Hage'onim Mitokh Hagenizah. Edited by Simchah Assaf. Jerusalem: Darom Press, 1929.

Toratan shel Rishonim. 2 vols. Edited by Chaim Meir Horowitz. 1881.

Urbach, E. E. "The Traditions about Merkabah Mysticism in the Tannaitic Period" (Hebrew). In *Studies in Mysticism and Religion Presented to Gershom G. Scholem,* edited by R. J. Zwi Werblowsky and Ch. Wirszubski. Jerusalem: Magnes Press, 1967.

Wallach, Luitpold. "The Beginning of the Science of Judaism in the Nineteenth Century." *Historica Judaica* 8, no. 1 (1946): 33–60.

Wacholder, Ben Zion, ed. *Jacob Mann's "The Bible as Read and Preached in the Old Synagogue."* New York: Ktav, 1971.

Wieder, Naphtali. "Birkat Yein 'Asis." *Sinai* 20 (1947): 43–48.

————. "Fourteen New Genizah Fragments of Saadiah's Siddur Together With a Reproduction of a Missing Part." In *Saadya Studies,* edited by E. I. J. Rosenthal. Manchester: Manchester University Press, 1943.

————. "Lecheker Minhag Bavel Hakadmon." *Tarbits* 37 (1967/68): 135–57, 240–64.

————. "The Old Palestinian Ritual: New Sources." *JJS* 4 (1953).

Yabetz, Ze'ev. *Sefer Mekor Haberakhot.* Berlin, 1910. Reprint. Jerusalem, 1976.

Zeitlin, Solomon. "The Liturgy of the First Night of Passover." *JQR,* n.s. 38 (1947–48): 431–60.

Zikaron Larishonim Teshuvot Hage'onim. Edited by A. Harkavy. 1886. Reprint Israel, 1965.

Zucker, Moshe. "Teguvot Litenu'at 'Avelei Tsiyon Hakar'im Besifrut Harrabbanit." In *Sefer Hayovel Lerabbi Chanokh Albeck.* Jerusalem: Mosad Harav Kook, 1963.

Zuckerman, Arthur J. *A Jewish Princedom in Feudal France: 768–900.* New York: Columbia University Press, 1972.

Zulay, Menachem. "Shemoneh 'Esreh Lerav Saadiah Gaon." *Tarbits* 16 (1944/45): 57–70.

Zunz, Leopold. *Die Ritus des synagogalen Gottesdienstes.* Berlin: Louis Lamm, 1919.

————. *Haderashot Beyisra'el Vehishtalshelutan Hahistorit.* Translated by Chanokh Albeck. Jerusalem: Mosad Bialik, 1954.

Index

239